From the Activities menu, choose Write Checks to display the Write Checks window and you're ready to go.

1 Account name

This tells you which account you're writing a check from.

2 Check date

Type the check date here or use the minicalendar to select a date.

3 Payee

Enter the payee here. If you've written a check to this payee before, as you type, QuickFill will fill in the rest of the payee's name for you.

4 List of payees

If you want, you can click this arrow to select the payee from a list of payees that you've written checks to before.

5 Check amount

The check amount goes here. If you need to make a calculation, click the minicalculator icon.

6 Payee's address

If you're using a window envelope to mail this check enter the payee's address here. To speed up your work, type a quotation mark (") on the first line to insert the payee's name.

7 Notation

Type a brief notation here.

Quicken register? Here's how.

11 Edit

Need to edit a transaction? Click this button to delete, restore, copy, paste, and so forth.

12 Splits

If you need to assign more than one category to a transaction, click here to open the Splits window.

8 Description

Add a brief description or notation here.

13 Scroll

Scroll up and down the register to see more transactions using the scroll bar.

9 Category

Be sure to assign a category to this transaction so that Quicken can track your income and expenses.

10 Record

Record your transaction by clicking this button.

Click the Register icon to display the register.

1 Account name

Here's the name of the account that you're currently working in.

2 Account selection bar

To select another account, click the account name from the Account selection bar.

3 Date

Enter the date of the transaction here.

4 Check number

Record the check number or other transaction reference.

5 Payee

Who is this transaction payable to? Enter the payee here.

6 Amount

Are you entering a payment or a deposit? Enter the amount in one of these fields.

7 Balance

Quicken automatically updates your account balance after each transaction that you enter.

5 for Windows

rite a check in Quicken!

que®

201 W. 103rd Street Indianapolis, IN 46290
(317) 581-3500
Copyright© 1995 Que Corporation

⑪ Splits
If you need to assign more than one category to the check, click here to open the Splits window.

⑫ Print
Ready to print this check? Click here.

⑬ Scroll
Scroll the checks you've just written using the scroll bar.

⑧ Category
Assign a category to your check transaction so that Quicken can track your expenses. Type the category name or click the arrow to select from the Category & Transfer List.

⑭ Balance
Quicken shows you how much you have in your checking account before you write this check.

⑨ Record
Click here to record your check.

⑩ Restore
Need to start over? Click this button to restore the check to its original state.

Using
Quicken 5® for Windows®

Using
Quicken 5® for Windows®

Linda A. Flanders

Gail Perry

Using Quicken 5 for Windows

Copyright© 1995 by Que® Corporation

Library of Congress Catalog No.: 95-71440

ISBN: 0-7897-0631-8

97 96 95   6 5 4 3 2 1

Interpretation of the printing code: the rightmost double-digit number is the year of the book's printing; the rightmost single-digit number, the number of the book's printing. For example, a printing code of 95-1 shows that the first printing of the book occurred in 1995.

All terms mentioned in this book that are known to be trademarks or service marks have been appropriately capitalized. Que cannot attest to the accuracy of this information. Use of a term in this book should not be regarded as affecting the validity of any trademark or service mark.

Screen reproductions in this book were created using Collage Plus from Inner Media, Inc., Hollis, NH.

Composed in *ITC Century*, *ITC Highlander*, and *MCPdigital* by Que Corporation.

Credits

President
Roland Elgey

Vice President and Publisher
Marie Butler-Knight

Associate Publisher
Don Roche Jr.

Title Manager
Kathie-Jo Arnoff

Editorial Services Director
Elizabeth Keaffaber

Managing Editor
Michael Cunningham

Director of Marketing
Lynn E. Zingraf

Senior Series Editor
Chris Nelson

Acquisitions Editor
Deborah Abshier

Production Editor
Thomas F. Hayes

Editors
Lynn Northrup
Linda Seifert

Assistant Product Marketing Manager
Kim Margolius

Technical Editors
Jan Snyder

Acquisitions Coordinator
Tracy M. Williams

Operations Coordinator
Patty Brooks

Editorial Assistant
Carmen Phelps

Book Designer
Ruth Harvey

Cover Designer
Dan Armstrong

Production Team
Steve Adams
Brian Buschkill
Jason Carr
Chad Dressler
Bryan Flores
DiMonique Ford
John Hulse
Daryl Kessler
Stephanie Layton
Michelle Lee
Julie Quinn
Kaylene Riemen
Kelly Warner

Indexer
Mary Jane Frisby
Debra Myers

To Scott, who always shows great confidence in me and who gave me the extra push to do this book.

About the Authors

 Linda A. Flanders is a Certified Public Accountant and holds a Bachelor of Science degree in Accounting from Indiana University. She has worked in public accounting for Arthur Andersen & Co., and private accounting for Mayflower Group, Inc., where she specialized in taxation. She currently operates a small individual tax practice. She is the author of Que's *Using Quicken Version 3 for Windows, Using Quicken Version 7 for DOS, Using QuickBooks for Windows,* and *Using Microsoft Money 2.0.*

 Gail Perry is a CPA and a graduate of Indiana University where she studied journalism and computer science. After working as an accountant in the real world, she returned to school to study accounting and taxes at Illinois State University. Gail spent several years in the trenches of the Chicago office of Deloitte Haskins & Sells (now Deloitte & Touche), learning the ropes of the tax profession. She has devoted the past several years to writing articles and books about taxes and computers including *The Complete Idiot's Guide to Doing Your Taxes 1996.* In addition, Gail teaches computer classes at the Indiana CPA Society.

Acknowledgments

Thanks to Kathie-Jo Arnoff, Chris Nelson, and Tom Hayes for helping me grow my "user-friendly" skills. And a special thanks to Gail Perry for helping me out in a pinch.

We'd like to hear from you!

As part of our continuing effort to produce books of the highest possible quality, Que would like to hear your comments. To stay competitive, we *really* want you, as a computer book reader and user, to let us know what you like or dislike most about this book or other Que products.

You can mail comments, ideas, or suggestions for improving future editions to the address below, or send us a fax at (317) 581-4663. For the online inclined, Macmillan Computer Publishing has a forum on CompuServe (type **GO QUEBOOKS** at any prompt) through which our staff and authors are available for questions and comments. The address of our Internet site is **http://www.mcp.com** (World Wide Web).

In addition to exploring our forum, please feel free to contact me personally to discuss your opinions of this book: I'm **76507,2715** on CompuServe, and I'm **karnoff@que.mcp.com** on the Internet.

Thanks in advance—your comments will help us to continue publishing the best books available on computer topics in today's market.

Kathie-Jo Arnoff
Product Development Specialist
Que Corporation
201 W. 103rd Street
Indianapolis, Indiana 46290
USA

Contents at a Glance

Contents

4 Tracking Income and Expenses with Categories 57

5 Introducing the Quicken Register 77

6 Writing Checks   99

7 Let Quicken Help Balance Your Checkbook 121

Part II Saving Time with Quicken

8 Nifty Quicken Shortcuts that can Save You Time   137

9 Speed Up Your Register Entries with Memorized Transactions 149

10 Scheduling Future Transactions 159

11 Paying Bills Electronically 175

12 Storing Addresses in Quicken   187

Part III Organizing Your Finances

13 Tracking Cash and other Assets   199

16 Creating Your Budget   243

Part IV Analyzing Your Finances

17 Staying on Top of Your Investments   263

Part V Planning for the Future

Part VI Managing Quicken and Banking Online

24 Making Quicken Work the Way You Want It To   353

25 Doing Your Banking Online   363

Index 371

Introduction

If you're like most people, you'd rather have a root canal than deal with your finances. Let's face it, financial management is one of those never-ending tasks that usually leaves you frustrated and depressed.

No matter how many hours you spend writing checks, balancing your checkbook, plugging away at your budget, or updating your investment portfolio, you're most certainly going to spend that many hours again next week or next month. It's kind of like dirty laundry; shortly after it's done, there's a new pile.

I'm sure that you'll find Quicken to be the answer. No, Quicken doesn't do your laundry for you, but it does make financial management a quick and easy process and a little bit fun, too. *Using Quicken 5 for Windows* provides the answers and solutions to making Quicken the financial package that solves all your needs.

What can Quicken do for me?

I've been using Quicken for the last seven years and have become quite dependent upon my system to keep my finances in order. You may think since I'm a computer-book author that I learn and use all kinds of programs, and that's true. But the program that I choose to use after lots of analyzing and comparing is Quicken. Because I know the ins and outs of Quicken and other programs, I have a better-than-average feel for which programs work the way they're supposed to and save the most time. Quicken's the one. Quicken 5 for Windows really can help you gain control of your personal or business finances.

If you use the program in the simplest way, Quicken can maintain your check register for you by deducting payments and adding deposits to your checking account balance. No need for long-hand math or burdensome calculators and you certainly won't have to worry about overdrawing your checking account because you made an arithmetic error. But the real value in Quicken lies in all the other great things it can do for you, like:

- Printing checks in just minutes

- Balancing your checkbook

- Reminding you to pay bills

- Accumulating data in the form of reports and graphs

- Keeping track of your cash and credit card expenditures

- Tracking your outstanding loans

- Budgeting your income and expenses

- Helping you gather your income tax information

- Updating your investment portfolio

- Forecasting your cash flows

- Calculating college and retirement needs

- Storing your financial addresses

- Keeping your home inventory

- And much, much more

What's neat about Quicken is that you can do as little or as much as you want to do with it. At first, you may use just the basic features. As time goes on, you may want to ease into the rest as you become more comfortable with Quicken.

What do I need to use Quicken 5 for Windows?

Quicken 5 for Windows is developed for use with Microsoft Windows 3.1 or 3.11. Your new version of Quicken also runs under Windows 95 but may not be totally compliant with some of the features in this new operating system.

The screen shots throughout this book were shot in Windows 95. However, most of these screen shots will look the same in Windows 3.1. Any differences in functionality are pointed out throughout the book. Also, you will need extra equipment like a modem to use online banking and a printer to print out checks and reports.

What's new in Quicken 5 for Windows?

If you're already using an earlier version of Quicken, let me tell you what new things you can expect to do in this version:

- Keep your financial addresses handy in the new Financial Address Book
- Create the most common reports about your finances with EZ Reports
- Update your investment portfolio and get customized stock news and information with Online Investor
- Do your banking online (like download your statement, transfer funds between accounts, and download credit card transactions) with QuickBanking
- Pay bills online with QuickBillPay
- Inventory your household items with Quicken Home Inventory
- Print a report on a single page (no matter how big the report is)
- Use EasyStep to help you set up those difficult investment accounts
- Specify new investment transactions: transfer shares between accounts, change corporate names, deal with corporate securities spin-offs and acquisitions, record stock dividends
- Link a checking account to an investment account so that you can write checks
- Sort the Scheduled Transaction list by description, amount, or next date
- Manage your tax schedule assignments with the TaxLink Assistant
- Use EasyStep to set up loans
- Save multiple budgets
- Hide inactive accounts in the Account list
- Display Quicken Tips with useful information on how to use Quicken

What makes this book different?

You don't need an advanced degree in computer science, accounting, or finance to read this book. If you can tell the difference between the left and right mouse buttons and between income and expenses, you've got all the technical background you need.

It's written in plain English, too. I promise not to bury you in detailed explanations and three-letter acronyms (TLAs). After all, you're not studying for a degree in computer science—you're trying to get your finances in order, with the help of an incredibly powerful program like Quicken.

With Quicken, there may be more than one way to do something. If you're planning to become a Quicken expert, you'd expect this book to give you step-by-step instructions for each of them. Not this book.

In this book, I focus on results. That means I'll tell you the best way to get each job done. There might be three other ways to do the same thing, but for most people, most of the time, the technique I describe is the one that will get results most quickly.

By the way, there's no quiz at the end of this book. Hope you're not disappointed.

How do I use this book?

This isn't a textbook. You don't have to start at page 1 and read all the way to the end. It's not a mystery novel, either, so if you want to skip to the last chapter first, be my guest.

You'll probably be surprised at some of the things that Quicken can do for you. That's why, if you have the time, it's worth flipping through the chapters, looking at the headings, and searching out the references to the things you need to do. The people who published this book went to a lot of trouble to make sure that those interesting ideas would leap off the page and catch your attention as you browse.

This book will come in especially handy when you're not sure where to begin. And if you get stuck, you'll probably find the way out in these pages.

How this book is put together

Some people will use every last feature in Quicken. Others will spend most of their time doing the same simple tasks over and over again. It doesn't matter which type you are—you'll find exactly what you're looking for. You could look at this book as a tool to help you learn how Quicken 5 for Windows can help you manage your finances more effectively. The sections are divided into chapters that get into the specifics of the program. Inside each chapter, you'll find tips, hints, and step-by-step instructions for getting your work done faster without having to ask what to do next.

Part I: Getting Started with Quicken

Here, you learn what Quicken looks like when you start it and how to do some of the more basic tasks with the program, like using the check register, writing checks, and balancing your checkbook. Find out where to get help and how to quit when your work is done.

Part II: Saving Time with Quicken

Want to really zip through your financial tasks? Come here to see all the neat shortcuts in Quicken that will make your life easier. See how minicalendars, minicalculators, and QuickFill help you fill fields with a click or a few keystrokes, while memorized and scheduled transactions help you fill in entire transactions.

Part III: Organizing Your Finances

Organization is what it's all about. Here, you'll learn how to be more organized than you ever thought possible. Once you're through this part you'll be tracking your cash expenditures, be right on top of those credit cards, and managing your debts. And don't forget about putting together a budget so that you know exactly where your hard-earned money is going.

Part IV: Analyzing Your Finances

Here's some good stuff that will help you quantify your financial situation and put it all in perspective. Managing your investments, printing reports, and creating graphs are what I talk about in this part. I also cover how to be ready, willing, and able at tax time.

Part V: Planning for the Future

"Live for today" may be your motto, but you've got to plan for the future if you hope to send those kids to college and retire while you can still punch the keys on your keyboard. Want to see your future cash flows? Want to see how much you need to sock away now to send little Ali to college? How about that investment you made in the 80's; how's it doing now?

Part VI: Managing Quicken and Banking Online

You really should keep your Quicken system neat and tidy. Don't let old files hang around and clutter up your program. Come here to learn how to manage your Quicken files and prevent any accidental loss of data; backups and passwords are the key. Can you change the way Quicken works and looks? Sure you can. Go ahead, change the screen color, register size, iconbar, and lots more.

Quicken's really keeping up with the times with its new online features. Take an adventure in QuickBanking or Online Investor for a real thrill.

Special book elements

This book has a number of special elements and conventions to help you find information quickly—or skip stuff you don't want to read right now.

 TIP **Tips either point out information often overlooked in the** documentation, or help you use your software more efficiently, like a shortcut. Some tips help you solve or avoid problems.

Sidebars are interesting nuggets of information

Sidebars provide interesting, nonessential reading, side-alley trips you can take when you're not at the computer or when you just want some relief from "doing stuff." Here you may find more technical details, funny stories, personal anecdotes, or interesting background information.

Cautions alert you to potentially dangerous consequences of a procedure or practice, especially if it could cause serious or even disastrous results (such as loss or corruption of data).

 ### *What are Q&A notes?*

Cast in the form of questions and answers, these notes provide you with advice on ways to solve common problems.

 ### *Plain English, please!*

These notes explain the meanings of technical terms or computer jargon.

Throughout this book, we'll use a common to separate the parts of a pull-down menu command. For example, to open a another Quicken file, you'll choose <u>F</u>ile, <u>O</u>pen. That means "Pull down the File menu, and choose Open from the list."

The underscore keys are hot keys and can be used as shortcuts.

We also put new terms in bold.

And if you see two keys separated by a plus sign as Ctrl+X, that means to press and hold the first key, press the second key, then release both keys.

Part I: Getting Started with Quicken

1

Welcome to Quicken

● **In this chapter:**

- Okay, I'm ready to start Quicken

- How do I choose a start date?

- Ready to set up my first account

- I need to keep my new Quicken file organized

- Time to stop working. How do I quit Quicken?

Quicken's time-saving features will make you wonder how you ever existed without it . . . . **>**

You will quickly discover how easy Quicken is to use and then wonder why you waited so long to computerize your personal finances. What the microwave oven did for preparing dinner, Quicken does for managing your finances. If you haven't used Quicken before, you may spend a little up-front time getting all of your information in the system, but after that, you're going to sail through all your financial tasks.

Your start date is important

So, you've decided to start using Quicken for your finances. Good for you! Now you need to give some thought to the best time to convert to Quicken. The day you convert is the day you stop using your old long-hand methods and begin using Quicken.

So when are you going to take the plunge and put away your paper, pencil, and calculator? This is an important question. In the next few sections, I'll give you some things to think about. After that, I'll show you how to start your program and what you need to do to start Quicken 5 for Windows.

 TIP   If you're just going to use Quicken to help you maintain your checkbook and print checks, the conversion date is not important. You can start using it at any time. But if you want Quicken to summarize your income and expenses, to help you with your budget, or to accumulate your tax deductions, you need a clean accounting cutoff point. From the cutoff date forward, Quicken handles all your financial information. Before the cutoff date, your manual system takes precedence.

Converting from your manual system to Quicken

Ideally, try to start using Quicken on January 1. This way you have a clean fiscal-year start. From January 1 on you will have all your income and expenses recorded in one place. But realistically, this timing probably doesn't work. It may be June 15 and you're ready to start now! Well, that's okay, too. You can start Quicken anytime you want, just try to pick a natural cutoff date that makes switching from your manual system to Quicken easy. A natural cutoff date might be the ending date of your last bank statement or the first day of the month. If it is June 15, you could start on June 1 and enter those transactions that have transpired between June 1 and June 15, or you could wait until July 1 to start; whichever works best for you.

If you can't start at the beginning of the year, try starting at the beginning of a month. That way you can stop your manual records at the end of one month and start Quicken at the start of the next. Combining the two at the end of the year is then a breeze.

Avoiding common errors when converting to Quicken

Okay, you've decided that on March 1 you're going to switch from your manual system to Quicken. You're already looking forward to stepping off the financial paper trail, and you'll be glad you did! But you want to make sure all your tracks are covered, so you need to keep a few things in mind.

One error that you might make when you start using Quicken and stop using your manual system is you may record the same transaction twice. If March 1 is your start date, you'll want to start using Quicken from March 1 on. However, you might have already recorded a couple transactions in your manual checkbook register that are dated March 1. Don't record those in Quicken, too.

Also avoid the common pitfall of not recording a transaction in Quicken that's dated March 1 because you think it's already in your manual register.

A thorough review of your transactions is the only way to avoid these errors. Make sure that all of your check numbers are accounted for. If your manual system stops at check 1234, make sure that all checks up to that number are also recorded in your manual system. Then, start with check 1235 in Quicken.

I'm ready to start the program now

The kids are in bed, the coffee's on, your checkbook register is sitting next to your computer, and you're ready to get to work with Quicken. If you haven't installed Quicken on your computer, you need to do that first. If Quicken's already on your computer, all you need to do is start it. You'll start the program in one of two ways, depending on whether you are running Quicken in Windows 95 or Windows 3.1.

TIP **If you already have an earlier version of Quicken on your** computer and you have created some files, you don't have to do much to start using Quicken 5. When you install Quicken, the program looks for any existing Quicken files and asks whether you want to convert them to the new version. Select <u>Y</u>es to convert your old Quicken files and you're ready to go in Quicken 5. When you start the program, Quicken 5 starts and opens the last file that you worked in. To learn how to open a different file, see Chapter 23.

I'm working in Windows 95

If you're running Windows 95, open the Start menu and choose <u>P</u>rograms (see fig. 1.1). Notice that your Programs menu will probably look different than mine, but if you've installed Quick 5 for Windows correctly, you should see Quicken. Choose Quicken and then select Quicken 5.

Fig. 1.1
When you click Start in Windows 95 and then select <u>P</u>rograms, you see a list of program groups, or folders, from your computer's hard drive. Your Quicken 5 for Windows files are located in the Quicken Deluxe program folder.

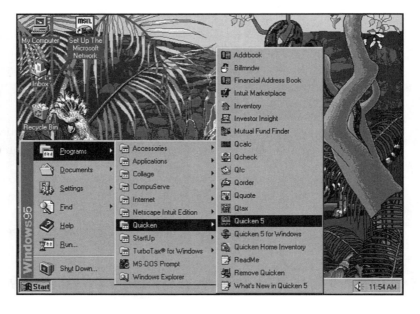

I'm working in Windows 3.1

For Windows 3.1 users, just double-click the Quicken icon from the Quicken Deluxe program group to start Quicken 5 for Windows.

I've never used Quicken before? What happens first?

If you've never used Quicken before, Quicken shows you the Quicken New User Setup dialog box. Figure 1.2 shows you what your screen looks like the first time. This dialog box helps you set up your first account (usually a checking account) in Quicken and choose the categories that you want to use. (Categories are explained in Chapter 4, "Tracking Income and Expenses with Categories.")

Fig. 1.2
Quicken shows you the New User Setup dialog box if you've never used the program before. From here you can set up your first account and choose which categories you want to use.

Here's where you start. You'll see the first EasyStep window that will get you started setting up your first account

You'll name your account and enter the starting date and balance for your account in the EasyStep windows displayed under this tab

Click this tab to review the account and categories that you set up in your Quicken file

This tab lets you select the categories that you'll use in your Quicken file

At the top of the Quicken New User Setup dialog box, you see four tabs with the topics that you need to go through as you're setting up Quicken for the first time. Since you've obviously already started the program, you've covered the Start topic so the Start tab is checked. You will work your way through the setup process by clicking each of the remaining tabs in turn and following the instructions.

Quicken displays a series of dialog boxes that help you walk through the things that you need to do to get Quicken set up the first time. Here's what's going to happen. First you'll set up an account to use (usually a checking account). You can't do anything in Quicken until you've got at least one account to work in. When you set up the account, you'll give it a name, enter the start date, and account balance. Finally, you'll choose how you're going to organize transactions in your new Quicken file.

Setting up your first account

You can't use Quicken until you've set up your first account. The first account that you set up is usually a bank or checking account. Because you're new to Quicken, you get a lot of help in setting up this account. Quicken displays a series of windows that prompt you for the information it needs to set up your account.

When you're ready to set up your first account, click the Bank Account tab in the Quicken New User Setup dialog box (refer to fig. 1.2). Now you'll see the first in a series of windows that Quicken displays to help you set up your account.

As you go through these windows, you

- Enter a name for your new account.

- Tell Quicken the start date for the account. This usually coincides with the ending statement date from your last bank statement.

- And finally, enter the account balance from your last bank statement.

This is all of the information that Quicken needs to set up an account.

 TIP   **After you've set up your first account, you'll be able to set up** others as you might need. In Chapter 3, I explain more about what accounts are, how they're used in Quicken, and how to set up more accounts.

Naming your new account

When you see the window with the Account Name box, (see fig. 1.3) type a name for your account. You can call it "Checking" or use the bank name, like "First National." Just remember that you can only use up to 15 characters and you can't use these characters in the name:

:][/? | ^

Fig. 1.3
Name your new account anything that you want, but you can only use up to 15 characters.

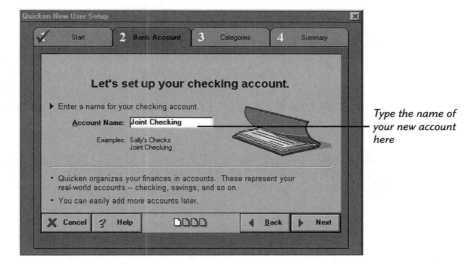

Type the name of your new account here

Now, click the Next button and then decide whether you're going to use the information from your last bank statement to set up your new account.

Do I use my bank statement information?

The date on your bank statement probably won't be January 1, or the first day of any month, for that matter. In this case, you won't use the account balance from your statement as the starting balance in the account. Instead, you'll use the balance shown in your manual checkbook register as of January 1 or the first of the month that you're starting.

If you haven't kept your manual checkbook up-to-date, well, you're like most people (at least those who aren't CPA's). No big deal. Use your last bank statement date and balance as the starting point for your new account, then bring Quicken up-to-date. Just enter in Quicken all uncleared transactions from your last bank statement.

TIP **Entering uncleared transactions is not difficult and not much** different than entering other transactions in Quicken. After you read Chapter 5, "Introducing the Quicken Registry," you'll know exactly how to enter any type of transaction, whether current or past.

So, if you're going to use the information from your last bank statement, select Yes and then click the Next button and you're ready to enter the bank statement date and account balance.

If you're going to use some other date, select No and then Next to continue.

Entering your account statement date and balance

The window in figure 1.4 is where you enter your account statement date and balance if you decided to use the information from your last bank statement. Enter the ending statement date in the Ending Statement Date box. Dates are entered in the MM/DD/YY format. So, August 16, 1995 is entered as **081695** (you don't have to enter the slashes).

Fig. 1.4
Use the information from your last bank statement to enter the starting date and account balance for your new account.

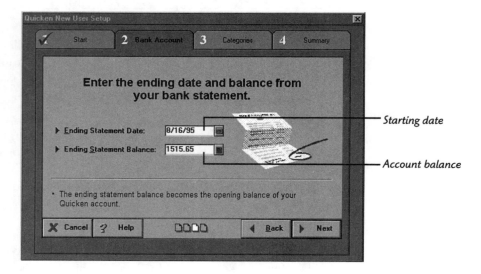

Now move to the Ending Statement Balance box and type the account balance shown on your last bank statement. Type the amount using the decimal point to separate dollars and cents, but no commas; for example, **1515.65**.

If you're not using the information from your last bank statement to start your account, Quicken automatically uses today's date and a $0.00 balance for your account. But don't panic, before you finish setting up your account, you'll get a chance to enter the date and account balance you want.

How should I organize my transactions?

After you've named your account and entered the starting date and account balance, select the Categories tab so that you can choose the categories that you want to use. Quicken gives you a little editorial on the importance of categories (believe me, they really are important!). Then, click Next until you get to the window that you see in figure 1.5. If you're using Quicken strictly for your personal finances, choose I Want Home Categories Only. But maybe you want to combine your personal and business finances into one Quicken file. If so, choose the I want both Home and Business Categories option.

Fig. 1.5
Quicken includes two predefined category lists; one for home use and one for home and business use. Choose which category you'd like to use in your new Quicken file.

Plain English, please!

You're probably wondering what **categories** are. A category describes and summarizes your income and expenses and tells you where your money comes from and how you're spending it—an important part of organizing finances.

Categories are simple to use. You can, for example, group your electric and water bills in a category called Utilities. Then at any time you can review all your utility bills by reviewing the Utility category.

There's a list of categories for home use and a list for business use. If you're using Quicken strictly for your personal finances, choose Home categories. If you want to use Quicken to keep the books for your small business, choose Business categories. Or, if you want to combine your personal and business finances into one Quicken file, you can choose both Home and Business categories.

Make sure everything is correct

Click the Summary tab in the Quicken New User Setup dialog box to see a summary of the information that you entered for your account (see fig. 1.6). If all your account information is correct, click the Done button. If not, move to the box with the wrong information and correct it.

If you didn't use the information from your last bank statement, this is the time for you to enter a new date and account balance. Just move to the Statement Date box and type in a new date and then go to the Ending Balance box to enter a different date. Then click Done to set up your new account.

Fig. 1.6
Review your new account information carefully. Now is the time to make changes to your new account information.

It's time to quit

I know you're just getting into working with Quicken, but eventually you have to quit and fix dinner, play ball with the kids, or just go to bed. When you're ready to quit, just select File, Exit and Quicken automatically saves your work in the current file.

2

Learning the Quicken Ropes

● **In this chapter:**

● **What's in a Quicken window?**

● **Learn how to do things in Quicken**

● **Move around in Quicken**

● **Where do I go for Help?**

Get comfortable with Quicken. Take a few minutes to explore Quicken and feel your way around . . . . ●

I f you're a new computer user, there may be a lot of components to the Quicken screen you need to familiarize yourself with. You're in the right place. This chapter describes everything you see on your screen and shows you how to get where you want to go.

Even if you've used computers before but have never used Quicken, a quick review of this chapter will make you a more confident user.

Now, how do I do things in Quicken?

So you've got the Quicken application window on your screen, what do you do now? There's a lot of activities that you can perform in Quicken, like writing checks, entering transactions in registers (like your checkbook register), balancing your checking account, setting up a budget, and so on. But before you can do any of these things, you need to tell Quicken what you want to do. Quicken is kind of like your chauffeur—it'll take you anywhere you want to go once you decide where that is.

The elements you saw in the Quicken application window (like the menu bar and the iconbar) will help you perform activities. But you can use special key combinations on your keyboard, too.

What do I do with these menus?

The main menu bar you see at the top of your application window is simply a list of choices you have while working in Quicken. When you choose something from the Quicken main menu bar, a pull-down menu appears (see fig. 2.1).

Think of the main menu bar as a long curtain rod with each individual menu hanging from it in a neat line. Each menu unrolls like an old-fashioned window shade to reveal the list of choices underneath. Getting to a pull-down menu is easy—just point to one of the menu items on the Quicken main menu bar and click the left mouse button to unfurl it.

Let's see what's in the Quicken application window

Like all other Windows programs, Quicken has a lot of different windows you can work in and have open at the same time. These windows are displayed within a bigger application window that shows the same things all the time. All the elements in the Quicken application window are there to help you perform tasks and work faster.

*The **Title bar** tells you the name of the application (or program), the file that you're currently in, and the name of the active window. Here, Quicken 5 for Windows is the active program, QDATA is the current file and HomeBase is the active window.*

In most windows, you'll see these handy buttons. The GoTo button lets you quickly move to other areas in Quicken, click Help to get assistance in the current window, and select the Iconbar button to enlarge the current window by hiding the iconbar.

Windows that you open in Quicken are shown beneath the iconbar, like the HomeBase window here.

If this button is flashing, then you've got some things to do in Quicken, like checks to print, bills to pay, or notes to review in your calendar.

*As with all windows programs, the Title bar contains **minimize, maximize (or restore)** and **close buttons**. Note that if you're working in Windows 3.1, these buttons will look different.*

*The **iconbar** includes (you guessed it) icons, or little pictures, that you use to select tasks or activities that you would normally select from a menu.*

*The Quicken **main menu bar** includes 10 different menus that you can choose from to do your work.*

Fig. 2.1
Everything you could possible want to do in Quicken, you can do from a pull-down menu. Use the File menu, for example, to open a file, start a new file, or even to back up a file.

66 *Plain English, please!*

A **file** is where Quicken stores your data. Quicken assigns a file name to each file. The file added to Quicken when you start it for the first time is named QDATA. Each of your Quicken files is stored in the directory (or folder) where you installed Quicken (such as C:\QUICKENW). 99

Main menu items or choices are fixed; that is, the available choices remain the same, no matter what you're doing in Quicken. Every time you start Quicken you see the same menu items—File, Edit, Activities, Lists, Reports, Plan, Add-Ons, Online, Window, and Help. Sometimes, however, the choices on a pull-down menu vary, depending on what you have selected or the activity you're performing.

Q&A *My mouse works, but I prefer the keyboard. How can I make menu choices without a mouse?*

Press the Alt key and the underlined letter of a menu name to open a menu or highlight a command. (To choose a menu that doesn't have an underlined letter, press the Alt key, press an arrow key to highlight the menu, and then press Enter.) Press the down arrow to move the highlight down the list of commands in a menu. Press Enter to choose the command, or Esc to close a menu.

TIP **Anything you can do in Quicken, you can do with the help of a**
menu. It might not always be the fastest way, but it's guaranteed to work. If
you're ever stumped at how to get a particular job done in Quicken, your
best bet is to look on every menu you can find—sooner or later, you'll find
the command you're looking for.

Sometimes, choosing a menu item does something right away. If you choose
Edit, Void Transaction, for example, the current transaction is immediately
voided. But sometimes a menu choice does nothing at all. You can point and
click until your finger falls off and nothing happens. What's going on? You've
stumbled on a menu choice that's temporarily unavailable. (Unavailable
menu items appear dimmed.) Maybe you selected Edit, Stop Payment and
nothing happens. That's because this menu choice is available only if you
have set up Quicken to pay bills electronically. If you haven't done this, you
can't, nor don't need to, use this menu item.

When you select a menu item followed by …(an ellipsis), a dialog box pops
up with more choices for you to make. For example, when you choose Edit,
Options, the Options dialog box pops up. Obviously, from here you can make
choices about the options you want to use in Quicken. When you select a
menu item followed by an arrow, a sub-menu appears with additional options.

Hey, I don't want these menus on my screen anymore! Well, get rid of them
by clicking the menu item in the main menu bar or press Esc twice.

These icons sure make Quicken easier to use

The row of icons, or pictures, that you see under the main menu bar is called
the **iconbar**. This row of icons represents some of the more common windows and activities you'll be using in Quicken. Clicking an icon to select a
window or activity is quicker and easier than going through the menu.
Although quicker, the end result is still the same.

Want to access the Account List? You can just click the Accts icon in the
iconbar and Quicken instantly displays the Account List on your screen.
Selecting Lists, Accounts does the same thing. If you really like using your
keyboard, you won't be able to use the iconbar; it's mouse-operated only.

Plain English, please!

An **icon** is a graphic image or picture that represents a Quicken window, list, or activity. Clicking an icon instantly opens a window, list, or performs an activity. **99**

Here are the icons that Quicken puts in your iconbar by default:

The icon	What it means in plain English
Registr	Display the register for the current account
Accts	Access the Account List
Recon	Start reconciling the current account
Reports	Put together a report
Online	Do your banking online
Calendar	Show the Financial Calendar
QFNet	Access Quicken's Financial Network
AddrBk	Look up something in the Address Book
Investr	Track your stocks with Investor Insight
Inventry	Inventory your household belongings
MutualF	Use the Mutual Fund Finder
Help	Give me some HELP!

If you can't see all of the icons in your iconbar, click the arrow buttons on each end of the iconbar to move the bar right or left.

 TIP **When you're using Quicken, you may find that you'd like other** activities and windows represented as icons so that you can choose them quicker. No problem. You can take out some of the existing icons and put in your own. And if you don't like the iconbar at all, you can delete it from your screen altogether. Take a look at Chapter 24 to find out how to change the iconbar.

I can use quick keys, too

If you want to use your keyboard to select a menu item or perform an activity, you can use **Quick keys**. Quick keys are a combination of two keys; usually the Ctrl, Alt, or Shift key with a letter key. To use a quick key, press and hold the first key while you press the second key. If I tell you to use a quick key to get something done, I'll show you the two keys separated by a "+", like Ctrl+A. Here are the quick keys you can use:

Quick key	What it does
Ctrl+A	Displays the Account List
Ctrl+B	Backs up the current file
Ctrl+C	Shows the Category & Transfer List
Ctrl+D	Deletes a transaction or account
Ctrl+E	Edits a transaction or account
Ctrl+F	Finds a transaction
Ctrl+H	Starts to set up a loan
Ctrl+I	Inserts a transaction
Ctrl+J	Displays the Scheduled Transaction List
Ctrl+K	Brings up the Financial Calendar
Ctrl+L	Displays the Class List

continues

Continued

Quick key	What it does
Ctrl+M	Memorizes a transaction
Ctrl+N	Starts a new transaction or account
Ctrl+O	Opens a file
Ctrl+P	Prints
Ctrl+R	Goes to the register
Ctrl+T	Recalls a memorized transaction
Ctrl+U	Switches to the Portfolio View
Ctrl+V	Voids a transaction
Ctrl+W	Goes to the Write Checks window
Ctrl+X	Goes to a transfer transaction
Ctrl+Y	Displays the Security List
Alt+Backspace	Undoes the last edit
Shift+Del	Deletes a transaction and puts it in the Clipboard
Ctrl+Ins	Copies a transaction to the Clipboard
Shift+Ins	Pastes a transaction to the Clipboard
F1	Gives you help on the current window or menu item

How do I get around in Quicken?

Getting around in Quicken is fast and easy. You can go from field to field, activity to activity, or window to window using several different "modes of transportation." It's like getting around in New York City. You may walk to get from place to place, but if you're going very far you'll take a taxi or the subway. (Certainly, getting around in Quicken is a lot easier than getting around in New York!)

Quicken provides several different "modes of transportation" through the program. Take a ride through Quicken using your mouse, the keyboard, new QuickTabs, and Quicken's HomeBase system.

Let's mouse around

As with any Windows-based program, using your mouse to move around and select menu items or activities is usually more efficient than using the keyboard. (Sometimes, however, using a combination of the mouse and keyboard makes sense.) The most important thing to remember when you use your mouse is to move the mouse pointer to the item that you want to choose first. In other words, make sure that the mouse pointer (that little arrow on your screen) is pointing to the menu item, icon, or transaction you want to choose. Once the pointer is where you want it, here's what you do next:

- *Click*. Selects an item or moves to where the mouse pointer (cursor) is pointing.

- *Double-click*. Also selects an item or enlarges a window or icon back to its original size.

- *Drag*. (Hold down the left button and move the mouse on your desk or mouse pad). Picks up an item, like an icon, and moves it. Dragging your mouse also highlights text so that you can move it.

How do I use my keyboard to travel?

You also can navigate your way around in Quicken using the keyboard. If you like using your keyboard, use these keys to move:

Which key to press	Where you go
←	One space left in a field
→	One space right in a field
↑	Previous transaction
↓	Next transaction
Page Up	Transaction at the top of the register window
Page Down	Blank transaction at the bottom of the register
Home	Beginning of current field
End	End of current field

continues

Continued

Which key to press	Where you go
Home (three times)	First transaction in the register
Ctrl+End	Blank transaction at the bottom of the register
Tab	Next field
Enter	Records the current transaction; moves to the next transaction

Move through open windows fast with QuickTabs

Want to move to the Write Checks window or the register or any other open window? Just click one of the new QuickTabs to get there. Each time you open a window, Quicken puts a QuickTab on the left side of your screen to represent that window. Figure 2.2 shows that you have several open windows you can quickly access by clicking a QuickTab.

Fig. 2.2
Use a QuickTab to go to any open window in Quicken.

QuickTabs

Q&A *What if I don't want or need QuickTabs on my screen?*

If you'd rather use the standard Windows method to activate open windows in Quicken, you can get rid of the QuickTabs by selecting one of the General Options that turns QuickTabs off. And, if you'd rather have open windows overlap each other on your screen, you can select another General Option that switches the QuickTabs function from one window shown at a time to multiple windows. You learn how to overlap windows later in this chapter and setting General Options is covered in Chapter 24.

TIP You can rearrange the order your QuickTabs are in by dragging a tab to where you want it and then releasing the mouse button. Quicken then rearranges the other tabs accordingly.

I want quick and easy access to Quicken tasks

Worried about getting lost once you're in Quicken territory? Don't be. If you're feeling a little uncertain, use Quicken's HomeBase system that gives you quick and easy access to most commonly used tasks and features.

To get to HomeBase click the HomeBase QuickTab in the left margin of your screen (refer to fig. 2.2). (Notice that the HomeBase QuickTab is always present in the left margin, even if you've closed all other Quicken windows.) Figure 2.3 shows what the HomeBase window looks like.

Fig. 2.3
Want easy access to Quicken's most commonly used tasks and features? Use HomeBase.

HomeBase QuickTab

Activity buttons

Exit button

With HomeBase open, choose an activity by clicking one of the buttons in the HomeBase window. To open and work in your list of accounts, click Account List; to open your check register, click Register, and so on. If you want a quick run down on Quicken's handy features and tools, click the feature Explorer button.

How do I work with all these windows?

If you don't really need a window open right now, click the Close button. If a window or list doesn't have a close button, double-click the Control menu box (in the upper left corner of a window's title bar). If you want to close all of the open windows, choose Window, Close All Windows.

Want to see some of each window that's open? You can make open windows more visible as you're working, by **cascading** them. To cascade windows, though, you first have to get rid of the QuickTabs on your screen. Remove QuickTabs by selecting the Options button, then General, and then click the Turn Quick Tabs Off option. When you click OK to save your option setting, you won't see QuickTabs anymore.

Now you can cascade your open windows. When you cascade windows, Quicken stacks them together in an overlapping manner. Just enough of each window still shows so you can see what it is. For example, if you're working in the register and want to write a check, you can cascade the two windows so that you always see a little of the inactive window. When you cascade windows, the window that's on top is the active window, or the one that you can currently work in. To cascade windows, choose Window, Cascade.

And if you do have any of your windows reduced to icons and want them in order at the bottom of your screen, just choose Window, Arrange Icons.

 TIP **If you're a creature of habit and would like to have the same** windows open in a particular order each time that you start Quicken, you can save your desktop (the arrangement of open windows). To learn how to do this, see Chapter 24.

Time to get a little help

Quicken's a pretty easy program to use, but there are going to be times when you have some trouble figuring out how to use a feature or what to do next. You can get all the help you need from this book, of course, but if you want online help from Quicken, there's lots available.

Here's a list of the types of help that you can get from Quicken:

Help available	What you get
QuickTour	Gives you a general overview of Quicken
Qcards	On-screen cues to help you complete a task
Quicken Tips	Hints on useful features in Quicken
Quicken Help	Library of helpful reference material on Quicken

And just to help you with Help, here's a brief look at what you'll find when you go to use it.

Let's take a QuickTour

Don't worry about getting up early to catch the tour bus. You can take a QuickTour anytime you want a brief, online tutorial of Quicken. If you're a new user, this tour is helpful because it gives a general overview of what Quicken can do and how it works. If you want a more specific tour (you really want to see how some of Quicken's features work), you can select from the eight different areas that you see in the QuickTour window in figure 2.4. When you select Balancing Your Checkbook, for example, the QuickTour takes you through the steps involved in completing this task.

Fig. 2.4
Take a QuickTour
anytime you feel like it
to get the rundown on
Quicken.

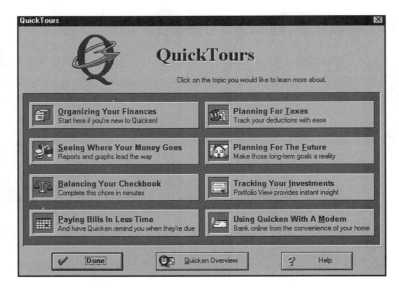

To start QuickTour, choose Help, QuickTours. When the QuickTour window
appears (refer to fig. 2.4), just click the topic or activity that you want to
know more about and the QuickTour begins. Click the Quicken Overview
button at the bottom for a summary of Quicken's major features. While
you're "touring" through Quicken you'll see a Next button at the bottom of
each window that you can click to move to the next window. If at any time
you want to cancel your tour, click the Cancel button at the bottom of each
window.

Qcards can give you a lot of help

Get on-screen cues from Quicken with Qcards. You've probably already seen
some of these cards pop up on your screen as you've been moving around in
Quicken windows. By default, Quicken assumes that you want to use these
Qcards and turns them on when you install the program. Don't worry
though—if they start to bug you they can be turned off.

Figure 2.5 shows you the Qcard that appears when you start to enter a
transaction in the register. This card stays on your screen until you perform
the action that it's telling you to. Then a new card appears with new instructions for the next action that you need to take. If you don't want to see the
card anymore, click the x box in the upper left corner, and then tell Quicken
if you want to turn Qcards off completely for this particular window.

Fig. 2.5
This Qcard tells you how to enter the date for a transaction in the register. Another Qcard appears after you've entered the date correctly and moved to the next field in the register.

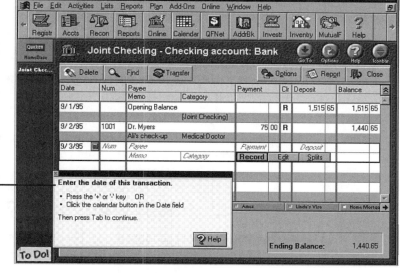

Qcard for entering a transaction date

If you don't ever want to see another Qcard again, turn them completely off by selecting Help, Show QCards.

These Quicken tips sure are helpful

Quicken 5 has a new feature that gives you a "tip of the day" each time that you start Quicken. Tips cover features of the program and hints for how to do things faster and easier. You might get a tip, for example, on how to find items in lists by pressing the first letter of the item that you want to find or how to enter dates in the register quickly by using the + and – keys.

Figure 2.6 shows a typical tip. Your tip, however, will probably be different. After you've read your tip, choose Done to remove it from your screen.

Fig. 2.6
Read Quicken tips for some great advice (straight from the source) on how to save time while you're working.

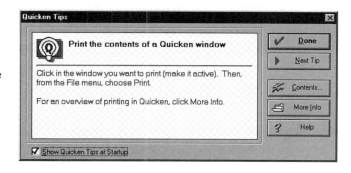

Anytime you want to see another Quicken tip while you're working, select Help, Quicken Tips. The Quicken Tips window opens with a new tip for you to read. If you want to read some more tips, click Next Tip.

Q&A   *I like these Quicken Tips, but I'd like to turn them off so I don't see them every time I start Quicken. Can I do this?*

You sure can. See the Show Quicken Tips at Startup checkbox at the bottom of the Quicken Tips window in figure 2.6 Just click the checkbox to remove the checkmark and Quicken Tips no longer appears when you start Quicken.

How does Quicken Help work?

As long as Quicken has been running under Windows, it's had a Help system that you're used to seeing in other Windows-based programs. Quicken Help assists with menu commands and options, provides definitions of terms that may not be familiar to you, explains how Quicken does things (like writing checks, printing, balancing your checkbook, and so forth), and gives you tips for using the program more efficiently.

There's an extensive library of helpful reference material in Quicken, mostly stored in the Help window. To access the Help window, select Help, Quicken Help. The information included in the Help window relates to the active window or menu item when help was selected. Figure 2.7 shows the Help window that's displayed when you ask for help from the Category & Transfer List.

  TIP   **Click the Help icon or press F1 to access the Help window.**

Fig. 2.7
You can find out a lot about Quicken and how to perform tasks in the Quicken Help window.

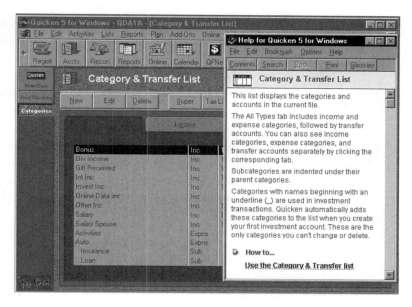

The information included in the Help window often includes additional topics you can select to see even more information. These topics appear in green and when you point to them with your mouse, the pointer changes shape to a pointed finger. To see additional information, point to the topic and click.

If you're unable to find the topic that you need help with, click the Search button and then enter the topic in the Search window (see fig. 2.8), or search through the list of topics.

Fig. 2.8
Every topic you would ever need to know about in Quicken is listed in the Search window

Once you're feeling Quicken-smart, close the Help window by selecting <u>F</u>ile, E<u>x</u>it (from the menu in the Help window), or click the Close button.

 TIP   **If there's too much help information to read on-screen, you can** print it by clicking the <u>P</u>rint button in the Help window.

 TIP   **Want to see some tips that Intuit has put together to solve** common problems that Quicken users have? At the bottom of most Help windows, click Troubleshooting topic (in green) to see a list of troubleshooting questions that relate to the Help topic that you're in.

Using Accounts to Store Your Transactions

● **In this chapter:**

- Figure out what all this talk about accounts is

- Add a new account

- Make some changes to an account

- Delete those accounts that you don't use anymore

- Hide an account in your account list

- Put your accounts in order

- Work with multiple accounts

Everybody's talking about the "Quicken" thing, so you just can't wait. Learn a few things about accounts first and you're on your way. . . . . ⊛

Accounts, accounts, accounts! Why do I keep talking about accounts? We're not setting up a bank here, are we? No, but from real life you already know about accounts, like checking accounts, savings accounts, credit card accounts (you know, VISA, MasterCard, American Express), brokerage accounts, and so on. You use these kinds of accounts in Quicken to keep track of your transactions. And don't forget about mortgages and car loans that also are accounts that represent our liabilities. You have to keep track of transactions in those accounts, too.

> ❝ *Plain English, please!*
>
> A **transaction** is any "action" you take that changes how much money you have or changes the value of things you own (like your house or any other investment). When you go to the bank machine to take out $20 for a movie and popcorn, that's a transaction because it changes how much money you have in your bank account. Or, when you spend $2,000 to add that new patio, that's a transaction because you changed the value of your house. ❞

What are accounts and how do I use them?

You set up your first bank account in Chapter 1. But you probably need many more accounts if you want to stay completely on top of your finances.

Here are the types of accounts that you can use in Quicken:

- **Checking account.** You're going to use this account to write checks. You should have set up this account in Chapter 1.

- **Credit Card account.** Even though your grandparents never use credit cards, you do. So Quicken lets you set up accounts to keep track of your purchases (no matter how frivolous), payments, and those dreaded finance charges. Flip to Chapter 14 for more on credit card accounts.

- **Money Market account.** If you keep cash in a money market account, keep track of it in—what else—a Quicken Money Market account. You can even write checks from this account. Money market accounts are set up the same way as other bank accounts, so stick with this chapter to learn more.

- **Asset account.** We all own something, right? So use this account to keep track of it—a house, a car, a boat, whatever. Chapter 13 tells you everything you need to know about asset accounts.

- **Savings account.** Whether you save your money under the mattress or at a bank, the savings account tells you how much you've socked away. Keep reading this chapter for more.

- **Cash account.** Reach into your pocket. There's probably some cash there right now. Well, don't forget about keeping track of it. Read Chapter 13 to see how.

- **Investment account.** These accounts are not for those who have weak stomachs. Venture into these accounts at your own risk; they're deep and a little confusing. For you risk-takers, use them to track your stocks, bonds, and mutual funds. Proceed cautiously to Chapter 17.

- **Liability account.** Admit it. You aren't without debt. We all have some. And Quicken's not going to let you forget it. Liability accounts help you keep track of your debts so that you know how much money you owe. Proceed to Chapter 15 to learn about amortized loans and liability accounts for unamortized loans.

 Plain English, please!

Liabilities are debts, or the money that you're "liable" for. If you buy a house and don't have enough money to pay for the whole thing (and who does!), you pay what you can (that's called a down payment) and borrow the rest (take out a mortgage). The mortgage is a liability because as long as you have the house in your possession, you are liable to the mortgage holder for the amount that you borrowed.

 But I don't want to use all of these accounts you keep talking about. All I want to do is use Quicken to print checks and balance my checking account.

You can use Quicken any way you want. You don't have to set up any other account if you don't want to. Quicken works with one account or as many as 64. And to be honest, when I first started using Quicken, I used it just for my checking account. Heck, I used it for two years without even printing checks.

I'm merely suggesting that you get acquainted with these other accounts so that you can expand your use of Quicken to gain a complete picture of your financial situation.

Should I set up more accounts?

You already have a checking account set up in Quicken, right? You'll use this account to enter all of your checking account transactions, like checks, deposits, and withdrawals. And if you have more than one checking account, you guessed it, you can set up a Quicken account for each. You also can set up a Quicken account for each of your savings accounts, credit union accounts, money market accounts, and maybe even accounts for certificates of deposit (aka CDs).

Don't go crazy setting up accounts, though. If you don't have much activity in an account, don't bother to set it up. It really depends on how much detail you want Quicken to have.

I need to add an account

Accounts are easy to add. You can add them at any time on any day. Here, I'm going to show you how to add bank accounts that include checking, savings, and money market accounts.

Quicken's EasyStep feature makes adding accounts a breeze. With EasyStep, you just answer a series of questions to get your account going. It's like talking to an online interviewer who asks you questions about your account in a logical manner. When you're ready to set up an account, EasyStep is ready to help. This feature is always active, so you don't have to worry about turning it on or off. It's there to make your work in Quicken easier.

So now let's add a savings account. (You already set up a checking account in Chapter 1, so for variety, we'll add a savings account now). The first thing that you need to do to add an account is choose Activities, Create New Account. When you do this, Quicken displays the Create New Account window (see fig. 3.1).

Fig. 3.1

You can add eight different types of accounts in your Quicken file and have up to 64 in all.

Next, select the type of account you want to add. Because we're adding a savings account, click Savings. You should see the EasyStep Savings Account Setup window (see fig. 3.2). Notice the tabs at the top of the window: 1 Start, 2 Account, 3 Online, 4 Optional Info, and 5 Summary. These tabs represent the topics that need to be addressed (or types of questions that need to be answered) as you're setting up your account. After you complete the window in a tab, click Next or the next tab to proceed to the next step.

Obviously, you've started setting up your new account, so the Start tab is already selected. Just choose the Account tab (or click the Next button) to proceed.

How much am I worth?

Ever heard of "net worth" and wondered what it was or thought that it only applied to the Donald Trumps of the world? Well, not true. Everyone has a net worth (it just may not always be a positive number). Your **net worth** is the difference between the total assets that you own and your total debts. So if your only asset is a house, car, and some cash worth $100,000 and your total debts are $50,000, then second grade math says your net worth is $50,000.

Quicken can figure out your net worth. Just set up an account for each of your assets and each of your debts, print out a Net Worth report, and there you have it.

Fig. 3.2
Adding a new account in Quicken is simple with the help of EasyStep Account Setup windows like this.

Name that account

Now you're ready to name your new account and perhaps add a brief description (optional) about the account. As you see in figure 3.3, EasyStep shows you what you need to do here. So type the name you want for this account, such as **My Savings**, **Joint Savings**, or just **Savings**—whatever you want. The only restrictions are that the name can only have up to 15 characters (including spaces) and *cannot* include any of these characters:

$$\rightarrow :] [/ | \wedge$$

If you want to add a brief description about your account, you can enter that now.

What's in a name?

Remember that you have only 15 spaces for your account name. You'll probably have to use abbreviations if you want to use the bank name as your account name—First National Bank & Trust can be 1st National or First Nat'l. If you use shorter names, you also can add the last four digits of the account number. This helps if you have more than one account at the same bank so that you can distinguish your accounts more easily. For example, you might name three accounts at the same bank as follows:

1stNatl-Sav for a checking account

1stNatl-Chek for a savings account

1stNatl-MM for a money market account

Fig. 3.3
Enter any name you
want for your new
account but make sure
it's quickly recogniz-
able to you.

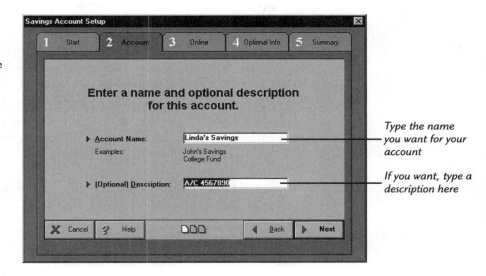

*Type the name
you want for your
account*

*If you want, type a
description here*

Enter your balance

Now click the Next button and tell Quicken if you have your last bank
statement. If you're going to use the balance from your last statement, select
Yes and then click the Next button so you can enter the ending statement
date and the ending balance as shown on your statement. If you're not using
the balance from your last statement, select No and then Next. Quicken will
use today's date as the starting date for your new account with a zero balance, but don't worry if this is not right. You can change the date and balance
when you get to the Summary window.

CAUTION **Don't use commas or dollar signs when you enter your bank**
account balance. If the balance for an account is zero, be sure to type **0**.
You can't leave the text box blank or Quicken will give you an error
message.

TIP **When you're entering your bank statement date, you see a little**
icon at the end of the text box. If you're wondering what this is, it's a minicalendar that you can click to see an on-screen calendar. When the
calendar is on-screen, you can click the date that you want to enter as the
Statement Date. In Chapter 7, I'll tell you more about the mini-calendar
and some other neat Quicken shortcuts.

Interested in banking online?

After you've entered the date and account balance for this new account, you can select the next tab, Online, where you tell Quicken whether you want to set up the account for online services, like QuickBanking or QuickBillPay. If you're not going to use these services, of course you can skip this. If you are, you'll need to specify which service, or both, you want to use and then provide the name of the financial institution, the routing number, the account number and type, and your Social Security number.

Q&A   ***What if I don't select these online options now? Can I do it later?***

Yes. You may not even know that you're going to use online services right now. That's OK. You can set up a bank account as a traditional account now, and then later change it to an online account by editing the account.

I want to keep track of some other bank information

To enter optional information about your account, you can click the Optional Info tab, select Yes, and then click the Next button. Figure 3.4 shows you the type of information you can add about your account.

Fig. 3.4
Here's all of the additional information you can enter about your new account.

This information is completely optional; only enter information that may be helpful to you later. When you're finished, click the Next button or the Summary tab.

Need to change anything?

When you're finished entering information about your new account, Quicken shows you two Summary windows that recap the information you just entered. The first Summary window shows the name, date, and account balance (see fig. 3.5). Review this Summary window carefully and make changes if you need to.

Fig. 3.5
Make sure all of the information about your account in the Summary window is correct. If it's not, change it here.

When you think the information in the first Summary window is correct, click Next. Then you see the second Summary window, where you're probably noticing that there's a Tax button but you didn't enter any tax information while you were setting up this account. This information is optional, but necessary, if you want to designate the earnings from the account as tax-deferred or if you want to designate a tax schedule to assign to transactions you enter in this new account. You learn about assigning tax schedules to accounts in Chapter 18.

After reviewing the second Summary window, click Done and you've just added a new account in Quicken.

Where can I see a list of all my accounts?

If you just added one new account or several new accounts, you may be wondering where you can go to see a list of all your accounts. Your accounts are all listed—in alphabetical order by account type—in the Account List. And you can see the Account List at any time by clicking the Accts icon in the icon bar or selecting Lists, Account. Figure 3.6 shows you what the Account List looks like.

You can make some
program changes by
clicking the Options button

Need Help in the
Account List?
Click this button

Fig. 3.6
All of your accounts
are listed in the
Account List.

Enlarge the Account
List window or
reduce it back to its
original size

The button bar
performs tasks in
the Account List

Click this button
to go to another
Quicken activity
or window

Use these tabs
to sort your
Account List by
account type

Do you want to see the
accounts that you've
hidden? If so, check here

Here's the total of
all your accounts in
the Account List

The button bar at the top of the Account List includes buttons you can use to work with accounts. You can use these buttons in place of the main menu to speed up your work. Instead of choosing Edit, New Account, you can click the New button in the button bar.

You can do all sorts of things to accounts from the Accounts List, like add a new account, edit an existing account, delete an account, sort the list, and even hide accounts that you don't want to show up in the list.

 TIP **If you need information fast, look at the Balance Total at the** bottom of the Account List. This is a quick way to view your net worth because this figure takes into account all your assets and liabilities and comes up with your current net worth. Looking at this figure eliminates the hassle of printing tons of reports.

Can I change an account?

You can change an account at any time. You can change the account name, description, any of the additional information you may have entered, tax schedule assignments, and activate or deactivate online services for an account. About the only thing that you really can't change about an account is its account type. For example, if you set up an account as a bank account, you can't change it to a credit card account or an investment account.

 CAUTION **If you discover that you set up an account as the wrong account** type, you'll need to delete the account and set it up again as the correct type. If you've already entered transactions in the account, however, you should first set up the new account and then copy the transactions to the new account register before you delete the incorrect account.

 If you need to edit an account, find the account in the Account List and click the Edit button in the button bar. Quicken displays the Edit Account window (similar to the Summary window that you saw in figure 3.5) with all the information that you can change for the account.

 TIP **If you only want to change some of the additional information you** entered for an account, just select the account and then click the Info button in the Account List button bar.

To make a change, move to the text box you want to edit and type over the existing characters. If you want to edit additional information, click the Info button; if you want to edit tax information, click the Tax button.

After you've made all your changes, click the Done button.

So, you don't want this account anymore

If you decide you don't want to track the transactions in an account anymore (or you've closed the account), you can delete accounts from your Account List.

CAUTION   **Be careful when deleting accounts. When you delete an account,** you delete all the transactions in that account. Obviously, if you've never used an account, it won't matter if you delete it.

So if you really want to delete an account, here's how:

1 Go to the Account List by clicking the Accts icon in the iconbar.

2 Find the account that you want to delete and click or highlight it.

3 Now click the <u>D</u>elete button from the Account List button bar.

4 Since deleting things is a serious matter in Quicken, you have to confirm that you really want to delete the account. Quicken displays a little warning box for you to confirm by typing **yes**. (If you change your mind, just click Cancel and Quicken will forget that you ever even thought about deleting this account.) Then click OK.

The account is instantly removed from your Account List. There will be no trace of this account left in your Quicken file—no account, no account register, and no transactions.

This account is inactive, but I don't want to get rid of it

In Quicken 5, you can hide accounts that you don't want to see in your Account List but you just can't part with. You're probably thinking that you're not so attached to any one account that you can't imagine when you'd need to use this feature. Well, how about when you've got some accounts that don't have any current activity but you don't want to delete them because they've got some past transactions that you want to keep. Or, maybe you want to hide some accounts to see how your Balance Total at the bottom of the Account List is affected without these accounts.

Whatever your reason, you can easily hide accounts from the Account List but still keep them in your Quicken file. To hide an account:

1 Select the account by clicking or highlighting it.

2 Then click the Hide button in the Account List button bar.

A message appears telling you this account will no longer be displayed unless you select the View Hidden Accounts checkbox at the bottom of the Account List. Click OK to hide the account. If the View Hidden Accounts checkbox is not checked, you won't see the account you just hid. If it is checked, you'll see the hidden account but there will be a little "black eight ball" next to the account name in the Account list to show that it's a hidden account.

If you don't want to hide an account anymore, just select the hidden account in the Account List and click the Hide button again to "unhide" it.

Putting your accounts in order

Quicken sorts your Account List alphabetically, by account type. Unless you specify otherwise, all of the account types are shown in your Account List. Bank accounts are listed first, followed by credit card accounts, then other account types like cash, asset, and liability account, and last, investment accounts.

If you'd rather have your Account List include only one account type, you can change the accounts shown in the list.

The tabs that you see below the Account List button bar let you decide which types of accounts are shown in the Account List. In figure 3.6, for example, all types of accounts are listed. So you see bank accounts, credit card accounts, a cash account, an asset account, and other liability accounts. But if you only want bank accounts to be listed, you can select the Bank tab and Quicken will hide all of the other accounts of other types and only list bank accounts. Sorting your Account List by type is helpful if you want to do a quick review of your accounts within each type. Or, if your list is too long, you may want to limit it to make it easier to find an account.

How do I work with all these accounts at once?

If you only have one account that you're using in Quicken, you never have to select which account you want to use. There's only one, so Quicken knows that it's the account you'll be using.

But what if you have lots of accounts? How does Quicken know which one you want to work in? Simple. You select the account in one of several ways.

If you're in the Account List, you just select the account from the list and click the Open button from the button bar. Quicken then opens the register for the account that you selected.

If you've been working in several accounts during your current work session in Quicken, then a QuickTab for each account that you've used appears in the left margin of your screen (remember, we talked about QuickTabs in Chapter 2). You then just click the QuickTab for the account that you want to work in.

Another way to choose to work in an account is to select the account from the Account selection bar in any register or the Write Checks window. Figure 3.7 shows the register for the Joint Checking account with the Account selection bar just below the transaction lines.

To select another account to work in, just click the button for that account from this bar. If you have a lot of accounts and all of them are not visible in the Account selection bar, click the scroll buttons at the ends of the bar to view the accounts that don't fit.

 TIP **You can rearrange the accounts in the Account selection bar so** that you always see the accounts you want to see. By default, Quicken arranges accounts by account type (just like they're arranged in the Account List). To switch account buttons, just drag (with the mouse, of course) the account you want to move to the spot where you want it. Then release the mouse button. If there are accounts that you use most often, you may want to rearrange the Account selection bar to group those accounts together so they show up on your screen all of the time.

Fig. 3.7
Each register in
Quicken has an
Account selection bar
so you can switch from
account to account
with just a click.

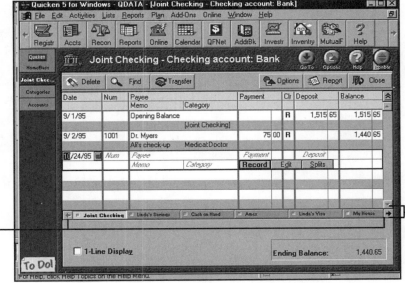

*All of your accounts are
arranged in this Account
selection bar.*

*Use these scroll
buttons to see
the accounts
that don't fit on
your screen.*

4

Tracking Income and Expenses with Categories

● **In this chapter:**

- ● **Find out what categories are and why they're important**

- ● **Figure out which categories you need**

- ● **Add a new category**

- ● **Add groups of categories at a time**

- ● **Get rid of categories you don't need**

- ● **See how subcategories work**

- ● **Shuffle the category list around**

- ● **Switch the category for transactions**

Categories are like electronic filing cabinets—use them to track everything you ever wanted to know about your money . . . . ▶

Do you stuff your receipts in envelopes or folders to differentiate all of the kinds of expenses you have? One envelope for utilities, one for groceries, one for entertainment, and so on. Well, get rid of that system and start using Quicken categories to track your income and expenses. Imagine having all of your expenses tracked in one place so that you can find out instantly how much you spent on clothes or dining out last month!

Sounds like a perplexing task, doesn't it? If I don't separate my receipts or fill out a multi-column ledger sheet, how can I possibly know how much I'm spending on utilities every year? Or, if I don't keep all of my dividend vouchers, how will I know how much dividend income I had last year?

Categories are just what you need. Using categories in Quicken makes it easy to track all your income and expenses. If you assign each transaction to a category, you know, at any given time, how much you're spending on everything. You know how much money you've made from that second job, how much interest income you've received, how much you're spending each month on clothing (or how much your spouse is spending), how much on dinner out, and so forth. These are the things we need to know if we're to gain control of our finances!

Why are categories important?

If there's one thing that I would advise you to use more than anything else in Quicken, it's categories. You can enter transactions in Quicken and not assign them to categories. But by doing this, you're really not using one of the real powers of Quicken. Categories group your income and expenses so that you always know exactly how much money you've made and from what source and how much money you've spent and on what.

By categorizing, Quicken can do the following difficult tasks:

- Break down checking account deposits and payments into groups of similar transactions so that you can summarize your income and expenses in reports and graphs

- Budget your income and expenses and then compare budgeted amounts with actual amounts

- Track and calculate your taxable income and tax-deductible expenses
- Project your future income and expenses

What categories should I have?

When you installed Quicken, you established your Quicken file with a set of categories. Quicken has two sets of categories already built into the program. One set of categories is strictly for home, or personal use. It has categories that you commonly use for your household finances, like Salary, Int Inc (for interest income), Childcare, Clothing, Entertain, Groceries, etc. Keep in mind that this is a general list of home categories and probably won't include every category you need. Don't worry, you can always add, delete, or change categories from the category list.

The other set of categories is for business. If you run a small business and want to use Quicken to keep the books for your company, there's a whole set of predetermined categories that you will find useful in business accounting. Some of the categories included in the business category set are Gr Sales (Gross Sales), Ads, Meals & Entertn, Office, Returns, and so forth.

If you're planning to keep your home finances and your business finances together in the same file, you can combine both sets of categories in your category list.

About the cash flowing in and out

Don't confuse all cash inflows as income. If you sell a stock, for example, the money that you receive is not income to you. Income from the sale is the difference between what you paid for the stock and what you sold it for (if the result is negative, you have a loss). Medical insurance reimbursements also aren't income; they just offset your medical expenses.

Sometimes, you might mistake the cash that you pay out as expenses. Money spent for the purchase of major assets, like cars, boats, or an addition to your home are not really expenses. These type of cash outflows are just transfers from one account (the account that you use to pay for the asset) to another (the account that you set up for the new asset).

CAUTION **I don't really recommend that you combine your home finances** with your business finances in the same Quicken file. It's better to set up a separate Quicken file for your home use and one for your business. That way, you can keep all of your transactions separate without danger of misclassifying income and expenses. There is one drawback to using two different files, however—you cannot enter transactions that affect both a business and a personal account. For example, if you transfer funds from your business account to your personal account, you'll have to enter a separate transaction in your business file and another in your personal file. If you were using just one file, you could easily enter one transaction that transfers funds from one account to the other.

So how do you know if the categories that are already in your Quicken file are the ones you need? The category list that's already there will probably be sufficient for most of your transactions, but we're all different and have different kinds of income and expenses. Personalize your category list by adding some new categories, changing some that are already there, or getting rid of some that you know you'll never use. It's that simple. If you have some farm income, you'll want to add a category like Farm Inc; if your kids take music lessons, you may want a category like Music or Piano Lessons; if you have expenses related to your pet cat, Felix, you may want a category called Pet or Pet Care, or even Felix Exp.

Where do I find my list of categories?

Your categories are stored in a list called the Category & Transfer List (just like you found with accounts that are stored in the Account List). You can access the Category & Transfer List anytime you want. Just select Lists, Category & Transfer and you see the Category & Transfer List like the one in figure 4.1.

This list is called the Category & Transfer List because it includes all of your categories (and subcategories) and all of your accounts (so that you can enter transfer transactions). (I tell you all about subcategories later in this chapter). Quicken keeps the Category & Transfer List in alphabetical order by category and account type. All income categories are listed first, then expense categories, followed by accounts (in order by account type). Subcategories are listed in alphabetical order under the category in which they relate.

You can make some program changes by clicking the Options button

Click here to go to other Quicken windows or activities

Need Help in the
Category & Transfer
List? Click this button

Enlarge the Category &
Transfer List window or reduce
it back to its original size

The button bar
performs tasks in the
Category & Transfer List

Fig. 4.1
All of your categories,
subcategories, and
accounts are listed in
the Category & Transfer
List.

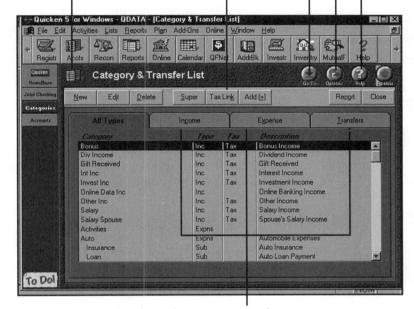

Use these tabs to sort categories by income or expense
or to just list accounts in the Category & Transfer List.

Q&A *I opened my Category & Transfer List but found I didn't
open any categories in the list. What happened and
what do I do now?*

Don't panic. When you installed Quicken, you must not have selected one
of the predefined category lists included in the program, so Quicken
thought that you wanted to enter all of your own categories. If this is not
the case, you can still add categories from the predefined lists. You learn
how to do this in the section, "What if I want to add a whole group of
categories?" later in this chapter.

TIP **If you've already opened the Category & Transfer List during this**
session, you'll find a Categories QuickTab in the left margin of the screen.
Just click the Categories QuickTab anytime you want to access the Category
& Transfer List again.

The button bar at the top of the Category & Transfer List includes buttons you can use to work with categories. You can use these buttons in place of the main menu to speed up your work. Instead of choosing Edit, New Category, you can simply click the New in the button bar.

You can do all sorts of things to categories from the Category & Transfer List, like add a new category, edit an existing category, delete a category, add a super category (you learn about these when you start budgeting in Chapter 16), assign tax schedules to categories, add or delete more than one category at a time, and even create a report on a category that includes all transactions assigned to that category.

TIP **It might be easier for you to review a printed copy of the Category** & Transfer List rather than scroll through the list on your screen. You can easily print the list by selecting File, Print List and then clicking OK. For more on printing lists, go to Chapter 19.

I want to add a new category

Okay, so you've decided there's a category you need that just isn't in Quicken's standard set of categories. It's easy to add any category that you want.

First, access the Category & Transfer List if it isn't already shown on your screen like in figure 4.1 (choose Lists, Category & Transfer). Then click the New button in the button bar to see the Set Up Category dialog box shown in figure 4.2.

Fig. 4.2
Just give your new category a name, an optional description, and tell Quicken whether it's an income or expense category or a subcategory.

As you can see from the Set Up Category dialog box, you need to name your category, give it a brief description (if you want), tell Quicken what type of category it's going to be, and, optionally, assign a tax form to the category.

So what should we call this category?

You can use whatever name you want for a new category. Just make sure there's not already a category with that name and that it's a name that is easy to recognize. You might not want to use many abbreviations in category names because you may not remember what they stand for six months from now. For example, if you want a category for Lawn Care, don't call it LC or LCare. Go ahead and use the full names for categories when you can. Quicken won't let you use more than 15 characters (you can include spaces) and you can't use any of these characters in the name:

:] [/ | ^

Now move to the Name text box and type the new category name. Then press Tab to add a description of the category. In figure 4.2, I set up a category called Music and then described it as Kids' music lessons so I know that this category is for my kids' music lessons expenses.

Next, you need to tell Quicken what type of category you're adding.

Selecting the category type

In the Type section of the Set Up Category dialog box (refer to fig. 4.2), you need to select which type of category you're setting up. As you can see, there are income categories, expense categories, and subcategories. If you're setting up a category that relates to income transactions (like wages or salary, interest income, dividend income, and so forth) then click the Income option. For categories that relate to your expenses (like rent, clothing, Childcare, groceries, etc.) click the Expense option.

The other type of category you can select is subcategories. **Subcategories** are a "subset" of categories. They simply break out your categories into more detail. Later in this chapter, there's a whole section devoted to subcategories and how to set them up. If you are adding a subcategory at this point, click the Subcategory Of option, and then tell Quicken which category your new subcategory relates to by clicking the down arrow and selecting a category from the list that drops down.

If you want, you can assign a tax form to the new category. Assigning tax forms to categories is optional. But if you want to accumulate your taxable income and tax-deductible expenses so that you can use this information for income tax return purposes, you need to assign tax-related categories to tax forms and schedules. Chapter 18 covers income taxes and assigning categories to tax forms and schedules.

Adding your new category

After you've named your category and selected the type for your new category, you've entered everything Quicken needs to add the category to your Category & Transfer List. You can stop now and add the category by clicking OK. Quicken inserts your new category in the Category & Transfer List in its proper alphabetical order by category type. In figure 4.3, you see the new Music category is now added to the list.

Fig. 4.3
When you add a new category to the Category & Transfer List, Quicken puts it in its proper order in the list.

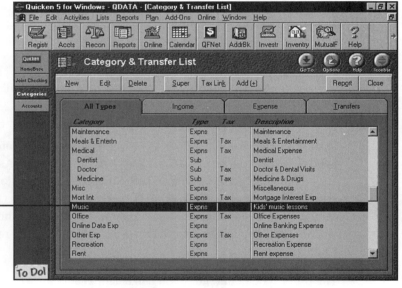

Here's the new Music category, placed alphabetically within all other expense categories

What if I want to add a whole group of categories?

Maybe you've decided that you don't really like some of the categories that are in the Category & Transfer List and you want to change the list. Maybe you want just some of the predefined home categories or a few of the business categories, too. It would take some time to individually add these categories one at a time, wouldn't it?

Quicken's new Add button in the Category & Transfer List button bar lets you add groups of categories at one time. Click the Add button to see the Add Categories window in figure 4.4.

Fig. 4.4
You can quickly add groups of categories from Quicken's standard home and business category sets.

Select either the Home or Business category sets

Here's the list of categories that you can add at one time

If you want to select all of the categories to add, click this button

Clear the checkmark from all of the categories by clicking this button

Quicken shows you the categories that you've selected to add

Click here to remove the selected categories from the Categories to Add list

Click here to copy the selected categories to the Categories to Add list

Selecting categories to add

To select categories from the home list, click Quicken Home Categories. Quicken lists all of the home categories in the Available Categories list. Or, click the Quicken Business Categories option to see all of the standard business categories in the Available Categories list.

Next, use the scroll bar in the Available Categories list to scroll through the category names to see which ones you want to add. Before you can add categories, you have to mark each one in the Available Categories list. Mark categories by clicking on the category name in the Available Categories list.

TIP **Select all categories in the Available Categories list by clicking** the Mark All button. Use the Clear All button to remove the checkmark from all of the categories. You may want to clear categories if you've reconsidered which categories you want to mark and want to start over.

Adding the categories

After you've marked the categories that you want to add, click the <u>A</u>dd button to copy the marked categories to the Categories to Add list. In figure 4.5, you see that I'm going to add five categories to my Category & Transfer List. If you're satisfied with these categories, just click the OK button and Quicken automatically adds the new categories to your Category & Transfer List and places them in their proper order.

Fig. 4.5
You'll see the categories that you've decided to add in the Categories to Add list. When you're ready to add them, just click OK.

I don't need this category in my list

What if there are some categories in your list that you know you'll never use? There's no need to have them there cluttering up your Category & Transfer List if you don't need them, so just get rid of them. If a category has subcategories, though, you can't delete it until you first change its subcategories into categories or move the subcategories to another category. I'll explain more about this when I get the section on subcategories. For now, just remember not to delete a category that has any subcategories.

CAUTION **You can delete most categories from the Category & Transfer List** except categories preceded by an underscore (_). These categories are automatically added to your list when you set up investment accounts in Quicken. You cannot delete these categories because they are needed to record transactions in your investment accounts.

When you're ready to delete a category, here's what you do. First, access the Category & Transfer List, then find the category that you want to delete and click or highlight it.

 TIP **You can move really fast through the Category & Transfer List to** find a category by using the Home key to move to the very beginning or the End key to move to the very end. Another speedy way to find a category is to type the first letter in the category name. Typing the first letter moves you to the first category in the list that starts with that letter. For example, when I type **S**, Quicken moves to the category called Subscriptions because it's the first category that starts with S.

Now, click the <u>D</u>elete button in the Category & Transfer List button bar. So that you don't make a rash decision here, Quicken gives you an opportunity to keep the category and not delete it. When Quicken displays its warning message, click OK to go ahead and delete the category. If you decide to keep it, click Cancel.

 CAUTION **Be careful that you don't delete categories that you've previously** assigned to transactions.

If you do, Quicken removes the category from all of those transactions; your transactions are NOT removed. So, you'll have transactions without an assigned category and you'll need to go back and assign a new category to them. If there is a category that you've assigned to transactions that you want to delete, recategorize the transactions first and then delete it. I'll tell you how to recategorize transactions a little later in this chapter.

 TIP **I just cautioned you not to delete categories that are assigned to** transactions. Right? Well, here's an easy way to see if you've assigned the category that you want to delete to any previous transactions. Just select the category from the Category & Transfer List and then click the Rep<u>o</u>rt button. If Quicken finds any transactions with the category that you selected, you'll see them in a QuickReport on your screen. If you want to know a little more about QuickReports, read Chapter 19.

This category needs a change

Like most things in Quicken, you can change them if you need to. So, if you need to change a category name or description, change the type of category it is, or change the tax form or schedule assigned to the category, you can do so at any time.

There's only one group of categories that you won't be able to change and they're the ones preceded by an underscore ( ). These are categories that Quicken automatically sets up when you add your first investment account. They are used for investment transactions and cannot be changed.

First, go to the Category & Transfer List and find the category you want to edit. Click or highlight the category name. Then, click the Edit button from the button bar. What you see next is the Edit Category dialog box. All of the information that you can change about a category is included in this dialog box.

Now, just move to the text box or option that you want to change and type over the existing information. When you're finished making changes to the category, click OK.

Do subcategories work like categories?

Earlier in this chapter you saw something called a "subcategory," and I know I only explained very briefly what it was. But now, we're ready to talk about subcategories, what they are, and how they work in Quicken.

A **subcategory** is similar to a category, but represents more detail than a category does. Subcategories are "subsets" of categories; they break down a category into smaller pieces. You might say that a category is a parent and subcategories are the children.

Take, for example, the category Utilities. The category Utilities is a general grouping for all of your utility expenses. And it's certainly okay to just group all of your utility expenses into this one category. But what if you want to know how much you spent on electricity last year or on water and sewer charges? If you have subcategories for each of these expenses under the general category of Utilities, then you can easily answer these questions. You could have the following subcategories for the category Utilities:

Electric

Water

Sewer

Gas

In this case, the subcategories of Electric, Water, Sewer, and Gas are subcategories of the parent category, Utilities.

Each time you pay an electric bill, you assign the subcategory Electric to the transaction. Then you can easily determine how much your electric bills were for any given time.

 TIP **Guess what? You can even have subcategories of subcategories.** These would even further break out the detail of a subcategory. There probably aren't many instances where you'll need these subcategories of subcategories. Here's one example. Say you have a subcategory called Condo Maint (for condominium maintenance) under the category Condo Exp (condominium expense). You could break out condo maintenance even further by creating subcategories called Cleaning and Lawncare. These would be subcategories of Condo Maint, which is a subcategory of Condo Exp.

Where do I find subcategories?

Subcategories are found in the same place you find categories—in the Category & Transfer List. You can tell which item in the list is a subcategory because it appears indented, right under its parent category, or the category to which it relates. In the Category & Transfer List shown in figure 4.6, notice that there are four subcategories for the category Auto: Fuel, Insurance, Loan, and Service. Then look in the Type column of the Category & Transfer List; Quicken shows Sub as the type of category these are.

Fig. 4.6
When a category has subcategories, Quicken lists them in the Category & Transfer List right under the parent category.

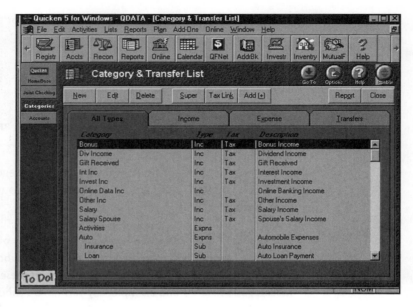

Adding, deleting, and editing subcategories

As I said earlier, subcategories are very similar to categories. And because they're similar, you add, delete, and edit a subcategory the same way that you do a category.

When you add a subcategory, follow the same instructions that I gave you for adding a category, but just be sure to click the Subcategory of option. Then click the down arrow and select the category that you're setting up the subcategory for, or the parent category, from the list that drops down.

Deleting a subcategory works just the same way as deleting a category. When you delete a subcategory that you've assigned to transactions, Quicken automatically merges the subcategory into its parent category. So, if you have a subcategory called Movies under the parent category called Entertn and you delete Movies, any transactions with Movies assigned to it will automatically be merged into the category Entertn and therefore be assigned to this category.

You can edit a subcategory the same way that you edit a category. You can change the name, description, and even the parent category of a subcategory.

So, if you decide you'd rather have the subcategory Art Fees under the category Activities instead of Recreation, you can change the parent category in the Edit Subcategory dialog box. I explain how to change a subcategory's parent a little later in this chapter.

Let's rearrange the category list

When I say you can "rearrange" your Category & Transfer List, I don't mean that you can put the categories in a different order. Quicken will always put your categories in alphabetical order by category type. All income categories are first, followed by expense categories, and then transfer accounts.

What you can do to your Category & Transfer List is change categories to subcategories (and subcategories to categories), change a subcategory's parent, and merge categories and subcategories together. The next few sections explain how to do this kind of rearranging of your list.

Changing a category to a subcategory and vice versa

Just like employees in corporate America, a category can lose its status and get demoted to a subcategory and a subcategory can climb the corporate ladder by getting a promotion to a category.

Let's say that you decide you've got a category called Fuel and you decide you want to group all of your auto expenses into a category called Auto. You'll have to demote the Fuel category to a subcategory of the category Auto.

To demote a category to a subcategory, first select it from the Category & Transfer List. Then choose the Edit button in the button bar so that Quicken displays the Edit Category dialog box (like the one in fig. 4.7). Next, change the category type to a subcategory by selecting the Subcategory of option. So now that the category is a subcategory, tell Quicken which category is the parent by selecting the category from the Subcategory of drop-down list. Click the OK button and the category gets the bad news and becomes a subcategory.

Fig. 4.7
You can demote a category to a subcategory in the Edit Category dialog box.

If you want to grant a promotion to a subcategory, first select the subcategory from the Category & Transfer List and then click the Edit button. When Quicken displays the Edit Category dialog box for the subcategory, change its type from a subcategory to either an income or expense category and click OK.

Whether you've been heartless and demoted a category or benevolent and promoted a subcategory, Quicken will automatically change all previous transactions that were assigned to the category or subcategory.

Changing a subcategory's parent category

There are probably a lot of teens out there that would like to change their parent from time to time, but they're out of luck. But in Quicken, you can easily change a subcategory's parent without any legal hassles. You may want to do this if a subcategory seems better suited for another category rather than its own parent category. For example, if you've got a subcategory called Auto Lease, you may want to move it from the Auto category to the Lease Expense category.

When you're ready to make the switch, choose the subcategory from the Category & Transfer List and then click the Edit button from the button bar. When you see the Edit Category dialog box, open the Subcategory of drop-down list by clicking the down arrow. Then just scroll through the list to pick another category. Click OK and Quicken changes the parent category. You see in the Category & Transfer List that the subcategory is now listed under the new parent category.

Merging categories and subcategories

Sometimes you may want to condense your category list by combining categories and subcategories together. When you merge two categories or subcategories, Quicken assigns the category or subcategory that you retain to transactions. For example, if you have a category to record interest income called Int Inc and you really don't want to break out your investment income out into this type of income category, then you could merge this category into your investment income category, maybe Invest Inc. After you merge the two categories, Quicken changes the category assignment of any transactions that were assigned to Int Inc to Invest Inc.

The first thing that you have to do when merging categories is to change the category that you want to merge into a subcategory (demote it). If you're merging a subcategory into another, make it a subcategory of the subcategory that you're merging with. You just learned how to promote and demote categories and subcategories, so you should be able to do this now.

Next, delete the subcategory that you want merged into its parent (either category or subcategory). Remember that when you delete a subcategory, Quicken merges it into its parent. So by deleting the subcategory, you're actually merging it into its parent category or subcategory. Any transactions that were assigned to the subcategory that was just merged will now be assigned to the parent category or subcategory.

How do I switch a transaction from one category to another?

Oh no! You just realized that you've been assigning the wrong category to your rent payments. Instead of assigning the category Rent, you assigned the category Lease (which applies to your car lease payments). What do you do now? It will take forever to go back and find each rent payment transaction and assign the proper category.

Well, you really don't have to go through this ordeal. Quicken makes it quick and easy by finding groups of transactions and replacing the category in all transactions that you select with the category that you want.

Finding transactions

The first thing that you need to do when you want to switch (or recategorize) a group of transactions from one category to another is to have Quicken search through the register for the transactions assigned to the wrong category. Do this by selecting Activities, Recategorize. Quicken displays the Recategorize window.

In the Search Category box, click the down arrow to display the list of categories and then select the category that you mistakenly assigned to transactions. In my example, I'd select the category Lease.

Then click the Find All button. Quicken searches the register for any transactions assigned to the category that you selected and displays them in the Recategorize window, like in figure 4.8.

Fig. 4.8
When Quicken finds transactions assigned to the wrong category, it displays them all in the Recategorize window.

Sometimes, a transaction has more than one category assigned to it. This is called a **split transaction**. Split transactions break out the transaction into different categories. I give you lots more detail on split transactions in the next chapter. If you have any transactions that you assigned more than one category to, you can show each category in the transactions by clicking the Show Matches in Splits checkbox at the bottom of the Recategorize window.

CAUTION   **Quicken will not switch the category of the top level of a split** transaction in the Recategorize window. A split transaction has two or more levels (or two or more categories assigned to the transaction). The top level is the first line of the split transaction. If you need to recategorize the top level, go to the transaction in the register and change the category. I tell you all about editing split transactions in the register in the next chapter.

Marking transactions to switch

Now that you've found all of the transactions that you assigned the wrong category to, you can switch the category in all of the transactions, or select transactions that you want to switch.

To select a transaction so that Quicken recategorizes it, mark it by clicking the transaction in the Recategorize window. Quicken places a checkmark next to each transaction that you select. Figure 4.9 shows three marked transactions.

Fig. 4.9

Quicken only changes the category for the transactions that you mark in the Recategorize window. Quicken places a checkmark next to a transaction to show that you've selected it to be recategorized.

If you want to mark all of the transactions in the Recategorize window, click the Mark All button; to clear all marked transactions, click the Clear All button.

Recategorizing transactions

Once you've marked the transactions that you want to recategorize, just tell Quicken which new category you want assigned to the transactions. In the

Replace With box, click the down-arrow to display the category list and select the replacement category. Then click the Replace button. Quicken displays a confirmation message telling you how many transactions will be recategorized. Click OK to recategorize the transactions.

Q&A   *When I look through the Lists menu, I see something called Class. Is a class like a category, and how do I use it?*

Classes are similar to categories in that they help to break out transactions into income and expense groups. But classes add a second dimension to your transaction data by breaking it out in different ways. For example, if you want to track an expense by job or project, by salesperson or product line, or by geographic location or functional company area, you can use classes to record the expense.

Classes are very useful to business users of Quicken; however, they probably serve no purpose for the Quicken home user.

Introducing the Quicken Register

● **In this chapter:**

- See what the register looks like

- Move around the register

- Record a transaction in the register

- Split a transaction

- Learn about transfer transactions

Quicken's register takes the hassle out of tracking all your facts and figures . . . . ❯

Quicken's registers look like the register you're used to seeing in your checkbook. You know, you write a check and then flip back to the register to record the date, check number, payee, and the amount of the check. We all are very diligent about recording each and every check that we write and we even subtract the check amount from the account balance so that we always know exactly how much money we have. Not! Most of us try to keep on top of our finances but with today's time constraints we don't always get the job done.

But now that you've decided to automate your finances, you can rely on Quicken to keep track of your transactions and do all the arithmetic for you. Never again will a simple math error cause you to bounce a check!

What's a register?

Quicken registers do just what the name implies: they "register" (or record) your financial activity in a ledger-like format. Quicken's register is the program's major component. Every other feature in Quicken depends upon the register to function. Look at how the register interacts with other features in Quicken:

- The check-writing feature records your checks in the register

- The bank account reconciliation feature uses the transactions in the register to balance your account

- The reporting and graph features uses the data from your register to create summaries of your transactions

- The tax features in Quicken rely on the information in your register

What do you do with a register?

Any financial activity you have can be recorded directly into a Quicken register. Sometimes you'll enter transactions directly into a register and other times Quicken enters the transaction in the register for you.

Here's when you're going to need to use a register:

- To enter checks you write manually

- To enter bank deposits and ATM (automatic teller machine) transactions

- To enter other types of transactions, such as interest you earn on a bank account or bank service charges

- When you want to review your transactions

- If you want to edit or delete a transaction

- To void a check or other transaction

- To find a transaction

- If you want to print transactions

Okay, how do I get to a register?

Open the account and Quicken automatically displays its register on your screen.

Let's review the different ways to open an account (and therefore its register):

- Click the Accts button from the iconbar to open the Account List. Then select the account from the list and click the Open button from the button bar (see fig. 5.1). Quicken opens the register for the specified account.

- If you've been working in several accounts during your current work session in Quicken, click the QuickTab (see fig. 5.2) for the account register that you want to open.

- If you've already got an account register open, select the account from the Account selection bar (see fig. 5.2) at the bottom of the register (you learned about the Account selection bar in Chapter 3). Open an account register by clicking the account name in the Account selection bar.

Fig. 5.1
Click the Open button
in the Account List to
open the selected
account's register.

*Click the Open button to
open the account register*

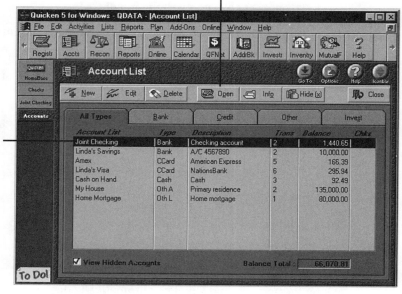

*Here's the account
whose register you
want to open*

Fig. 5.2
There's a QuickTab for
every register that
you've worked in
during this session.
Click the QuickTab for
the account whose
register you want to
open.

*QuickTabs appear for
every register or
window that you've
opened during this
session*

*The Account selection
bar includes a button
for all of your accounts*

- If you're working in the Write Checks window for an account, you can open the account's register by clicking the Register button from the iconbar.

What you'll find in the register

Registers in Quicken look much like the register in your checkbook. Format aside, the information that you're used to entering in your checkbook is the same for a Quicken register.

Button bar
Use these buttons to perform tasks in the register, like deleting a transaction, finding a transaction, entering a transfer between two accounts, changing register options, creating a QuickReport of transactions with the same payee, and closing the register.

Account selection bar
Quickly switch account registers by clicking another account button on the Account selection bar.

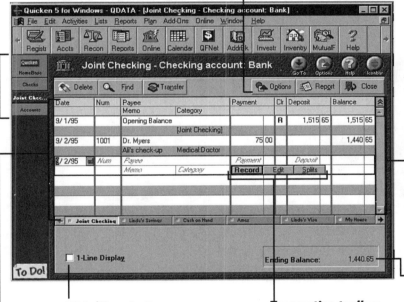

Scroll bar
Use the scroll bar to move through the register. To move up one transaction at a time, click the up arrow; to move down one transaction, click the down arrow. Drag the scroll box up or down to move quickly through lots of transactions. As you drag the scroll box, Quicken shows you the date and check number of the current transaction.

Balance
Quicken always shows you the balance in your account.

Hide/Show button
Click this button to hide the register button bar so that you can see more transactions in the register.

Transaction toolbar
Use this toolbar to record a transaction, change a transaction, or split a transaction (assign more than one category to it).

Transaction lines
Here's the guts of the register, where you enter the date, identifying transaction information (like the check number), the payee for a check or the source of a deposit, the amount of the transaction, an optional memo, and assign the category.

Seeing more transactions in the register

Quicken shows you two lines of information for each transaction in the register. This is called **two-line display**. With this format, you can't see very many transactions at a time. Click the 1-Line Display check box so that more transactions fit in the register (see fig. 5.3). Don't worry, you haven't lost any of your transaction data; it's just hidden from view.

Fig. 5.3

If you want to see more transactions in the register at one time, select the 1-Line Display check box.

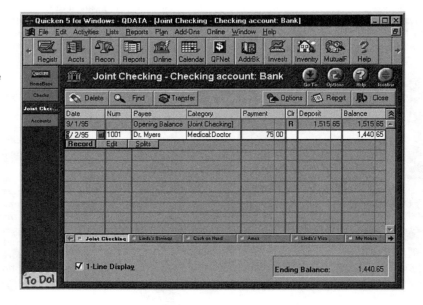

Of course, you can change the register back to displaying two lines per transaction by clicking the 1-Line Display check box again.

Entering a transaction is easy

Before entering a transaction in the register, make sure you're working in the appropriate account. If you're entering transactions for checks you've written from your 1st Natl checking account, make sure that the 1st Natl checking account register is the one that's open on your screen.

Moving to a blank transaction line in the register

It's probably obvious that you want to move to a blank transaction line first before you start to enter a transaction. Just make sure you do. If you start entering a transaction where one already exists, Quicken will write over the old transaction and you'll lose it.

The first blank transaction line is always at the end of the register, so move to a blank transaction line by pressing Ctrl+End.

TIP **You also can get to a new transaction line by choosing Edit, New** Transaction or pressing Ctrl+N. You also can insert a blank transaction line between two existing transactions. Figure out where you want to insert the transaction and highlight the transaction below the one that you want to insert. (Quicken inserts transactions above the highlighted transaction.) Then choose Edit, Insert Transaction or press Ctrl+I.

If the current field (the one with the flashing cursor) is not the Date field, press Home twice to get there. The date is the first piece of information you'll need to enter.

 Plain English, please!

A **field** in a register is a blank area where you enter information. The current field is the one with the blinking cursor. Usually, pressing the Tab key moves the cursor from field to field. **99**

Entering the transaction date

After arriving at the Date field in the blank transaction line, you'll notice that Quicken already has today's date entered. Quicken automatically enters the system date in the Date field. You can enter any date you want by typing over the date that's already there. The date you'll want to enter is the date of the check or other transaction. If your check's written on 10/15/95, you'll enter this date in the MM/DD/YY format. You don't have to type the slashes though, so just type **1015** (entering the year isn't necessary either because if it's the current year, it's already entered for you).

Here's two other quick ways to enter dates in the Date field in the register:

- Press the + or – keys on the numeric keypad to change the existing date one day at a time. So, if the date that's already entered is 11/14/95, just press + once to change it to 11/15/95 or press – twice to change it to 11/12/95.

- Click the calendar icon in the Date field (see figure 5.4) to see Quicken's minicalendar. Then click on a date in the calendar to enter it in register. I explain more about the minicalendar in Chapter 8.

Fig. 5.4
Quicken's minicalendar appears when you click the calendar icon in the Date field.

Click the calendar icon to see the minicalendar

You can select any date from Quicken's minicalendar

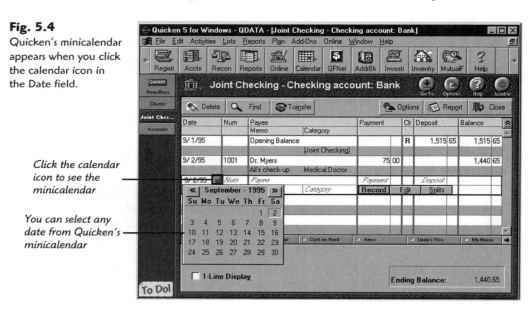

After you've entered the transaction date, press Tab to move to the next field to enter the check number or other identifying symbol.

Recording the transaction (check) number

If you're entering a transaction for a check that you've written, enter the check number in the Num field. If you've already entered some checks in the register, Quicken automatically enters the next check number in the Num field for you. If that number's correct, just press Tab to move on. If it's not the correct number, type over it with the right one.

There are two other ways to enter the check number:

- Press the + and – keys on the numeric keypad to change the check number one at a time. So if the check number entered is 1345 and you press + twice, the check number changes to 1347. If it's 1345 and you press – twice, it changes to 1343.

- Select Next Chk# from the drop-down list that appears when you move to the Num field . Quicken automatically adds one to the last check number entered in the register.

There are several options in the Num field drop-down list. Here's when to use them:

- **<Edit>** When you want to change one of the items in the Num field drop-down list. Just select and make your change.

- **<New>** If you want to create a new item in the Num field drop-down list.

- **ATM** To enter an Automatic Teller Machine transaction.

- **Deposit** Used for deposit transactions.

- **EFT** To enter electronic funds transfers.

- **Next Chk#** To have Quicken automatically add one to the last check number entered in the Num field.

- **Print** To tell Quicken to print a check for the transaction you are entering.

- **Send** To send payment instructions for electronic bill paying.

- **Transfer** To enter a transfer of funds from one Quicken account to another.

TIP **Typically, you enter checks you want Quicken to print for you in** the Write Checks window (which I get to in the next chapter). Checks you write by hand (or manually) are entered directly into the register. You also can enter checks that you want Quicken to print into the register if you select Print in the Num field (so Quicken knows to print it).

Once the Num field is filled, press Tab to move to the Payee field.

Who's the payee in this transaction?

Now you're ready to fill in the Payee field. Quicken uses the term **payee** generically to describe transactions in the register. Obviously, the payee in a check transaction is the person or business to whom you are writing the check. But there really is no payee for a deposit transaction or a withdrawal from the ATM. So just consider the Payee field as a description of the transaction that you're entering. For a deposit transaction, for instance, you could enter the source of the cash, like **Weekly Payroll** or **Stock Dividend**. For an ATM withdrawal, you could describe it as **Cash Withdrawal** or just **Cash**.

You can type the entry in the Payee field (using up to 31 characters) or you can select it from the drop-down list that appears when you move there. The list that you see is comprised of every other payee that you've entered in Quicken registers. So if you write a check to Municipal Utilities every month, you're going to see Municipal Utilities in the drop-down list.

Q&A *When I start typing a payee's name in the Payee field,* *Quicken finishes entering the name for me. What's* *happening here?*

You've just discovered QuickFill. QuickFill is a feature that saves you tons of time. When you type a few characters in a field, Quicken searches previous transactions in the register and in the Memorized Transaction List (you don't know about this list yet, but you can turn to Chapter 9 if you're dying to know) to find a match. When Quicken finds a match, the QuickFill feature fills in the rest of the field. I explain a lot more about QuickFill in Chapter 8.

Now you're ready to enter the amount of the transaction.

What's the amount of the transaction?

So, is this a payment that you're making or a deposit? If it's a payment, Tab once from the Payee field to arrive at the Payment field. If the transaction is a deposit, Tab twice to get to the Deposit field.

Now, enter the amount of the transaction. You can enter amounts using up to 10 characters and as large as $9,999,999.99 (the decimal point counts as one character, but the dollar sign and commas do not). By the way, you don't have to type dollar signs or commas.

 Q&A   *I want to add several amounts together to figure out how much my deposit is. Is there a calculator I can use in the Deposit field?*

Yes. As a matter of fact, Quicken's minicalculator is available from both the Payment field and the Deposit field. Just click the calculator icon (see fig. 5.5) to make it appear on-screen. Then, perform your calculations and press Enter to record the result in the Payment or Deposit field. The chapter on Quicken shortcuts, Chapter 8, tells you more about the minicalculator.

Fig. 5.5
Need some help figuring out amounts to enter? Use Quicken's minicalculator to help by clicking the calculator icon from the Payment field or the Deposit field.

Q&A **What's the Clr field and what do I enter here?**

This is the Clear field and shows whether a transaction has been recorded by the bank, or cleared. When you're entering current transactions, you don't enter anything in this field. When you balance your account (which we get to in Chapter 7), Quicken enters a C in this field to show that you've marked the transaction as cleared. Once you complete the reconciliation process, Quicken changes the C to an R to show that the transaction is cleared and reconciled with your bank statement.

If you are entering past transactions in Quicken that have already cleared, enter an * in the Clr field (this is the only character Quicken accepts from you). After you reconcile your account, Quicken changes the asterisk to an R.

Need a memo?

The Memo field is completely optional. If you want to enter a transaction memo, press Tab to move to this field and type up to 31 characters. I use memos to provide as much information about a transaction as I can. If I write a check for something unusual or to someone I may not remember six months later, I usually enter a memo to describe what the check was for, like Birthday gift for mom, or Recover chair.

Assigning a category is important

Here's one of the most important fields that you need to complete in a transaction. The Category field is where you assign the category, subcategory, or other account (for transfers) to a transaction. If you don't assign something here, the transaction does not get classified into an income or expense category. It just ends up in an Other category and you won't know what it's made up of.

Q&A **How can I make sure that I assign all of my transactions to a category? Quicken doesn't make me do this, does it?**

Quicken will record a transaction in your register whether or not you've assigned a category. If you want to make sure that a category has been assigned to your transactions, there's a register option you can select in Quicken to help you remember. When you select this particular option, Quicken displays a warning message when you try to record a transaction that's uncategorized. Later in this chapter, I talk about how to set register options, and this option is one of them.

Press Tab to move to the Category field. When you get to the Category field, you see another one of those drop-down lists. Included in this list is all of your categories, subcategories, and accounts so that you can just select one to enter in the Category field. (If the drop-down list doesn't automatically appear, just click the down-arrow.)

If you'd rather just type in your category, start typing the category name. Again, you'll notice that after you've typed a character, Quicken fills in the rest of a category name for you. This is QuickFill at work.

By the way, if you're assigning a subcategory to a transaction, you also can select it from the drop-down list or type the parent category followed by a colon (:) and then type the subcategory name.

TIP **If you're entering a transaction and decide that you need a** category that's not in the Category & Transfer List, you can add the new category *on the fly* by just typing the new category name in the Category field. When Quicken doesn't find it in the Category & Transfer List, the Set Up Category window appears so that you can add it now. The category appears in your Category & Transfer List.

You also can assign an account to a transaction by selecting or entering the account name in the Category field. This is called a *transfer transaction* which transfers funds from one Quicken account to another. Later in this chapter, I talk more about transfer transactions and how to enter them.

You're almost finished entering your transaction. The only thing left to do is record it so that Quicken saves the data in the register.

Recording your transaction

After you've filled in all of the information for a transaction, you can record (or save) it in the register by clicking the Record button from the Transaction toolbar or pressing Enter.

When you record a transaction, Quicken places the transaction in the proper order (by date) in the register and updates your account balance accordingly. If the balance is too large (wouldn't we love that!), Quicken displays asterisks in the Balance field. If the balance is negative, a minus sign precedes the amount and for color monitors, the balance appears in red.

I've got a transaction that affects two accounts

When you have a transaction that affects two accounts, in essence it's a transfer of funds from one account to another. This is called a **transfer transaction**. Suppose that you go to the ATM and transfer $500 from your savings account to your checking account. You would have to enter a transfer transaction to show the transfer of funds from your savings account to your checking account. It really wouldn't matter which account you entered the transfer transaction in. When you enter this type of transaction in one account, Quicken automatically enters a corresponding transaction in the other account (the account that you select or enter in the Category field).

There are two ways to enter a transfer transaction:

- In the register for either one of the accounts, enter the transaction like any other, except select Transfer in the Num field (and Quicken enters TXFR) and select the other account in the Category field.

- In the register for either one of the accounts, click the Transfer button from the button bar. Quicken displays the Transfer Money Between Accounts dialog box that you see in figure 5.6. Fill out the date, description, the amount of the transfer and then select the account to where you're transferring funds. Click OK to record the transfer transaction in the register.

Fig. 5.6
Here, I'm transferring $500 from my savings account to my joint checking account.

 TIP If you want to see the corresponding transfer transaction in the other account that Quicken enters, highlight the transfer transaction and press Ctrl+X.

Go ahead, assign more than one category

When you see a transaction line in the register, you see only one field for assigning a category. But that doesn't mean you can only assign one category to a transaction. As a matter of fact, you can assign up to 30 different categories to a single transaction. Assigning more than one category to a transaction is called **splitting a transaction** because you're splitting the amount of the transaction between two or more categories.

Here's a good example of a split transaction. Let's say you go to Wal-Mart and write a check for $129.55 to cover your purchases. So what did you buy? Probably a lot of different things that fit into different categories, like toiletries, household items, a CD, hardware, and some grocery items. When you enter the transaction in your Quicken register, you'll need to break out the transaction to reflect the appropriate expense categories, maybe something like this:

Amount	Category
$24.67	Toiletries
$19.88	Household Items
$14.99	Music
$33.19	Hardware
$36.82	Groceries

So the single transaction for the check to Wal-Mart can be broken out into five different categories.

 TIP **If you want to track your expenses closely, enter split transactions** for all of your expenditures. If you just dump some of your expenditures into a catch–all category, like Miscellaneous, you really won't know where all of your money is going. Keep your receipts from department stores and discount stores so that when you're ready to enter the transaction in Quicken, you can look at the receipt to figure out which categories to assign.

Splitting a transaction

You already know how to enter a transaction in the register and assign one category. Assigning two or more categories (splitting a transaction) only requires a few more steps.

Here's how you split a transaction:

1 In the register, fill in the Date, Num, Payee, Amount, and Memo fields as usual.

2 Click the <u>S</u>plits button from the transaction toolbar to open the Splits window (see fig. 5.7), which contains 30 lines for you to assign categories.

Fig. 5.7
You can assign up to 30 different categories to a transaction in the Splits window.

3 Begin entering or selecting categories in the Category field, enter an optional memo, and then enter the amount for each category. Press the Tab key to move from field to field in the Splits window.

4 When you're finished assigning categories, click the OK button to return to the transaction in the register.

Then you'll need to record the split transaction in the register by clicking the Re<u>c</u>ord button.

After you record a split transaction in the register, Quicken inserts —Splits— in the Category field to show the transaction is split between two or more categories (see fig. 5.8).

Fig. 5.8
Here's what a split transaction looks like in the register after it's recorded.

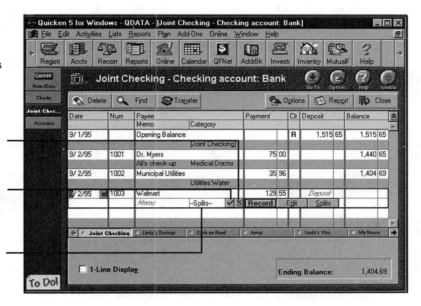

Click the X button to clear all split lines in a split transaction

Use the check button to go back to the Splits window to edit a split transaction line

Quicken inserts— Splits—to show this is a split transaction

TIP **Use the Adj. Tot. button in the Splits window to calculate the** amount of a transaction. Perhaps you have several invoices from the same payee and each represents a different type of expense. If you don't already know the total amount of all the invoices, let Quicken calculate it for you. Open the Splits window (select Splits) before entering the transaction amount; then enter all your categories and amounts for all of the invoices. When you're finished, click the Adj. Tot. button in the Splits window to have Quicken calculate the total of all the amounts you just entered. When you click OK in the Splits window, Quicken returns to the register and enters the total amount of the transaction for you.

Changing a split transaction

If you need to change one of the categories or an amount in a split transac-tion, just click the check button to go back to the Splits window. Press Tab to move to the split line that you want to edit and then make your change. When you're finished editing the Splits window, click OK to return to the register and then click Record to record your changes.

CAUTION   **If you change an amount in the Splits window, your transaction**
may no longer balance (the total in the Splits window won't equal the
transaction amount). If you need to change the transaction amount anyway,
click the Adj. Tot. button to recalculate the transaction. If the original
transaction amount is correct, change one of the other split line amounts so
that the transaction balances.

Undoing a split transaction

If you enter a split transaction and later decide that you want just one
category assigned to the transaction, you can undo the split by clicking the X
button in the transaction line in the register. When you click the X button,
Quicken asks whether you want to clear all split lines. Select Yes to delete all
the split lines in the Splits window and then select the single category from
the drop-down list (displayed automatically by Quicken) that you want to
assign.

Let's look over our transactions

It's a good idea to review the transactions you enter (especially if you're new
to Quicken) to make sure that you've entered everything correctly. You also
may want to review the transactions in your register to confirm whether a
payment was made or if you've recorded a deposit.

To review transactions, just use the scroll bar or the keyboard arrow keys
(like I explained earlier in this chapter) to go move through the register to
see the transactions that don't fit on your screen.

Even though you've already recorded a transaction, at any time you can edit
the transaction, delete it, or void it. The next few sections explain how to
perform these actions on transactions.

I see a mistake, is there a way to change it?

Want to make changes in a transaction? Maybe you entered the wrong payee
or the wrong check number. Or, maybe you entered the wrong amount or
entered a payment transaction that should have been a deposit.

It's easy to edit a transaction. Just highlight the transaction that you want to change and then move to the field that's wrong. Either type over the existing information or select a new item from the drop-down list. Then, click the Re**c**ord button to record the changes to the transaction.

The E**d**it button in the transaction toolbar opens an Edit menu that can be used to make changes to transactions.

Q&A *What if I'm editing a transaction and then decide it shouldn't be changed?*

While you're editing the transaction, you can change it back to the way it was originally by selecting E**d**it from the toolbar in the transaction and then selecting **R**estore Transaction. Quicken restores the transaction to the way it was before you started editing it.

TIP **If you need to copy a transaction from one account to another,** highlight the transaction and choose E**d**it, Cop**y** Transaction. Then, go to the account register where you want to enter the copied transaction, go to a blank transaction line, and select E**d**it, Pa**s**te Transaction.

I think I need to get rid of this transaction

If you enter the wrong transaction in an account register or a transaction in the wrong account, you can easily delete it. Be sure you want to delete it because once you do, it's removed permanently from the register.

CAUTION **Don't mistake deleting a transaction with voiding a transaction. If** you inadvertently enter a transaction that you never should have entered, you delete it. But, if you enter a transaction for a check that you've written and you later lose the check or stop payment on the check, you void the transaction. When you delete a transaction, you remove all record of the transaction. But when you void a transaction, Quicken retains the transaction information in your register, but not the amount. The next section explains how to void a transaction.

Once you've decided that you do indeed want to delete a transaction in the register, here's what you do. First, select the transaction that you want to delete. To show it's selected, it should be highlighted. Then, click the Delete button from the button bar. Quicken won't let you make hasty decisions so it displays a confirmation message to make sure that you really want to delete the transaction. If you do, click <u>Y</u>es. If you don't want to delete it, click <u>N</u>o and the transaction remains untouched.

If you delete a transaction that is part of a transfer transaction (where you transferred funds from one Quicken account to another), the corresponding transaction in the other account is also deleted.

When deleting a transfer transaction that is part of a split transaction, you have to delete the transaction from the account where the transaction was originally entered. If the transfer transaction between your savings and checking accounts also was a split transaction and was entered in your savings account register, you have to delete the transaction from the savings account register.

And I need to void this transaction

You may need to void a transaction in the register for a check that you've already written. You now want to:

- Stop payment on the check

- Replace a lost check

- Print another check to replace a misprinted check

So what's the difference between voiding a transaction and deleting one? When you void a transaction, Quicken keeps your transaction information in the register but erases the amount and adjusts your account balance. In contrast, when you delete a transaction, Quicken wipes out the transaction completely. You have no record of the transaction in your register.

To void a transaction, highlight the transaction in the register and then choose <u>E</u>dit, <u>V</u>oid Transaction. Quicken inserts **Void** in the Payee field (just before the payee name), erases the transaction amount, and places an R (for reconciled) in the Clr field. Then click the Re<u>c</u>ord button to record the voided transaction.

When Quicken erases the amount in a voided transaction, the account balance is adjusted accordingly. Voided transactions do not increase or decrease your account balance.

TIP **You can change the way your register appears on-screen, how you** enter information in the register, and how the QuickFill feature works in the register. Click the Options button in the Register button bar to open the Register Options window. The Register Options window includes three tabs (Display, Miscellaneous, and QuickFill) so that you can select the type of register options you want to change. Read Chapter 24 to learn more about customizing your register.

6

Writing Checks

● **In this chapter:**

- **Order pre-printed checks**

- **See what a check looks like on your screen**

- **Write a check**

- **Print checks**

Forget those two hours you spent paying bills last month. With Quicken's printing feature, you can now pay your monthly bills in less than half the time . . . . ❯

You're well aware of how long it takes to write checks each month, record the checks in your checking account register, and then update your account balance. What a tedious job. Right?

Well, now that you're using Quicken you can speed up this process significantly. Using Quicken's check-writing feature, you can write a whole month's worth of checks in just a few minutes. Quicken not only prints your checks, but also records them in your checking account register and automatically updates your account balance. And your printed checks are ready to sign, stick in envelopes, and mail.

What kind of checks should I use?

So you've decided that you want to use Quicken to print checks. Great! But first you need to order preprinted computer checks from Intuit that are compatible with your printer. You'll have to decide the check size, style, color, and whether you want multipart or voucher checks.

The best way to decide which checks work best for you is to review the Intuit Check Catalog that was included in your Quicken Deluxe package.

 TIP **When you order preprinted checks, you have to tell Quicken the** check number that you want to start with. If you're still using your manual checks, start your computer-printed checks with a number that won't overlap your manual checks. For example, if the next check number in your manual checkbook is #2890, then start your computer checks with the number #4000 or even #5000.

Ordering checks from Intuit

Order checks or any other Quicken supplies online through Intuit Marketplace or more traditionally by fax or mail.

You can order online

If you've got a modem, it's quick and easy to order your Quicken checks online through Intuit Marketplace. You can access Intuit Marketplace from Windows 95 by selecting the Marketplace program from the Quicken Deluxe program folder in Windows 95. If you're using Windows 3.1, just click the Intuit Marketplace icon in the Quicken program group to open the Intuit Marketplace window that you see in figure 6.1.

Fig. 6.1
Use Intuit Marketplace and your modem to order checks and other supplies.

Click this button to order checks

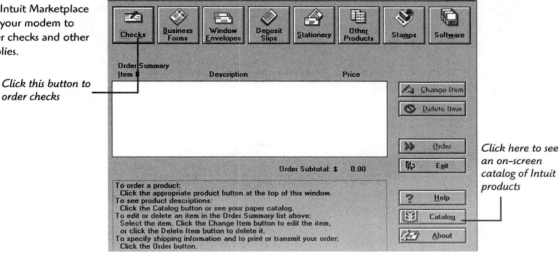

Click here to see an on-screen catalog of Intuit products

Click the Checks button to order checks. Click the Continue button in each of the next dialog boxes, to enter information about your bank, printer, and the size and style of checks that you want to order.

Computer checks are going to cost you more!

Preprinted computer checks are going to cost more than manual checks you order through your bank. You might expect to pay about $39.95 for 250 wallet-sized checks through Intuit and around $15 for manual checks. Of course, the time you'll save with computerized checks is worth something; however, you'll have to weigh the benefits.

After you've entered all the information Intuit needs to process your check order, review the Verify Check Order window (see fig. 6.2) to make sure that all the information is correct.

Fig. 6.2
Review this window carefully so that your checks get printed correctly. If you need to make a change, click the Ba**c**k button to get to the window with the wrong information and then correct it.

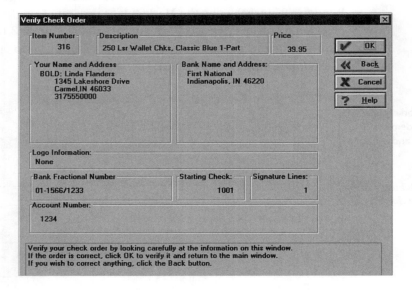

When you're ready to send your order, click the <u>O</u>rder button. Then select the <u>M</u>odem option for ordering and tell Quicken how you intend to pay for your checks. You have to pay by credit card when you order through Intuit Marketplace. So, be sure to provide a valid credit card number and expiration date and then click OK to send Intuit your check order.

TIP **You also can use Intuit Marketplace to print an order form to mail** or fax to Intuit. Just enter check information as you would if you were sending your order by modem, but choose Mai<u>l</u> or FA<u>X</u> as the ordering option instead. Then select the <u>P</u>rint button to print the completed order form.

Order by mail or fax

If you don't have a modem, you can fill out the order form in the Intuit Supplies Order Form found inside the Supplies Catalog. Send your completed order form to Intuit:

- By mail to:

  Intuit Supplies
  P.O. Box 50810
  Palo Alto, CA 94303

- By fax to:

  1-415-833-6455

- Or phone in your order to Intuit's customer service staff from 8:00 a.m. to 5:00 p.m. in your time zone at:

  1-800-433-8810

Where do I go to write checks?

Remember back in Chapter 5, you entered manual checks in the check register. But now that you're using Quicken to print checks, you should use the Write Checks window to enter check information.

You can only write checks from bank accounts that you've set up in Quicken (like your checking account, savings account, or money market account). Obviously, you can't write checks from a credit card account or an asset account. If you have more than one bank account set up in Quicken, then you'll want to make sure you're using the appropriate account when you open the Write Checks window. After I show you how to open the Write Checks window, I'll tell you how to select the bank account you want to use with it.

You can get to the Write Checks window a few different ways:

- Click the Check icon from the iconbar.

- If you've already opened the Write Checks window during this Quicken session, click the Checks QuickTab on the left side of the screen.

TIP **If you like using the register better than the Write Checks window,** you can still enter checks that you're going to print in the register. Just be sure to enter "Print" in the Num field so that Quicken knows it needs to print a check for the register transaction. After you print checks, Quicken replaces the word "Print" with the appropriate check numbers.

What you find in the Write Checks window

Here's what the Write Checks window looks like when you open it. Notice the check in the middle of the window that looks just like one of your personal checks. And it's just as easy to fill out.

On-screen check
Write a check by filling in this on-screen check

Current bank account
Here's the bank account that you're currently using to write checks

Scroll bar
The scroll bar helps you flip through the checks you've written (but not yet printed). To see the previous check, click the up arrow; to see the next check, click the down arrow. Drag the scroll box up or down to move quickly through lots of checks

Command buttons
These buttons are used to record a check, restore a check to the way it originally appeared, split a check transaction (assign more than one category to it), and print any checks that have already been written in the current account

Quicken always shows you the balance in your account after checks have been written

Button bar
Use this button bar to perform tasks when you're writing checks, like deleting a check, finding a check, viewing scheduled transactions and online payees, changing check options, creating a report of checks with the same payee, and closing the Write Checks window

Category
Assign a category to your check transaction

Account selection bar
The Account selection bar lets you quickly switch to another bank account to write checks from by clicking another account button

Payee's address
If you want to use window envelopes to mail checks, type the payee's address here

Moving around the Write Checks window

In addition to the scroll bar, and your mouse, you can use these keys to move around the Write Checks window quickly:

Press this key...	To move here...
Tab	Next field
Shift+Tab	Back one field
Home	Beginning of the current field
Home (two times)	First field in the check
End	End of current field
End End	Last field in the check
Ctrl+→	To the next word in a field
Ctrl+←	To the previous word in a field
Page Up	Previous check written
Page Down	Next check written or blank check
Home (three times)	First check written (but not yet printed)
End (three times)	To a blank check

Ready to write a check?

You've opened the Write Checks window and there's a blank check staring you in the face. To write a check in Quicken, just fill in the on-screen check in the Write Checks window and then record it.

Before writing your first check, make sure that you're writing the check from the appropriate account. If you're writing a check from your joint checking account, make sure that the Write Checks window for Joint Checking is the one that's open on your screen. In figure 6.3, you know that you're using the right account because Quicken shows the name Joint Checking in the Write Checks window. If you need to change the account, just click one of the account buttons in the Account selection bar.

Here's the name of the account that
you'll be writing checks from

Fig. 6.3
When this Write
Checks window is
open, you'll be writing
checks from the Joint
Checking account.

Select another
account to write
checks from by
clicking an account
button

Entering the check date

Usually, when you open the Write Checks window, the cursor is already
positioned in the Date field. If it's not there, press Tab to move forward one
field at a time or Shift+Tab to move backward.

When you're safely in the Date field, type the date of the check. Enter dates
in the MM/DD/YY format. So, to enter 4/15/96, type **415** (Quicken automatically enters the current year so you won't have to type 96 in this example if
the current year is 1996).

Here's two other quick ways to enter check dates in the Date field:

- Press the + or – keys on the numeric keypad to change the existing date
  one day at a time. So, if the date that's already entered is 11/14/95, just
  press + once to change it to 11/15/95 or press - twice to change it to
  11/12/95.

• Click on the calendar icon in the Date field (see fig. 6.4) to see Quicken's minicalendar. Then click on a date in the calendar to enter it in the Date field. I explain more about the minicalendar in Chapter 8.

Fig. 6.4
Quicken's minicalendar appears when you click the calendar icon in the Date field.

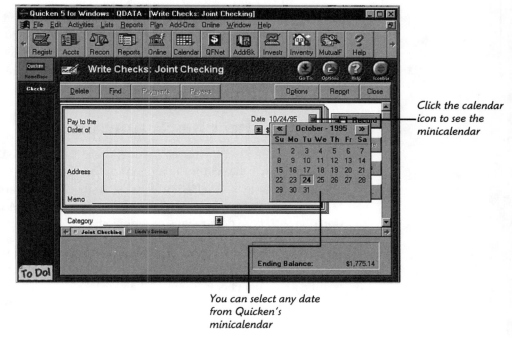

Click the calendar icon to see the minicalendar

You can select any date from Quicken's minicalendar

After you've entered the check date, press Tab to move to the Pay to the Order of field.

Who do you want to pay?

Obviously, the payee is the person or business to whom you are writing the check.

You can type the entry in the Pay to the Order of field (using up to 40 characters) or you can select it from the drop-down list that appears when you move there. The list that you see is comprised of every other payee that you've entered in the Write Checks window or in Quicken registers. So if you write a check to Public Service, Inc. every month, you're going to see Public Service, Inc. in the drop-down list.

Q&A *What's going on here? When I start typing a payee's name in the Pay to the Order of field, Quicken finishes entering the name for me.*

When you type a few characters in a field, Quicken searches previous transactions in Quicken registers and in the Memorized Transaction List (you don't know about this list yet, but you can turn to Chapter 9 to find out about it) to find a match. When Quicken finds a match, the QuickFill feature fills in the rest of the field. I explain a lot more about QuickFill in Chapter 8.

What's the check amount?

After you've entered the payee's name, press Tab to go to the $ (Amount) field so that you can enter the amount of the check. You can enter check amounts as large as $9,999,999.99 using up to 10 characters (the decimal point counts as one character, but the commas do not). And by the way, you don't have to type dollar signs or commas.

After you've entered the check amount and pressed Tab, Quicken writes out the amount on the next line of the check just as you would do if you were writing a manual check. Some of the words in the written amount may be abbreviated by Quicken to save space; like "Hundred" is **Hndrd**, "Thousand" is **Thsnd**, and "Million" is **Mill**.

 TIP   **See the calculator icon in the $ (Amount) field in the Write Checks window?** You can click this to open Quicken's minicalculator and use it to calculate the check amount. For example, if you have several invoices payable to the same payee, you can add the invoice amounts together with the minicalculator and then press Enter to record the result in the $ (Amount) field. The chapter on Quicken shortcuts, Chapter 8, tells you more about the minicalculator.

Filling in the payee address

You can enter the payee's address on checks if you want to use window envelopes to mail checks. When you enter an address for the payee in the Write Checks window, Quicken prints the address on the check so that it shows in the envelope window. You can type up to 5 lines in the address and use up to 30 characters in each line.

If you're going to enter the payee's address, press Tab to move to the Address field in the Write Checks window. Then begin typing the payee's name and address. Use the Tab key to move to the next line.

TIP **Here's a little time-saver for you. If you want the payee name in** the address to be exactly as it is entered in the Pay to the Order of field, type an apostrophe (') or quotation marks (") in the first line of the Address field and then press Enter. Quicken copies the name from the Pay to the Order of field and puts it in the first address line. Since the Pay to the Order of field has space for 40 characters and the address line has space for only 30, the last 10 characters of the payee's name may get cut off.

Adding a memo

The Memo field in the Write Checks window is completely optional. If you want to enter a check memo, type up to 31 characters in the Memo field. I use memos to provide the payee of a check with information so that he can match my check to an invoice. I may enter the invoice number, my account number, or just **April Rent** to identify my check.

Q&A *Does the memo that I enter in the Write Checks window get printed on the check?*

Yes. So, if there's information that you don't necessarily want the payee to see, don't enter it as a memo in the Write Checks window. Instead, you can omit the memo, print the check, and then go to the register where Quicken records the check transaction and enter the memo there.

Assigning a category to a check

If you read Chapter 4, you know how important I think it is to use categories in Quicken to track your income and expenses. Assigning a category to a check tells Quicken the type of expense the check is being written for, such as utilities, interest expense, entertainment, clothing, etc. The Category field is where you assign the category, subcategory, or other account (for transfers) to a check. If you don't assign something here, the check does not get classified into an expense category. It just ends up in an Other category and you won't know what it's made up of.

When you get to the Category field, you see another one of those drop-down lists. Included in this list is all of your categories, subcategories, and accounts so that you can just select one to enter in the Category field. (If the drop-down list doesn't automatically appear, just click the down-arrow to see it).

If you'd rather just type in your category, start typing the category name. Again, you'll notice that after you've typed a character, Quicken fills in the rest of a category name for you. This is QuickFill at work.

By the way, if you're assigning a subcategory to a check, you can also select it from the drop-down list or type the parent category followed by a colon (:) and then type the subcategory name.

Q&A *What if the category that I need to assign to the check that I'm writing doesn't exist? How do I add it from here?*

If the category that you need to assign to a check isn't in the Category & Transfer List, you can add the new category *on the fly* by just typing the new category name in the Category field. When Quicken doesn't find it in the Category & Transfer List, the Set Up Category window appears so that you can add it now.

You also can assign an account to a check by selecting or entering the account name in the Category field. This is called a *transfer transaction* which transfers funds from one Quicken account to another. I talked about transfer transactions in more detail in Chapter 5.

Q&A *Do I use the Splits button to assign more than one category to a check?*

Yes. Remember in Chapter 5 when I talked about splitting transactions so that you can assign more than one category to a transaction? Splitting a check is done in just the same way. Just click the Splits button to open the Splits window and assign categories to your hearts content (but only 30, please!). If you're not feeling quite sure how to split a transaction, go back to Chapter 5 and read the section, "Go ahead, assign more than one category."

Recording a check

When you've filled in the check in the Write Checks window, you're ready to record it. Review the check first to make sure the amount is correct and that you've written it to the appropriate payee, and then click the Record button.

When you record a check in the Write Checks window, Quicken enters the check transaction in the register for the account that you wrote the check from. Figure 6.5 shows a check that I just wrote and figure 6.6 shows you the check transaction in the register after it's recorded.

Fig. 6.5
Here's a check I wrote in the Write Checks window from the Joint Checking account before it has been recorded.

Q&A ***Wait a minute! I didn't enter the check number any-where. Don't I need to?***

No. You don't enter the check number when you're writing checks. When you're ready to print the checks that you've written, Quicken asks you to enter the next check number from your preprinted checks. It then assigns the appropriate check number to the checks that you print. So don't worry about check numbers until you get ready to print.

After you record a check, it scrolls off your screen and a blank check appears so that you can write another one. After you've written and recorded a check, it's ready to print. I'll tell you how to print your checks a little later in this chapter.

Fig. 6.6
Here's the check transaction that Quicken enters in the Joint Checking account register after I recorded the check.

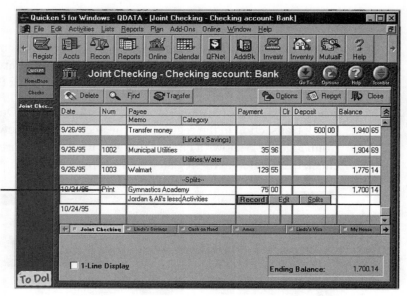

Quicken inserts the word "*Print*" here to show that this is a check that needs to be printed

Want to review the checks you've written?

If you want to look over the checks you've just written, now is the time to do it. Don't wait until they're already printed because you may waste some of your preprinted computer checks.

Quicken stores the checks that you write in the Write Checks window UNTIL you print them. Once you print the checks that you've written, they're no longer in the Write Checks window. Instead, Quicken records them in the register for the account that you wrote them from. You can always review them in the register, but again, if they're in the register then they have already been printed and perhaps wasted if there are mistakes.

Q&A *Can I change a check back to the way it was before I started editing it?*

While you're editing a check, you can change it back to the way it was originally by clicking the Res_t_ore button. The check now looks the way it did before you started editing it. The Res_t_ore button only works if you click it before you record the changes to your check. Once you click the Re_c_ord button to record changes to a check, you cannot restore the check.

I don't really want this check

What if I wrote a check for a bill that I've already paid? How do I get rid of it? I certainly don't want to print it. Well, since checks in the Write Checks window have not been printed yet, (because if they had been, they wouldn't be there; they'd be in the register) you can delete the check at any time.

First, flip to the check that you want to delete so that it's the one shown in the Write Checks window. Then click the Delete button from the button bar. Quicken won't let you make hasty decisions so it displays a confirmation message to make sure that you really want to delete the check. If you do, click Yes. If you don't want to delete it, click No and the check will remain untouched.

Do I void a check from here?

No. You don't void checks from the Write Checks window. And here's why. Checks in the Write Checks window have NOT been printed yet. They're just the checks that you've just written but have not gotten around to printing. Because you never need to void a check that hasn't been printed, you don't void checks from the Write Checks window.

Make sense? Well, let's look at an example. Let's say that you write a check in the Write Checks window to M&M Plumbing for $165.00 to repair your leaky water faucet. You then discover that your husband already paid M&M by credit card. If you haven't printed the check yet, it's still in the Write Checks window and you can just delete it (like you learned in the last section).

But, if you did print the check to M&M Plumbing, you will need to void it so that it can't get cashed. You'll void the check in the register for the account you wrote the check from. You already learned how to do this in Chapter 5, so turn back if you need to review voiding transactions again.

 TIP **When you void a check, make sure that you write VOID in big** letters on the printed check so that it can't mistakenly get cashed.

Let's print checks now

So you've written a few checks in the Write Checks window that you're ready to print. Don't press the print button yet.

Is Quicken ready to print?

You have to give Quicken some information about your printer and your checks before you can begin printing, like:

- Which printer you're using

- How checks are fed into your printer

- What kind of preprinted computer checks you'll be using (standard, voucher, or wallet)

- And how you'll load partial pages of checks into your printer

Give Quicken the information about your printer by selecting File, Printer Setup, Check Printer Setup. You'll see the Check Printer Setup window, like the one in figure 6.7, where you can begin setting up Quicken to print checks.

Fig. 6.7
Tell Quicken everything it needs to know about your printer and checks in the Check Printer Setup window.

Tell Quicken which checks you're using by selecting from the drop-down list of check types

Quicken can detect the type of paper feed your printer uses

Select your installed printer from the drop-down list in this box

Click the Font button to change the font style and size for check printing. Quicken includes several fonts and styles for you to choose from

Use the Align button to adjust the print on checks

Want a logo printed on your checks? Click the Logo button to select the .BMP file with your logo

If you print checks from a partial page of checks (where one or more have already been torn off), select the way the partial page gets loaded in your printer

To change other printer settings, like the paper tray, paper size, orientation, and number of copies printed at a time, click the Settings button

When you've entered the printer information that Quicken needs, click OK in the Check Printer Setup window and you're one step closer to printing those checks.

Now, let's align my checks

These preprinted computer checks were more expensive than the checks you're used to carrying around with you. So you certainly don't want to waste any of them because the print isn't properly aligned.

So let's take a little time and align your checks so that you don't have to scrap any of them because they weren't printed correctly. The best way to make sure your checks are properly aligned is to print a sample check. You can use the sample checks that Quicken enclosed in the Quicken Deluxe software package so that you don't have to use one of your own preprinted checks.

 Q&A ***Am I going to have to go through this alignment process every time I print checks?***

No, no, no. Quicken would never have you waste your time like that. You'll just have to align your checks once. Quicken saves the alignment settings so that they stay the same each time you print.

Now, go ahead and insert Quicken's sample checks into your printer. Then select File, Printer Setup, Check Printer Setup to get back to the Check Printer Setup window that you saw in figure 6.7. What happens next depends on the type of printer that you have.

Aligning continuous-feed checks

You should be looking at the Check Printer Setup window right now. So click the Align button so that we can start getting your checks aligned. In the next dialog box, select the method that you want to use to align your continuous-feed checks. Select Coarse alignment to adjust the text on your printed checks by one line or more; select Fine to make small horizontal or vertical alignments.

If you selected Coarse alignment, select OK next to print a sample check. Don't do anything right now to the checks in your printer. Just let the sample check print and then remove it so that you can see how the text was printed on the check. You'll now see the Coarse Alignment window (see fig. 6.8) on your screen where you can give Quicken some feedback on the sample check so it knows how it printed.

Fig. 6.8
Tell Quicken how well, or not so well, the text was aligned on the printed sample check.

Click OK

Find the POINTER LINE on the sample check and its position number from the check form's pin-feed strips and enter it here

If the text isn't properly aligned, Quicken automatically adjusts the checks in your printer and prints another sample check. If the text is aligned correctly, you're set. Just make note of the position of the checks in your printer and reload them the same way the next time you print checks.

If you selected Fine alignment, use the Fine Alignment dialog box to move the checks in your printer by increments of 1/100 of an inch (see fig. 6.9).

Fig. 6.9
Fine-tune the alignment of your continuous-feed checks by making very small adjustments.

Click to print a sample continuous-feed check with grid lines to help you figure out how much the text needs to move

Click these arrows to move the text up or down in increments of 1/100 of an inch

When the text is properly positioned on the checks, make a note of the position of the checks in your printer and reload them the same way the next time you print checks. Click OK in the Check Printer Setup window to save your alignment settings.

Aligning single-sheet or laser checks

For those of you with single-sheet printers, like laser, inkjet, PostScript, or other page-oriented printers, your job in aligning checks is not so involved. You'll be performing only the fine alignment of your sample checks.

Start from the Check Printer Setup window and then click the Align button. You see the Align Checks dialog box next (see fig. 6.10). Even if your checks come three to a page, you won't always have a full sheet of checks in your printer to print checks on. You have to give Quicken the alignment settings for one, two, or three checks per page.

Fig. 6.10
Ready to align your single-sheet checks so they print correctly? Select the number of checks per page that you want to align.

Tell Quicken how many checks per page you want to align by clicking one of these buttons

These settings are the ones currently used by Quicken to print your checks

Click OK if you know the alignment settings are correct

If you need to adjust the alignment settings that were shown in the Align Checks dialog box, click the button for the number of checks that you want to align. For example, to align a full page of checks, click the Full Page of Checks button; to align a page with only one check, click the One Check on Page button.

Now Quicken displays the Fine Alignment dialog box (shown earlier in fig. 6.9) where you can adjust the way text prints vertically and horizontally on checks. If the text on your single-sheet checks is not aligned properly, adjust the text vertically or horizontally in 1/100 of an inch increments.

To determine how the text will print on your preprinted computer checks, insert one of Quicken's sample checks into your printer or plain paper and click the Print Sample button. Quicken prints a grid on the sample check that you can use as a gauge for text alignment. After the sample check prints, check the alignment of the text. If you printed a sample check on plain paper, overlay it on top of one of your preprinted checks to check the alignment.

Each box in the alignment grid represents 10 units of height and 10 units of width. So, if the text is too high by one grid box, subtract 10 from the Vertical field value. If the text is too far left one-half grid box, increase the Horizontal field value by 5.

Print as many sample checks as you need to get the text aligned properly. After you've made the adjustments you need to get the text aligned, click OK twice to return to the Check Printer Setup window. Then click OK again to save your alignment settings.

Ready, set, print

Now you're ready to see how fast Quicken prints all those checks you just wrote. You're not going to believe how fast this whole process is. Since you're not going to have to align your checks anymore (you only have to do it once), writing and printing checks is a snap.

After you've written and reviewed your checks, just click the Print button in the Write Checks window when you're ready to print and Quicken shows you the Select Checks to Print window like in figure 6.11. Then tell Quicken the check number of the next blank, preprinted check, which checks you want to print, and print away.

Select to print all the checks you've written, only those checks that are dated through a certain date, or just the ones that you specify

Fig. 6.11
When you're ready to print checks, tell Quicken the next check number to use and then select which checks you want to print

Here's where you tell Quicken what the next preprinted check number is. Press the + or the – key to change the check number by increments of one

Select this option to print a logo on your check

If your computer checks are on single sheets, tell Quicken how many checks are on the first page of checks it will be printing to

Make sure the correct check style appears here. If it's not, select the right one

If you want to print more than one copy of a check, select this option

Selecting checks to print

Unless you specify otherwise, Quicken prints all of the checks that you've written in the Write Checks window. Notice in the Select Checks to Print window in figure 6.11, the All Checks option is already selected when you open the window. When this option is selected, Quicken prints all written checks when you click the OK button.

But what if you don't want to print all checks right now. Maybe you wrote checks for the entire month and only want to print the checks due through the 15th. Or, you may just want to print one or two checks right now and print the rest later.

To print checks dated through a certain date, click the Checks Dated Through: option and then enter the date. For example, entering **12/15/95** means that Quicken will only print checks with dates prior to 12/15/95.

If you want to hand-pick the checks that Quicken prints, click the Selected Checks option and then click the Choose button. Quicken displays another window, that lists all the checks that you've written but not yet printed.

Click each check that you want to print or highlight the check and press the spacebar. When you select a check, Quicken puts a check mark in the Print column to show that it will print. Click the Mark All button to select all checks, or click the Clear All button to remove all of the check marks from the Print column and start over selecting checks. When you've selected the checks that you want to print, click the Done button to return to the Select Checks to Print window.

Printing checks

After you've selected the checks that you want to print, you're ready to begin printing. From the Select Checks to Print window, click the OK button to print all of the selected checks now. If you want to see how the first check looks before printing all of them, click the Print First button to print only the first check.

Quicken prints your check(s) and asks whether they printed correctly. If they did, click OK. If one or more of the checks didn't print properly, type the number of the first check that didn't print right and then click OK. Quicken goes back to the Select Checks to Print window so that you can reprint the checks that didn't print correctly.

TIP   **If you lose a check that you've printed or a check gets misprinted** or destroyed somehow, you can just reprint. First, find the check transaction in the register for the account that the check was written from. Then, move to the Num field and type the word Print (or select Print from the drop-down list) over the check number. This tricks Quicken into thinking that it has not printed a check yet for this transaction. When you go to the Write Checks window and select the Print button, Quicken will reprint the check. Now don't forget though that you'll have to enter a voided transaction for the check that got lost or destroyed so that all of your checks are accounted for.

7

Let Quicken Help Balance Your Checkbook

● **In this chapter:**

● **Learn why balancing your checkbook is important**

● **Mark cleared transactions**

● **Balance your checkbook**

● **Print a reconciliation report**

● **Make adjustments so your checkbook balances**

Save yourself bounced check fees and some stress by letting Quicken help you balance your checking account this month . . . .

I know a lot of people who don't ever balance their checkbooks. They proclaim that it's a waste of time and that they don't need to do it; and certainly, you won't get arrested if you don't. But it's my contention that you can't really have a handle on how much money you have in your checking account if you don't do the balancing act.

Balancing your checkbook is like going to the dentist. You know you have to do it, but you put it off and dread every minute of it. Well, with Quicken, balancing your checkbook really doesn't have to be so frightful. (And I'll assure you it'll be more appealing than your dental checkup!)

Why do I need to balance my checkbook?

We all make mistakes. Right? Financial institutions, like your bank, aren't always perfect either. So when you balance your checkbook, you're performing a "check" of *your* records against the *bank's*; you're comparing the transactions and balance in your checkbook register against the transactions and balance shown on your bank statement. If you or your bank has made a mistake, you'll catch it when you balance your checking account.

One of the most common mistakes people make in their checking accounts, including me, is forgetting to record withdrawals from the ATM. It's easy to forget these transactions; there's no check involved so you usually don't have your checkbook register handy when you step up to the machine. So, if you've forgotten about $500 in withdrawals, how are you going to remember to account for them down the road? You'll think you have more money in your checking account than you really do. And what if that causes you to bounce a check?

 Plain English, please!

If you're not sure what I mean by **ATM**, it's the Automated Teller Machine that enables you to transact electronically with your bank.

If you balance your checkbook on a regular basis (each time you receive your bank statement), you'll catch forgotten withdrawals or other transactions before they cause you headaches later. And if your bank has made a mistake by omitting a deposit to your account or debiting your account for an erroneous amount, you won't know about these errors unless you balance your account. It'll be easier for you to catch errors and omissions if you balance your account each time you receive your bank statement.

Let Quicken do the hard jobs

When you use Quicken to balance your checking account, it does all the hard jobs for you. All you have to do is enter the information from your bank statement and let Quicken do the rest.

Here's what you'll need to do so that Quicken can balance your account:

- Choose the account you want to balance

- Enter the opening and ending statement account balances

- Enter the amounts and dates of other transactions shown on your bank statement, like service charges and interest earned

- Mark the transactions that have cleared your bank (the ones that are shown on your bank statement)

The next few sections teach you how to perform your part in the balancing act. When you're done, hopefully, your account will balance to the penny!

Tell Quicken which account you want to balance

You can balance, or reconcile, any bank account you have in Quicken. You can reconcile checking, savings, or money market accounts. When you reconcile an account, you're simply comparing the transactions and balance in your Quicken account register with the transactions and balance from your bank statement.

 Plain English, please!

When you **reconcile** a bank account, you're comparing the cleared balance that the bank says you have in your account with the cleared balance shown in your Quicken records. The **cleared** balance is the amount left in your account after all transactions have been presented to the bank.

If you have more than one bank account in Quicken, you need to tell Quicken which one you want to balance. If you're already using the account that you want to balance (like if you have the account's register open or the Write Checks window for the account), just click the Recon icon from the iconbar. Quicken assumes you want to reconcile the account that you were working in when you clicked the Recon button. Because Quicken already knows the account you want to reconcile, the Reconcile Bank Statement window opens with the name of the account at the top.

If you're not working in an account right now, (maybe you're working in the Category & Transfer List, the Financial Calendar, or in HomeBase), you'll need to tell Quicken which account you want to balance. So, when you click the Recon icon, Quicken displays the Choose Reconcile Account dialog box. Click the down-arrow in the Account box to see your list of bank accounts and then select one. Click OK to open the Reconcile Bank Statement window.

The Reconcile Bank Statement window is your starting point for balancing your account. Here is where you enter the information from your bank statement that Quicken needs for its balancing computations.

Now what does the bank say your balance is?

Let's look over your bank statement carefully to familiarize yourself with the information that appears. Here's some of the important stuff you should see:

- Your bank account number
- The beginning and ending statement dates
- The beginning and ending account balances
- Interest earned during the period, if any
- Bank fees charged during the period, if any

Your statement may include other information like the annual percentage yield on interest bearing accounts, interest paid to date, your taxpayer ID number, and so forth. This information is not important to the reconciliation process.

So now you're ready to tell Quicken what your bank statement balance is.

The Reconcile Bank Statement

Here's the Reconcile Bank Statement window for the account that you want to balance.

Any bank fees or service charges should be entered here.

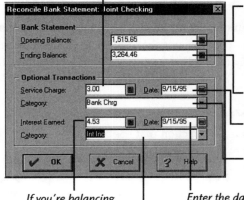

Quicken enters the ending balance from the last time it reconciled the account as the opening balance this time. If you've never balanced the account before, the opening balance is the balance that you entered when you set up the account in Quicken.

Enter the ending statement balance here.

The date that your account was debited for bank fees or service charges is entered here.

Select the category that you want to assign to service charges.

If you're balancing an interest-bearing account, enter any interest earned for the period.

Enter the date that the interest was credited to your account.

You should assign a category to bank transactions, just like any other transaction. Select the category to assign to interest income from this bank account.

When the Reconcile Bank Statement window is complete, click OK and you're ready to start marking cleared transactions.

CAUTION **If you haven't balanced your account in a while, don't just pick up** the last bank statement and start balancing from there. You need to go back to each bank statement you haven't reconciled and start from there. If you try to reconcile only your latest statement, you won't know which checks had cleared previously and you won't know if there were any balancing differences in previous periods. Balancing your account this time will become a nightmare!

Just click to mark cleared transactions

Moving from the Reconcile Bank Statement window where you enter bank statement information Quicken displays another Reconcile Bank Statement window listing all of your transactions in your bank account register that have not yet cleared (see fig. 7.1).

 Plain English, please!

A **cleared transaction** is a transaction that has been debited or credited to your account by your bank. **99**

If you need to add a new transaction while your reconciling, click the New button

You can make changes to a transaction by highlighting it in the list and clicking the Edit button. Quicken goes to the transaction in the register so that you can edit it

Delete transactions that shouldn't be in the list by clicking the Delete button

Want to go back to the first Reconcile Bank Statement window to see the statement information that you entered? Click the Info button

Fig. 7.1
Quicken lists all of the transactions that have not yet cleared the bank. From this list, mark the transactions that your statement shows as cleared.

The Mark button is used to mark the highlighted transaction as cleared

This option sorts your transactions by date, instead of by check number

As you mark transactions as cleared, Quicken updates these balances

When you successfully balance your bank account, the Difference amount will be $0.00 (zero)

Quicken 5 for Windows - QDATA - [Reconcile Bank Statement: Joint Checking]

File Edit Activities Lists Reports Plan Add-Ons Online Window Help

Registr | Accts | Recon | Reports | Online | Calendar | QFNet | AddrBk | Investr | Inventry | MutualF | Help

Reconcile Bank Statement: Joint Checking   Go To Options Help Iconbar

Mark | New | Edit | Delete | Info... | Help | Close

| Payments and Checks | | | | | Deposits | | | |
Clr	Date	Chk #	Payee	Amount	Clr	Date	Chk #	Payee	Amount
	9/ 3/95	ATM	Cash	-150.00		8/16/95	DEP	Brown & Co.	1,919.52
✔	9/ 6/95		Servic...	-1.00		8/22/95		Transfer Mon...	500.00
	8/21/95	1001	C&C Prop...	-600.00	✔	8/29/95		Interest E...	3.00
	8/22/95	1002	Municipal...	-35.00		9/ 3/95	DEP	Brown & Co.	1,919.52
	8/22/95	1003	Walmart	-129.55					
	8/28/95	1004	Gymnasti...	-75.00					
	8/28/95	1005	St. Elizab...	-25.00					
	9/ 6/95	1006	C&C Prop...	-600.00					
	9/ 7/95	1007	Municipal...	-32.88					

1 check, debit   -1.00   1 deposit, credit   3.00

☐ Sort by Date

Finished | Finish Later | Cancel

Cleared Balance:	100.00
Bank Ending Balance:	102.00
Difference:	-2.00

Now you're ready to mark the transactions that have cleared your bank. All cleared transactions appear on your bank statement; if they're not there, they haven't cleared. To mark a transaction as cleared, use the up and down arrow buttons to highlight it and then click the Mark button in the button bar. When you click this button, Quicken puts a check mark by the transaction in the Clr column and moves down to the next transaction. If that transaction has cleared, click the Mark button again, and so on.

 TIP **You also can mark a transaction as cleared by clicking the transac-** tion. When you mark a transaction this way, however, the highlight bar doesn't move to the next transaction after you click.

Notice that in the list of uncleared transactions, any transactions you entered from the bank statement (like interest earned or services charges) are already marked as cleared.

 TIP **Your bank statement usually lists the check number next to each** cleared transaction. If there are several checks in sequential order that have cleared, say 1234 to 1249, you can quickly mark a range of transactions as cleared, instead of marking them one by one. Just click the first transaction in the range that you want to mark, then move to the last transaction and press the Shift key as you click.

 Q&A ***What if, by mistake, I mark an uncleared transaction as cleared?***

That's easy to fix. Just click the transaction to "unmark" it and remove the check mark. Toggle between marking and unmarking transactions by clicking.

 TIP **If you discover a transaction on your bank statement that you** haven't entered, just click the New button to insert it in the register. You can also edit and delete transactions while you're reconciling by clicking the Edit and Delete buttons.

 Q&A ***Something just came up and I don't have time to finish balancing my account. I'm in the Reconcile Bank Statement transaction list right now. What do I do?***

Quicken lets you quit balancing your account even if you're not finished. See the Finish Later button at the bottom of the Reconcile Bank Statement transaction list in figure 7.1? Just click this button and Quicken saves your work in the Reconcile Bank Statement transaction list. When you're ready to resume balancing your account, just select the account and click the Recon icon in the iconbar.

CAUTION   **Don't leave the Reconcile Bank Statement transaction list by** clicking the Cancel button. When you select Cancel, Quicken does *not* save your work and you'll have to start over the next time.

Look! My checkbook balanced

Hopefully, now is your moment of triumph. You've entered all your bank statement information and marked all cleared transactions. You may have even added a transaction or two or edited a transaction while you were reconciling your account. So how do you know if your account balanced? Look at the Difference amount at the bottom of the Reconcile Bank Statement window. The Difference amount should be $0.00, which means that the cleared balance that you show in your account register is the same as the ending balance on your bank statement.

When the Difference amount is $0.00, you've successfully balanced your account and you're finished. So click the Finished button. Quicken congratulates you (and so do I) in figure 7.2 and asks if you want to print a reconciliation report.

Fig. 7.2
Let me congratulate you, along with Quicken, on balancing your account. Good work! Now decide whether you want to print a Reconciliation Report.

TIP **After you balance your account, you won't be aware of this at the** time, but Quicken puts an R (for reconciled) in the Clr column of each cleared transaction in the register.

Printing a reconciliation report

After you finish balancing your account, you can print a report that shows the details of the reconciliation you just did. As shown in figure 7.2, Quicken asks whether you want to print a reconciliation report. Click Yes if you want to print the report and Quicken displays the Reconciliation Report Setup window (see fig. 7.3) for you to complete.

 Plain English, please!

A **Reconciliation Report** is a printed record of the reconciliation you just performed. It lists all the cleared transactions and also lists all checks and deposits still outstanding.

Fig. 7.3
Complete the
Reconciliation Report
Setup window if you
want a printed report
of your account
reconciliation.

*Click this option if you
want your savings goal
transactions to appear
in the Reconciliation
Report*

⌐*Enter a title for your report using up to 25
characters*

⌐*Quicken inserts today's date here or you can
enter a different date*

*Choosing all transactions gives you all the
details of every transaction, cleared or uncleared; if you want Quicken to summarize
cleared transactions but give detail of
uncleared transactions, choose to include
summary and uncleared transactions*

└ *Click this button to open the Print Report window where you
tell Quicken more about printing the Reconciliation Report*

When you click Print from the Reconciliation Report Setup window in figure 7.3, Quicken displays the Print Report window. This is the generic print window that Quicken always displays when printing reports. Complete the Print Report window and then select OK to begin printing the Reconciliation Report.

Oh no! My checkbook didn't balance

If your account didn't balance (the Difference amount in the Reconcile Bank Statement transaction list window is any number other than $0.00), don't get uptight. Maybe you marked a transaction as cleared that really hadn't cleared the bank. Or vice versa. Or, maybe you recorded the wrong amount for a transaction in your register. Or, you may have inadvertently entered the wrong amount as the ending balance on your statement (with all the amounts shown on your bank statement, this is easy to do). So check the amounts you entered carefully, as well as the transactions that you marked as cleared. If you can't find the discrepancy after your review, you may have to enter an adjustment transaction so that your account balances.

There are two types of adjustment transactions—one for an opening balance difference and one for other differences.

 CAUTION   **If your account didn't balance the last time you performed a** reconciliation with Quicken, then you can't expect it to balance this time. Don't let balancing differences build up. The first time your account doesn't balance, look for the difference. If, after much deliberation, you don't find it, go ahead and make a balance adjustment. Then, the next time you balance your account, you should have no differences.

Do I adjust the opening balance?

Remember when you started balancing your account? You saw the Reconcile Bank Statement window that asked for the bank statement ending balance and other transactions from your bank statement. And remember that Quicken automatically entered the opening balance for you. The amount that Quicken used here was the ending balance from the last time you balanced your account. But if you didn't balance your account, Quicken uses the starting balance from when you set up your account as the opening balance.

Well, what if you changed the opening balance amount when you started balancing your account to match the balance shown on your statement? If you did, Quicken shows an Opening Bal. Difference in the Reconcile Bank Statement window, like in figure 7.4.

Fig. 7.4

When you change the opening balance, Quicken shows an Opening Bal. Difference that's the difference between the balance you entered and the one that Quicken thinks you should have.

Here's the opening balance difference that may cause your account not to balance

Here are some reasons why you may have an opening balance difference:

- This is the first time you've balanced your account with Quicken so Quicken is using the starting balance in your checking account as the bank statement opening balance. If you didn't use the ending balance from your last bank statement as your starting balance when you set up your checking account, this may be the difference.

- You're not reconciling your account with the right statement. Maybe you haven't balanced your account in a while. If you pick up your latest bank statement and start to reconcile it, your opening balance will be way off. Go back to the first bank statement you haven't reconciled (even if it's six months ago) and start with it. Then balance your account with each subsequent statement until you're up-to-date.

- When you started using Quicken, you may have entered some transactions in the register that had already cleared the bank but that you hadn't marked as cleared. This really messes up your opening balance. If you're entering old transactions in Quicken, be sure that you mark them as cleared if they have shown up on previous bank statements.

When you click the Finished button to complete the reconciliation and you have an opening balance difference, Quicken asks if you want to create an adjustment to make your account balance. If you do, enter the date for the adjustment transaction and click <u>Y</u>es.

Or do I adjust for other differences?

If Quicken shows a Difference amount in the Reconcile Bank Statement window that isn't related to an opening balance difference, you may want to make a balance adjustment as a last resort.

 Plain English, please!

> A **balance adjustment** means that Quicken creates a transaction in your account register that forces your account to balance with your bank statement. Let's say that when you balance your account there's a $1.28 difference. You've looked all over the place for this difference and can't find it. It's a pretty immaterial difference, so you can get your account to balance by making a $1.28 balance adjustment. **"**

So, you're finished balancing your account and you have a difference. When you click the Fini<u>s</u>hed button, Quicken asks whether you want to enter a balance adjustment for the difference (see fig. 7.5).

Fig. 7.5

Here's where you can tell Quicken to make a balance adjustment so that your account balances. Just select the date for the transaction and Quicken enters it in the account register for you.

Enter the date for the balance adjustment transaction, click the <u>A</u>djust button, and Quicken enters it in the register for you. Then tell Quicken if you want to print a Reconciliation Report; click <u>Y</u>es to print the report or <u>N</u>o if you don't want a report.

After you print the reconciliation report, you'll see the balance adjustment transaction in the register, like the one in figure 7.6.

Fig. 7.6

Quicken enters the balance adjustment transaction in the register for you. If you want, you can change the balance adjustment transaction, but your account will not balance if you change the amount.

Part II: Saving Time with Quicken

8

Nifty Quicken Shortcuts that can Save You Time

● **In this chapter:**

- Forget the wall calendar! You've got one on-screen!

- Forget the desk calculator! You've got one on-screen!

- Let Quicken type for you

- Did you pay the electric company? Quicken's Find feature searches for transactions

I'll bet there are plenty of fun things you could do if only you had some spare time. Quicken's shortcuts can reduce your work time and add free time to your day . . . . ▶

When you start taking advantage of the shortcuts Quicken provides, you'll feel like you have a personal assistant at your side, second-guessing your needs, handing you whatever tools you require, and even ready to type transactions for you.

Quicken provides you with the next best thing to a personal assistant— shortcuts like a pop-up calculator and a calendar only a mouse-click away, magic before-your-eyes typing initiated by a couple of keystrokes, and a filing system that never loses anything!

Never type a date again

You know how irritating it is to type **10/18/95**—you search all over the keyboard for the number keys, you can never remember if you're supposed to type the slashes or if this is one of those programs that does the slashes for you (it is), then if you try to enter slashes your fingers trip over the slash and hit the period instead. And which slash key are you supposed to use, anyway?

Forget all that nonsense about typing dates. Quicken makes date-entering easy!

Today's date is a natural

When you open the check register, Quicken is ready for you to type a new transaction—and this program is one step ahead of you in the date department. Today's date is already waiting for your approval, as shown in figure 8.1.

To accept today's date as the date you want to use, just advance to the next field (the NUM field) in this manner:

- Click with your mouse in the NUM field.

Or

- Press the TAB key to move to the NUM field.

Fig. 8.1
Today's date magically
appears when you
open a register.

Today's date
appears at the
start of a
transaction ——

Click here to
advance to the —
NUM field

TIP   **To quickly enter today's date in a date field that has been**
changed to a different date, simply strike the T (for Today) on your
keyboard.

Q&A   *I'm entering several checks that are dated yesterday.*
Will I have to change the date from today's date for
each check?

Nope. When you enter a series of transactions, Quicken repeats the last
date you used until you change the date yourself. In this case yesterday's
date will repeat for each transaction.

Changing the date is a "plus" or "minus" away

Say you don't want to use today's date, but today's date is the date that's
staring at you from the screen. How do you switch to a new date?

For starters, forget about typing a different date, that's the hard way. If you're
not going very far with the date—just a few days in either direction—just use
the plus and minus keys on your numeric keypad to make the date advance
or retreat.

- Each time you press + the date advances one day.

- Each time you press – the date goes back one day.

Making significant date changes with the pop-up calendar

You can press + or – until your fingers ache, but if you want to change the date in a big way (say you're entering last year's transactions) you need to bring in the big guns.

Look closely next to the date, and you'll see a little box with spots in it—that's supposed to represent a calendar (see fig. 8.2). Click this little box and a baby calendar appears on your screen!

Now you've got the centuries at your fingertips.

- Click any visible date in the calendar and Quicken types that date on-screen.

- Click the arrows to the right or left of the month in the calendar to move the calendar forward or backward a month (see fig. 8.2).

Let your fingers do the walking

There are keyboard shortcuts for changing your date. While in the date field, instead of typing a date, you can type one of these letters to place a date on the screen.

Key	Action
t	Today
m	First day of month
h	Last day of month
y	First day of year
r	Last day of year

• Hold down your mouse button while pointing to one of the month arrows to rapid-fire your calendar into the future or back to the past—several months will fly by before your eyes.

Clicking an actual date puts the date on your screen and takes the calendar away.

Q&A ***What if I just want to use the calendar to check on what day of the week my birthday will fall, but I don't want to change the date on-screen?***

You can look up whatever date you want in the calendar and then press Esc. This takes the calendar away and leaves the date on-screen the way it was before you started poking around.

Fig. 8.2
An on-screen calendar is only a click away.

Click this little button and get this little calendar

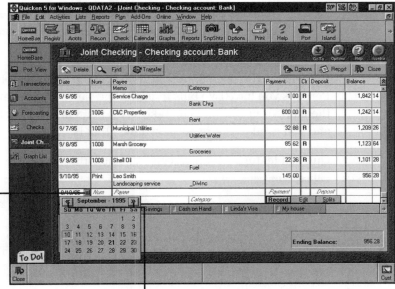

Click one of these buttons to change the month

The price of bread and other useful things you can figure out with Quicken's on-screen calculator

You've entered the date, you've entered the name of the payee or payer—now you need to enter an amount.

First of all, there may already be an amount entered for you. If Quicken has been trained to fetch the amount from the most recent transaction with this payee (or payer), that's what you'll see in the amount position. If that's the right amount and you don't need to make a change—you're finished here and ready to go to the next field.

 TIP Quicken's ability to automatically recall previous transactions is part of a feature called **memorization** and is discussed in Chapter 9.

But what if you need to do a little figuring in order to determine an amount? Perhaps you have two bills to pay to the same supplier and you need to add them up, or maybe you can take a two percent discount for an early payment and you need to figure out how much that is.

Quicken features an on-screen calculator that can come to your mathematical rescue.

To pull up the calculator directly from a number field:

- Click the little calculator icon in the Payment or Deposit fields (see fig. 8.3).

Or

- Press the + key on your keyboard (either press Shift and + on the main keyboard, or use the + on the numeric keypad).

Enter calculations in the calculator by using the number keys on your keyboard (or numeric keypad) or clicking on the numbers on the calculator with your mouse. Use the following mathematical symbols to perform operations:

+   addition

-    subtraction

*   multiplication

/   division

All of these math operators are represented by keys on the pop-up calculator so you can either click them on the calculator or type them from the keyboard. Finishing your calculation with the = sign (either type it or click it) or pressing Enter on the keyboard will put the answer on your screen and close the calculator.

There may come a time when you want to use the calculator but you aren't in a field that sports a calculator button. Maybe you're ready to type in the date field but you want to quickly do some calculations to figure out how much money you're going to have after next month's bills are paid. Instead of using a pop-up calculator, you can bring Quicken's calculator to the screen anytime by clicking on the Activities menu and selecting Use Calculator. The Quicken Calculator appears on-screen (see fig. 8.3).

Drag here to move the calculator

Click here to close the calculator

Fig. 8.3
Use Quicken's calculator to perform any standard mathematical operation.

The Quicken Calculator (as opposed to the pop-up calculator) stays on-screen until you don't want it anymore. In fact, you may want to slide it off to the side (use your mouse and drag the title, "Quicken Calculator" off to the side of the screen) and keep it available for whenever you need it (refer to fig. 8.3). Remove the calculator from your screen by double-clicking the calculator's control bar in the upper left-hand corner of the calculator.

 TIP   **After performing a calculation in the Quicken Calculator you can** paste an amount from the calculator into your register so you don't have to type it. First, click in your register where you want the amount to appear. Then, click the Paste button on the calculator.

Let Quicken do your typing for you

You don't have to perform any special tricks, nor do you have to click any little boxes to let Quicken do your typing for you. As long as Quicken is set up to memorize transactions (and, by default, it does this), you just have to start typing the payee or payer in a transaction in the Quicken register and Quicken will finish typing the name for you.

You can put your calculator on the iconbar!

If clicking on the Activities menu and then on Use Calculator is just too many clicks for your taste, you can add a button for the Quicken Calculator to your row of icon buttons at the top of the screen. To add the calculator to your icon buttons, follow these steps:

1 Choose Edit, Options.

2 Click the Iconbar button.

3 Click the New button.

4 In the Icon Action list, click Use Calculator. (Note that the items on this list are not presented in alphabetical order, so you may have to search a bit to find Use Calculator.)

5 Click OK, then click Done, then Close.

From now on, just click the Calculator button on your iconbar whenever you want to use the calculator.

TIP **Quicken may be smart but it's not a mind reader. If you're typing** in a payee's name you haven't used before, you'll have to type the full name. Once you've typed the name, Quicken will recall it as soon as you start typing the first letters of the name.

For example, as soon as you type a **P**, Quicken enters the first "P" company from your list of names you've typed previously, which may be "Poseiden Shipping Co." If the company you are really trying to type is "Pranitis Heating and Cooling," continue typing. By the time you have typed **Pr**, Quicken will have filled in the rest of the name for you. You don't have to type anything more. Click or press Tab to continue to the next field.

Q&A *My transactions aren't filling in the way you described. I know I've typed this company's name before, but I still have to type the full name in each time I want to use it.*

Your transactions aren't getting memorized as you type them. Go to the Edit menu and select Options. Click the Register button, then click the QuickFill tab. Make sure the first two boxes, Automatic Memorization of Transactions, and Automatic Completion of Fields, are checked, as illustrated in figure 8.4. (For more on this memorization feature see Chapter 9, "Speed Up Your Register with Memorized Transactions.")

Fig. 8.4
This is the QuickFill tab in the Regular Options window.

Make sure these two boxes are checked if you want Quicken to automatically fill in your transactions

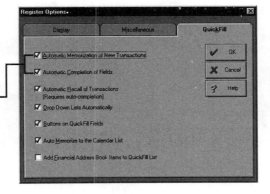

Quicken can help you find lost transactions

Use Quicken to search through your transactions and help you find something you entered in the past. Say you've got a statement in front of you from the electric company and you can't remember whether or not you paid it. Click the Find button, right above your register (or press Alt+I), and Quicken opens a box in which you can enter pertinent information about the transaction for which you are searching.

In the F̲ind box, type in the text or an amount from the transaction you want to find. If you only want Quicken to search in a particular field, click the down arrow across from S̲earch and choose the field you want to examine (see fig. 8.5). Or you can have Quicken look in all fields for your missing transaction information.

Fig. 8.5
Quicken can Find missing transactions for you.

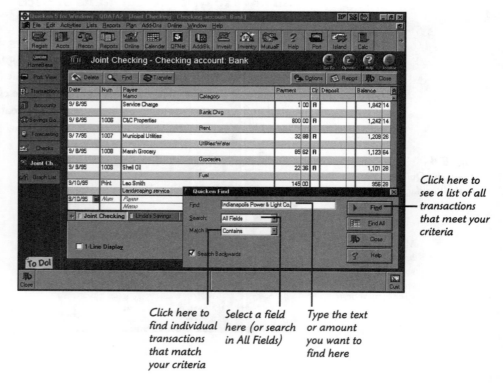

Click here to see a list of all transactions that meet your criteria

Click here to find individual transactions that match your criteria

Select a field here (or search in All Fields)

Type the text or amount you want to find here

Click the Find button to find the first transaction in your register that matches what you typed. Clicking Find again and again will take you through your register, one item at a time, finding every item that matches your criteria.

Click the Find All button and Quicken gives you a list of all the transactions in your register that match the text or amount you typed. Double-clicking any item in the list takes you to the place in the register where you entered that item.

TIP **When using Quicken's Find feature, you don't have to type the** full name from a transaction. Say you're searching for a payment made to Dr. Vosicky. Typing **Dr. V**, then clicking the Find button will take you to the first Dr. V transaction in your register. That may be Dr. Vosicky or it may be Dr. Voorhees, but it gets you close and saves you some typing. Keep clicking the Find button until you reach the transaction you're searching for, or click Find All to display a list of all the Dr. V transactions.

9

Speed Up Your Register Entries with Memorized Transactions

● **In this chapter:**

● **I can recall a transaction with QuickFill and make changes in it**

● **I can repeat an earlier transaction using the Memorized Transactions feature**

● **What if I need to change a memorized transaction?**

● **I'll never type this transaction again. Can I erase a memorized transaction?**

Tired of typing the same entry over and over? With Quicken, you never have to type the same entry twice! . . . . ▶

Once you enter a transaction in Quicken you never have to take the time to retype a similar transaction. This is an incredible time saver. Pay the mortgage, enter it once, tell Quicken to memorize it, and Quicken will send it back to you, each month, whenever you ask for it. Write a check to your doctor, and the next time you pay the doctor all you have to do is type a couple of letters of the doctor's name and change the amount. Quicken fills in the rest of the information—the doctor's whole name and the expense category. You don't even have to worry about correct spelling!

QuickFill repeats an earlier transaction

What a time-saver for entering payments! Enter the date and the check number (using the shortcuts you learned in Chapter 8), then start typing the name of the payee. It's like a guessing game for Quicken. You tell the program to find the first payee starting with a particular letter. If the payee Quicken finds is not the one you want to use, give Quicken another clue by typing the second letter of the payee. Continue typing until Quicken has enough clues to fill in the entire name.

Here's what happens. As soon as you type the first letter, "p" for example, Quicken searches through the names you've previously typed and finds the first one, alphabetically, that begins with "p," and fills in the rest of the name. If that's the correct payee, you're finished! Click the amount field (or press Tab to move to that field) and enter the amount. But what if "Pancake House" isn't the payee you wanted? Type another letter, "r" for example, and Quicken continues the search until it gets to the first "pr" payee (see fig. 9.1).

Of course, if this is the first time you have entered this payee, Quicken won't be able to guess the name you want. You'll have to type the entire name—but only this one time. The next time you enter a payment to this payee the name will be familiar to Quicken and on the list of names that can be recalled.

TIP **Capitalization isn't important when you expect Quicken to recall** a payee using the QuickFill feature. Type in lowercase and save the time it would take to type capital letters. However, if you are entering a payee for the first time, type carefully, watch your spelling, and use correct capitalization. This way Quicken is sure to recall the name later and present it just the way you want.

Fig. 9.1
Quicken searches
through your list of
previously entered
payees, trying to find
one that starts with the
letters you type.

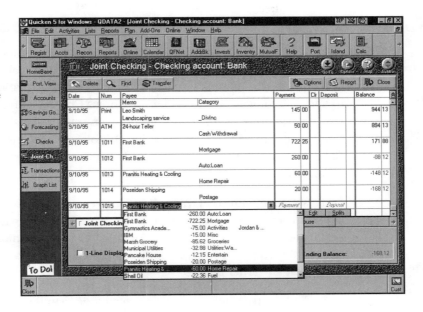

Notice that when Quicken uses QuickFill, not only the payee name is recalled, but the entire last transaction is recalled—the amount, the category,
and the memorandum. If everything stays the same, just click the Record
button and you're ready for your next transaction.

TIP If it appears that the QuickFill feature isn't working, it has probably
been turned off. To turn on QuickFill, click the Options button, click the
QuickFill tab, and make sure the first two boxes on this screen are checked.
For more information about QuickFill, see the shortcuts in Chapter 8.

Recall frequently repeated transactions

QuickFill is a super tool for saving you typing time. Quicken has an even
nicer feature for entering transactions that are the same every time, like
monthly loan payments or your bi-weekly paycheck.

The **Memorized Transactions** feature is a powerful tool that lets you
effortlessly repeat transactions. You can even teach it to enter transactions
for you on specific dates.

I want to memorize this transaction

Here's how Quicken's memorized transactions work. You enter a transaction in the register. Say it's a monthly payment for a leased car. You type the name of the payee, the amount, and any memorandum information you may want to add, including a category. Then you press Ctrl+M (or choose Edit, Memorize Transaction). Quicken flashes a box on-screen that says, "This transaction is about to be memorized." Click OK to accept the memorization or Cancel if you don't want to. A few little beeps signify that you've memorized a transaction!

You also can memorize a transaction you've previously entered. Maybe you entered your payment for cable television last month, it's time to pay cable again, and you realize that you're going to pay the same amount this month (and next month and so on). Here's how you memorize a transaction you entered at an earlier date:

1 Find the transaction you want to memorize in the register (you can use the Find Transaction shortcut you learned in Chapter 8).

2 With your cursor in any field on this transaction, press Ctrl+M.

3 Answer OK when the box appears on-screen.

Now I want to use my memorized transaction

Just as when you use QuickFill, you can begin typing a new transaction and, as soon as Quicken recognizes what you're typing, the rest of the transaction will fill in automatically.

Q&A *I don't get it. What's the difference between QuickFill and a Memorized Transaction?*

There are a lot of similarities between the QuickFill and Memorized Transactions. But there are a couple of significant differences:

- You have the option of turning off the QuickFill feature and not using it—but even if you've done that, your memorized transactions are still available.

- With QuickFill, each time you change a transaction (for example, your electric bill changes each month), Quicken remembers the

last entry you made when it recalls the transaction. With a memorized transaction, the entire transaction you memorize is the one
that sticks. Even if you make changes in it (say you memorized your
mortgage payment but this month you paid an extra amount
toward your principal so the amount changes), the next time you
recall it the fields you originally memorized are recalled.

You also can pull up to the screen a list of all your memorized transactions.
Just press Ctrl+T to see the list. Double-click a transaction you want to recall
and it is added to your register. Quicken automatically enters the transaction
and uses the next available check number. You can use memorized transactions in credit card and investment registers too.

CAUTION **Be sure you are ready to enter a new transaction when you begin**
to recall a memorized transaction. If your cursor is placed on an existing
transaction and you call for a memorized transaction, the existing transaction is replaced with the memorized one and you lose the transaction that
was there in the first place.

The list of memorized transactions that comes to the screen includes all the
transactions Quicken remembers, either because you specifically memorized
them or because you've had the QuickFill feature remembering them for you.
Transactions you specifically memorized are marked with a little padlock
(see fig. 9.2).

Fig. 9.2
Transactions with
padlocks are transac-
tions you told Quicken
to memorize.

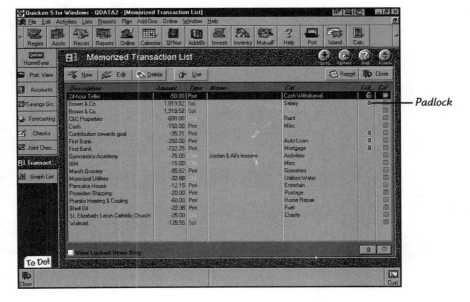

What's a locked transaction, anyway?

Locked transactions, the ones you told Quicken to memorize, are the unchanging transactions. You can record all the transaction and it always comes back the way you memorized it, even if you make changes when you enter it.

For example, say you frequently withdraw $50 cash from the ATM machine at your bank. When you enter an ATM withdrawal of $50, you memorize the transaction so you won't have to re-enter it each time. But this time you need extra cash and you withdraw $100. You recall the memorized transaction, it comes up with $50, and you change it to $100 before recording it.

The next time you want to enter an ATM withdrawal and you call up your memorized transaction, what amount do you think will appear? If you said $50, you're right. If you do the same thing using QuickFill, the $100 transaction would appear because it was the last transaction you used with your ATM account.

To see only the locked transactions when you display the list of memorized transactions, click the little View Locked Items Only box at the bottom of the transactions list (see fig. 9.3). From now on, the only transactions you see on this list are the ones you put there intentionally, by pressing Ctrl+M.

Fig. 9.3
Quicken's list
of memorized
transactions.

*Click here to display
only the transactions
you told Quicken to
memorize*

How can I change a memorized transaction?

Memorized transactions aren't written in stone. Maybe your monthly car payment has changed, or you now regularly take $70 from the ATM instead of $50. You can easily change a memorized transaction.

To change a memorized transaction, just enter the transaction the way you now want it to appear. Press Ctrl+M on the revised version of the transaction, and the "This Transaction is about to be Memorized" box appears. Click OK.

This time you see an additional box that reads: "Transaction Already Memorized." You can click Replace and your new transaction replaces the old one.

If you prefer, you can choose Add and your new revised transaction is added to the list but the old one also remains on the list. You'll then have two memorized transactions with the same payee from which to choose. (Thereafter, when you begin to enter a transaction to that payee, the two memorized transactions come up in alphabetical order, by category. As soon as you see the first one in the Payee field, the down arrow on your keyboard will take you to the second memorized transaction to the same payee.)

Click Cancel if you want to change your mind and not memorize the new transaction.

You can edit an existing memorized transaction by following these steps:

1 Choose Memorized Transaction from the Lists menu.

2 Choose the memorized transaction you want to change from the Memorized Transaction List that appears.

3 Click the Edit button.

4 Make desired changes in the Edit Memorized Transaction window that appears (see fig. 9.4).

5 Click OK when finished editing, and then click Close to close the Memorized Transaction List.

Fig. 9.4
You can edit a memorized transaction by clicking on the transaction, then clicking on the Edit icon.

My car's paid off! I don't need this memorized transaction anymore!

When you don't need a memorized transaction anymore, you can remove it from your list.

To remove a memorized transaction, follow these steps:

1 Open your memorized transaction list (press Ctrl+T).

2 Click the transaction you no longer need to select it.

3 Click the Delete button. A window appears with the statement: "You are about to Delete a Memorized Transaction."

4 Choose OK.

The transaction is deleted from the list of memorized transactions.

Other cool things you can do with memorized transactions

One of the nicest features you'll find in the memorized transactions list is the QuickReport feature. Click any item in your memorized transactions list, then click the Report button that appears right above your list (see fig. 9.5), and voilà! You get a report on-screen showing all the transactions you've had with that particular payee.

Click here to produce
a QuickReport

Fig. 9.5
Quicken can print a
QuickReport of your
transactions with one
payee.

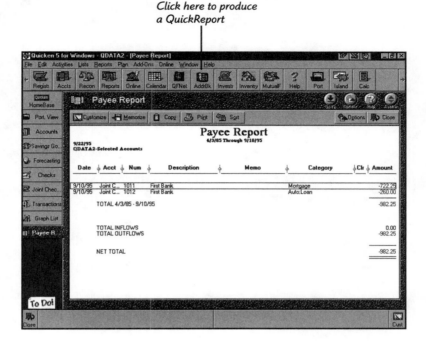

Say you want to see a total of how much you've paid your dentist. Just find
his name on the list, click it, click the Report button, and there before your
eyes is a list of every payment you've made to your dentist from your entire
register. Need a hard copy? No problem, just click the Print button at the top
of the report, then click the Print button from the Print Report box that
appears on-screen, and a copy of your report is sent to your printer.

TIP **Do you use a memorized transaction frequently? Consider placing**
an icon for that transaction on the iconbar—your memorized transaction will
be only a click away!

10

Scheduling Future Transactions

● In this chapter:

- ● **Create a scheduled transaction**

- ● **Pay the bills (and other neat tricks) with scheduled transactions**

- ● **Can I take a vacation and still pay the bills?**

- ● **Groups of scheduled transactions**

- ● **Quicken tells me when the rent is due**

- ● **Never miss a loan payment again**

Quicken's calendar feature takes care of scheduling financial events for you, giving you more time to relax! . . . . ●

Every month I pay the mortgage—same amount, same day of the month. I also make a monthly car payment. And then there are those pesky quarterly tax payments that creep up, not every month, but four times a year. When you stop and think about it, there are lots of things that repeat during the year. And it's not only expenses. Do you get a regular paycheck directly deposited in your checking account?

Whether it's income or expenses, let Quicken save you the trouble of remembering to record and remembering to pay. It's just one fewer factor that you have to remember in your busy life.

What's this about scheduling transactions?

Quicken's Scheduled Transactions feature is a tool you can use to either remind yourself when particular financial events are about to happen, or actually record and process the checks and/or deposits that occur regularly.

With Scheduled Transactions, you tell Quicken when a payment or deposit is supposed to occur. Give Quicken all the details about that transaction, including the amount, the date, the payee, the category, and any memorandum information you may want to include. Then decide whether you want Quicken to take care of processing the transaction or just remind you to process it yourself.

You won't ever have to worry again about missing an important payment due date or forgetting to enter your income in your check register (unless, of course, you forget to turn on the computer for a week or two—Quicken is good, but it's not that good).

How do I set up a scheduled transaction?

Before you start telling Quicken what to do, decide for yourself what kinds of things you can schedule into your Quicken account system so that you won't have to think about them any more:

- Mortgage payments
- Loan payments

- Rent

- Recurring monthly utility bills (even if the amount changes each month!)

- Lease payments

- College tuition and housing

- Tax payments

- Salary income from a job

- Your mother-in-law's birthday (I'm not kidding!)

Basically, anything you can plan for in advance, you can schedule into Quicken and take advantage of the Scheduled Transaction feature.

To set up a Scheduled Transaction, choose Lists, Scheduled Transaction (or press Ctrl+J). You see the window shown in figure 10.1.

Fig. 10.1
You can view, select, and edit scheduled transactions from the Scheduled Transaction List.

Click here to enter a new transaction

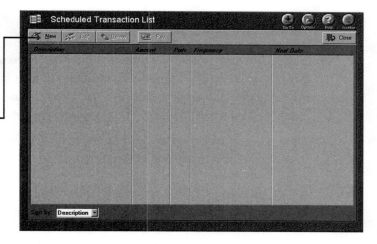

When you ask for a new transaction, a window opens (see fig. 10.2) in which you can enter all the pertinent information about the transaction you want to schedule.

Fig. 10.2
The Create Scheduled Transaction window.

Choose the account in which this transaction occurs

Select the date of the next scheduled payment (or deposit)

Is this transaction a payment or deposit, do you want Quicken to print a check, or are you using an on-line payment service?

Click here to see a list of the companies you've entered previously in Quicken.

There are several steps involved in setting up your scheduled transaction. Complete these steps once and you never have to repeat them again:

1 In the Next Scheduled text box, set the date for the next effective date of this transaction.

2 In the Account drop-down list, choose the account (usually your checking account) in which this transaction occurs.

3 In the Type drop-down list, select whether this transaction is a payment that you want to record in the register (but for which you will write a check yourself), a deposit, a payment for which Quicken will print a check, or an on-line payment you will perform electronically.

4 In the Payee drop-down list, choose the name of the payee (clicking the down arrow next to the payee space will drop down a list of all the payees in the file).

As soon as you select a payee, Quicken fills in the information from the last time you paid or received money from this payee. You can accept the rest of the information Quicken has filled in, or you can make changes. This additional information includes:

- **Memo.** Enter memorandum-type information for your own use. Anything you enter here will not ultimately appear in the list of Scheduled Transactions, but if you come back to this screen to edit or view the details of this transaction you will see the memo.

- **Category.** Enter the account category into which this transaction falls.

- **Amount.** Enter the amount of the transaction—this amount becomes part of the scheduled transaction, but you have the right to override this field (or any other field, for that matter) when you actually implement the scheduled transaction.

- **Frequency.** Is this transaction monthly? weekly? quarterly? a once-only event? You decide how often you want this transaction to occur.

- **Register entry.** Do you want Quicken to enter this transaction automatically (for example, if your paycheck is direct-deposited, you would want that entered automatically so you'll always have the correct balance when you open Quicken), or do you want to be prompted so that you can examine the transaction and be reminded to write a check? Choose Automatically Enter or Prompt Before Enter depending on what you want Quicken to do.

- **Number of Payments**. If the transaction is ongoing (like you hope your paycheck is, or like the monthly cable television bill), leave the number of payments at 999. This just means the transaction will continue to repeat itself, endlessly, with the frequency you requested. If there is a fixed number of payments (like your car loan that has only 18 months left), then change the number of payments to fit your needs.

- **Days in advance.** By default this is set at zero, but you can change it so that Quicken gives you a reminder that a transaction is forthcoming. In order to have a little advance warning that those nasty quarterly income tax payments are coming due, you might want to set this at 14 days to give you two weeks to prepare yourself. For a monthly transaction, you probably don't need much of a reminder.

In addition to several boxes to fill in regarding your scheduled transaction, there are some buttons along the side of the window that allow you to customize this transaction further (see fig. 10.3).

- **Splits**. Click this button to split the amount of your transaction among two or more categories. For example, you may split your paycheck so that all the withholding such as taxes and medical insurance gets divided among the proper categories.

Fig. 10.3
Buttons give you additional options for your scheduled transaction.

Split your transaction among several categories

Apply a payee's address if you use Quicken to write your checks

Add this transaction to a group

- **Address.** If you use Quicken to write your checks, including this scheduled transaction, click address and choose the address of the payee. That address will print on the Quicken check (see Chapter 6, "Writing Checks," for information on writing checks with Quicken).

- **Group.** You can make this transaction part of a group of transactions that are all executed at the same time. See "Using Transaction Groups" later in this chapter for more information about groups.

Once you've completed all the information for your scheduled transaction, click OK to add this transaction to your list of scheduled transactions (see fig. 10.4). From here on, on the designated date (or how ever many days in advance you asked to be prompted), Quicken prompts you with a window on-screen, reminding you of your scheduled transaction.

Fig. 10.4
It's official! Your scheduled transaction gets added to the Scheduled Transaction List.

I want to pay a scheduled transaction

Now that you've entered some of your scheduled transactions, what happens when the due date for one of these transactions comes around?

As soon as you start Quicken, you see a reminder of your scheduled transaction (see fig. 10.5). You can rely on Quicken to keep you current with your payments. If you are in the habit of starting Quicken daily, you will receive your reminders in a timely fashion. To learn how Quicken can remind you of your transactions when you don't start the Quicken program, see the section "Let Quicken Give You Reminders," later in this chapter.

Fig. 10.5
Time to make a payment! The Scheduled Transactions Due reminder box pops up on your screen as soon as you open Quicken.

Paying your scheduled transactions on time (or choosing not to pay)

So you've got this reminder on the screen. Now what? Actually, you've got several choices:

- **Record.** Click this button if you are ready to add the transaction to your register. If you plan to write a manual check, now's the time to do it. It's dangerous to record transactions when you mean to write the check sometime in the future. If you're not ready to write the check, save the "Record" option for later.

- **Edit.** Choose Edit to go back to the Create Scheduled Transaction window and make some changes. For example, if your scheduled transaction is your mortgage payment and the bank charged you extra (because last month you hadn't set up your scheduled transaction yet and you made your payment late), you can edit the amount to include the penalty.

Q&A *If I choose to edit a transaction from the pop-up scheduled transaction reminder box, will that editing affect the scheduled transaction in the future?*

When you edit a scheduled transaction from the reminder box your edit only affects the current payment of that transaction, not any of the future payments. To change a scheduled transaction for all future occurrences, open the Scheduled Transaction List (choose Lists, Scheduled Transaction). Any changes made here will affect all future occurrences of the transaction.

- **Delete**. Choose this option to skip this month's scheduled transaction. Don't click Delete if you are merely delaying payment of this transaction—only use this option if you want to skip the transaction entirely. Deleting a scheduled transaction from the pop-up Scheduled Transactions Due box will not delete the transaction permanently—you will still be reminded of this transaction next month.

- **Done**. Choose this option to take a pass on the transaction for now. Clicking Done closes the Scheduled Transactions Due window without entering the transaction, but the next time you open Quicken you will receive the same reminder about this transaction.

Can I pay a scheduled transaction in advance?

You always have the option of paying your Scheduled Transactions early. Because you're paying before the due date you won't see the reminder box on-screen. Instead, you have to go get the scheduled transaction in order to make the payment.

To pay a scheduled transaction early, open the Scheduled Transaction List (choose Lists, Scheduled Transaction), click the transaction you wish to pay, and click the Pay button at the top of the window. The Record Scheduled Transaction dialog box opens. You can enter any changes you might want to make before paying (for example, maybe you want to write the check today but plan to postdate it, or maybe you get to reduce the amount by paying early). Click Record (see fig. 10.6) and the transaction occurs.

Fig. 10.6

You can make changes to your scheduled transaction in the Record Scheduled Transaction dialog box.

Click here if you're ready to record this transaction

What if you change your mind and decide not to pay this transaction early? Just click Cancel and the window disappears but your regularly scheduled transaction is not disrupted. If you decide you're not going to pay it at all and don't want to be reminded of the payment on the due date, click Skip. Quicken will come back next month (or whenever this transaction falls due again) to remind you to make a payment.

Using transaction groups

A transaction group is just that—a group of transactions, scheduled transactions that is. Put several transactions that occur on the same day in a group and that group can be executed all at once. No matter how many transactions you put in one group, they all execute at the same time.

You don't need to set up your transactions as scheduled transactions before you put them in a group. In fact, if you do schedule transactions and then add them to a scheduled group, you need to delete the individual transactions from your scheduled transaction list, otherwise the transactions will be duplicated.

To set up a transaction group, open the Scheduled Transaction List window (choose Lists, Scheduled Transaction), and then select New. Ignore the choices in this window for setting up a scheduled transaction, and click the Group button. The Create Transaction Group window opens (see fig. 10.7).

In the Create Transaction Group dialog box, select the date of payment, the account, and the Group Type. The Group Type choices are Regular and Investment. Choose Regular for now. You can read about investment groups in Chapter 17, "Staying on Top of Your Investments."

Fig. 10.7
Use this dialog box to designate a group of transactions that you will pay as one.

Select a name for your group. The name can be no longer than 28 characters and it can include spaces. Call your group something that will give you a clue about what goes in the group. The example in figure 10.7 is "15th of the Month Payments." You can use a name like the one I've chosen, or maybe you want to create a group name that identifies payments that are of a similar type, such as "Utility Payments." It doesn't matter what name you pick as long as you pick a name that is meaningful to you.

After you name your group, select the frequency of payments, whether or not you want to be prompted for these payments, the number of payments (for something like a utilities group you would just leave the number of payments at 999 to indicate ongoing payments), and the number of days (if any) in advance of the due date that you want a reminder message. Fill in these items just as you did with a single Scheduled Transaction.

After you fill in all the information in the Create Transaction Group window, click OK and a window opens listing all your QuickFill transactions (basically, all the payees in your register). From this list you can select the payees you want to add to your group. To select a payee for inclusion in the group, click the name of a payee, and then click the Mark button at the top of the Assign Transactions to Group dialog box (see fig. 10.8).

Each group you create is given an identifying number by Quicken. This number appears in the Grp (Group) column at the right side of the Assign Transactions to Group window, alongside each payee's name that is included in the group.

Click the Mark button to include the payee in your group

Fig. 10.8
Assign transactions to
your scheduled group
in this dialog box.

*Click the name of a
payee you want to
include in your group*

*The group number in which
this payee is included*

CAUTION **Be sure you don't duplicate scheduled transactions. If you origi-**
nally set up a transaction to be scheduled by itself, then later added it to a
group, go back and delete the original scheduled transaction from your
Scheduled Transaction List. Otherwise Quicken will try to execute both the
original, single scheduled transaction, and the group that includes that
transaction. You don't want to pay the mortgage twice!

You can change the contents of a group by opening the Scheduled Transaction List, selecting the group you want to change, and clicking Edit. To add
to the items in the group or to remove an item from the group, click the OK
button and the list of QuickFill transactions appears with the Group designa-
tions in the right column. Simply click an item you want to add to the group
and click on the Mark button to add a transaction. To remove a transaction
from the group, click the item you want to remove, and again click the Mark
button. The Mark button turns on and off the group designation each time
you click it.

When it is time for your scheduled group of transactions to be executed,
Quicken pops up a reminder message, just as it did for a single Scheduled
Transaction. Selecting Record from the reminder window will have the effect
of recording every item in the group at once.

You can schedule transactions quickly using the financial calendar

Now that you understand how scheduled transactions work, you can speed
up the process a little and make it more visual. When you use Quicken's

Financial Calendar, you see an actual calendar on-screen and you can enter your scheduled transactions right on this calendar.

To open the Financial Calendar, choose the Activities menu, and then choose Financial Calendar. On your screen you see the current month calendar showing your transactions for the month. To the right of the calendar is a list of your QuickFill payees (see fig. 10.9).

Fig. 10.9
Use your mouse with this cool calendar to drag your transactions right onto the dates on which they should occur!

Drag an item from this list right onto a specific date on the calendar

To create a new a Scheduled Transaction, select one of your payees from the list on the right side of the screen and, using the mouse, drag the payee onto the calendar on the date on which you want to make the payment (you can change the pages of the calendar by clicking on the arrow buttons at the top of the calendar screen).

When you drag a transaction onto the calendar, the New Transaction dialog box opens (see fig. 10.10). To make this a Scheduled Transaction, click the Scheduled Transaction button at the top of the New Transaction window. Otherwise you are entering a one-time-only payment right into your register. All the rest of the Scheduled transaction options appear just as they did when you created a new Scheduled Transaction from the menu earlier in this chapter.

Fig. 10.10
This New Transaction dialog box opens in response to your dragging a transaction onto the calendar.

Select Scheduled Transaction to enter a future transaction

Can I change a transaction in the calendar?

You can change any transaction from the Financial Calendar, whether it is a transaction you entered in your register or a Scheduled Transaction. Just point with your mouse to the transaction you want to change and double click on it. A little window opens on-screen (see fig. 10.11) listing all the transactions for that day—register and scheduled. Click the transaction you want to change, then click the Edit button at the bottom of the window to make changes.

Fig. 10.11
You can add, edit, remove, and pay transactions from this little window.

Notice you also can Delete a transaction from this window, and request that a transaction be paid now. You also can enter a New transaction from this little window. In fact, another way to enter a new transaction on the Financial Calendar is to double click on any day of the calendar. This little Transactions window opens, even if there is nothing entered on that day, and then you can click on the New button to add a transaction.

If you double-click a date that is a scheduled transaction, you'll see the scheduled transaction listed in the transactions window. You can request an early payment of that transaction by clicking the Pay Now button, and Quicken executes your scheduled transaction, even though you're paying it before the due date.

I'd like to see how my accounts are doing

You can see a visual rendition of the way in which your checking account is holding by clicking the View button at the top of the Financial Calendar and selecting Show Account Graph. What you get when you make this selection is a bar graph at the bottom of the screen that displays the daily balance in your checking account, based on the transactions entered in your register and the projected scheduled transactions. Click any one of the bars, hold down your mouse button, and you see the actual amount that was or will be in your checking account on that particular day.

Use this bar graph (shown at fig. 10.12) to see in an instant if you're going to need some additional cash to cover a particular transaction.

Select View/Show Account
Graph to display the bar graph

I'm going to have a problem on September 15 when my tax payment is due. I'll need to deposit more money into the account or decrease the payment

Fig. 10.12
View the Account Graph to see at a glance how your checking account balance is holding up.

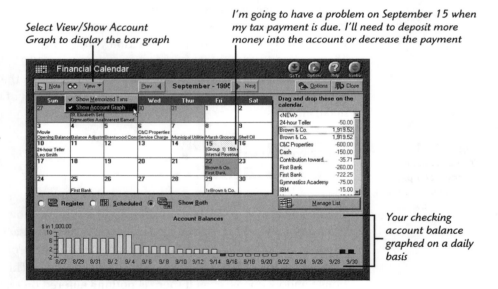

Your checking account balance graphed on a daily basis

Neat! I can make notes in the calendar!

You can add any text you want to your Financial Calendar—after all, it's *your* calendar. To add a reminder note to yourself, click on the day on which you want to be reminded, then click the Notes button at the top of the Financial Calendar window. A box pops on-screen in which you can write notes (see fig. 10.13). Click Save to keep the note, Delete to remove a note, Cancel to change your mind and close the box. These notes don't actually appear as text on the calendar, instead they appear as a little box in the corner of the calendar day (see fig. 10.14). Click the little box to see the note inside.

Fig. 10.13
Type your note in this box.

Click here to preserve your note

Fig. 10.14
Your notes appear on the calendar as little boxes.

Click here to read your note

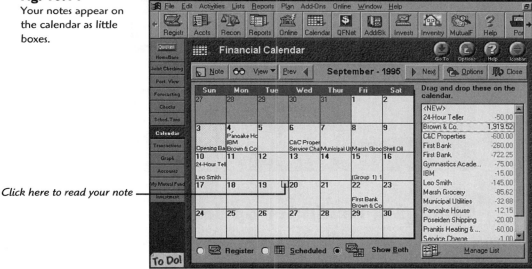

Let Quicken give you reminders

Now that you've entered all these Scheduled Transactions and Notes into Quicken, take advantage of Quicken's ability to remind you of all these things. You've already seen how your Scheduled Transactions come up on-screen each time you start Quicken. You also can make Quicken present you with your notes each time you start the program. After all, what's the use of entering your mom and dad's anniversary into the calendar if you aren't reminded of it when the time comes?

What's more, you can have Quicken remind you of all these important transactions and events without your even starting the Quicken program.

Getting reminders from Quicken

Check the Show Reminders on Startup box in the Reminder Options window and Quicken brings a window to the front of the screen each time you start Quicken, showing you the current reminder notes you typed in your financial calendar (see fig. 10.15).

Fig. 10.15
Reminder notes are presented on your screen when you start Quicken.

Click here to see a list of your current Scheduled Transactions

Changing reminder options

You can quickly change the display of reminder notes. When the Quicken Reminders window is open, click the Options button to open the Reminder Options window. From this window you can turn off any of the reminder features that are currently turned on.

To change Reminder options when the Quicken Reminders box isn't showing on your screen, choose Reminders from the Activities menu, or click the little To Do! button that appears in the lower left corner of your screen.

11

Paying Bills Electronically

● In this chapter:

- Set up your bank account electronically

- You don't have to rely on the postal service for timely payment

- Get your bills ready for payment

- Send your payments hurtling into space

- Stop payment on a bill

Forget the Western Union, you can now send money from the comfort of your living room by simply clicking a few buttons! . . . . ▶

I've been dreaming of electronic bill-paying for years. It seems I frequently wait to open my bills on the day they are due —sometimes even later—then I have to run out to make payments in person instead of relying on the "comfortable pace" at which our mail service moves. Sometimes I even have to make some phone calls explaining why my payment may be a couple of days late.

But now in the days of automatic teller machines and banking by phone, you can pay bills and send money in the comfort of your living room. Welcome to the 1990s.

How do I set up Quicken for electronic bill payment?

Wouldn't it be nice if we could just snap our fingers and tell Quicken, "Pay my bills electronically, I'm going on vacation." With electronic payments, that concept is closer than you think.

Quicken offers a service called Online Bill Payment, which is an electronic bill-paying service. To use this service, you must have a modem, and you must sign up with your bank.

First, let's set up my modem

What do you do first? Before you can even contemplate sending payments electronically, you need to have some way to transmit the payments. You need a modem.

A **modem** is a piece of equipment you add to your computer that allows you to communicate with the world via your telephone line.

 TIP   **Installing an internal modem is not as daunting as it sounds, so** don't be put off by the fact that it goes inside your machine. If you are concerned about messing around with the inside of your computer, you can probably find a neighborhood teenager or a less timid adult friend who will gladly put the modem in for you.

Once you've gotten your modem attached to your computer, turn on Quicken and follow these steps to set up your modem:

1 Select Set Up Modem from the Online menu.

Quicken searches around in the recesses of your computer and its plug-in ports until it finds something resembling a modem. Next Quicken tells you the modem has been configured and it asks you to test your modem by trying to register Quicken online, order supplies or software from Quicken, or update your portfolio prices online (see fig. 11.1).

Fig. 11.1
You will see this window on your screen when Quicken is finished figuring out what type of modem you have.

2 Click OK to continue to the next step.

3 Quicken displays a Set Up Modem—Intuit Online Services window (see fig. 11.2). The information in this window describes the location and speed of your modem. You don't have to change anything in this window, just click OK to close the window and return to your main Quicken screen.

Fig. 11.2
Click OK in this window to complete the modem installation.

TIP **If you've already registered your software by mailing the card that** accompanied the software, skip steps 4, 5 and 6. Pick up again with step 7.

4 Test your modem by registering your software online with Intuit (the folks that make Quicken). Select Software Registration from the Online menu in Quicken.

TIP **Make sure your modem is plugged into your telephone line before** running the modem test—you'll have a lot better luck this way!

5 In the Quicken 5 for Windows Software Registration box, fill in your vital statistics (see fig. 11.3). If any of the items don't apply to you (for example, if you don't have an Internet address), just leave those sections blank. Click OK when you're finished.

Fig. 11.3
Fill out this information to register your program.

Quicken 5 for Windows Software Registration

Online software registration is an alternative to sending in the printed registration card. If you register online, do not mail the card.

Name/Address
Title: ● Mr. ○ Ms. ○ Mrs. ○ Miss
First Name: [   ] Initial: [ ] Last Name: [   ]
Address: [   ]
City: [   ] State: [ ] Zip: [   ]
Company: [   ]
Internet Address: [   ]

Phone
Day: [   ] Evening: [   ]

✔ OK   ✗ Cancel   ? Help

6 Oops! Not finished yet! Quicken asks you some survey questions (see fig. 11.4). Using the drop-down lists, select answers to these questions, and then click the Register button to put your modem to work.

When you click Register, Quicken calls Intuit and registers your software. All you have to do is watch the screen and you'll get a message when you're finished that the software has been successfully registered.

Fig. 11.4
Quicken uses the
answers to these
questions to get a feel
for who its users are.

7 Go back to Quicken's Online menu and pick Intuit Membership, and then Setup. You have to be a member of the Intuit society of Quicken online users, or whatever you want to call it, in order to use the online services, like paying bills.

8 Choose Set Up New Intuit Membership from the window that appears on your screen.

9 The Intuit Membership Setup window appears on your screen. A lot of the information will already be filled in if you have registered online with Quicken (steps 4-6, above). Make sure all the appropriate categories are filled in, and then click OK.

10 You need a personal password in order to use Quicken's online services. Quicken lets you set your password in the Set Intuit Membership Password window.

TIP **If you don't complete this screen, you will have to type in your** password each time you want to go online with Quicken. Enter a password in the first box of the Set Intuit Membership Password window. Your password can be from four to 16 characters long. Quicken recommends that you use some kind of keyboard symbol (an asterisk, a dash, the ampersand, for example) to separate words in your password. You won't be able to read your password while you are typing it. When you have entered the password, press Tab or click on the second box. Enter the password again in order to double-check that Quicken and you are in agreement about what that password is. If you forget your password, you can call Quicken's Online Services Product Support (phone number is in your manual) to get a new password.

Quicken also asks that you type in your mother's maiden name to help verify your identity if you forget your password.

11 Click Connect, and Quicken calls up the membership services department and gets you set up to use online services. Quicken assigns a membership number to you. Click OK to complete the membership.

You need the Intuit Membership Number if you call Intuit Online Services Product Support or Customer Service. To view the number again, you can choose Intuit Membership, View Detail from the Online menu.

Congratulations! You're registered with Quicken's Online services and you're almost ready to begin banking from your computer!

CAUTION   **If you have more than one Quicken file (for example, perhaps you** have your personal financial records in one file and you keep the accounting records for your business in a separate file) and you want to use online banking services for both files, you have to register with Quicken's membership services twice—once for each file. Just go through the same procedure (starting at step 8, above) to enroll your second Quicken file with the membership department.

Next I need electronic bank accounts

So far you've given Quicken the information it needs in order to set up your membership. In order to actually use your online banking features, you have to jump through a few more hoops.

Contact your bank. Explain that you want to use Quicken's online electronic banking services to access your bank account and write checks electronically. Your bank will provide you with a "welcome package" that includes the numbers you need to connect your computer to this online banking service. The numbers you obtain from the bank include a 9-digit routing number and a 4-digit identification number.

If the person you talk to at your bank doesn't seem to be able to help you get set up to use Quicken's online banking service, you can order Quicken's bill-paying service, Online Bill Payment, directly from Intuit Services Corporation. You'll find an order form in the package that came with your Quicken software. Fill out the form, include a voided check from your checking account, and mail it to the address on the form.

To set up your Quicken program to communicate electronically with your bank and your bank account, choose Online, Set Up Bank. Quicken leads you through the steps necessary to enter your bank account number, the bank's routing number (this is provided in the welcome package from the bank), and a new PIN number. Your PIN number is your Personal Identification Number. This number is like a password that gives you access to your bank account information.

When you receive your welcome packet from your bank you will get a PIN number assigned to you. When you sign yourself up with Quicken to use the online banking services, you are asked for the pin number that the bank gave you, then you are asked to replace that number with one of your own choosing. Verify your new PIN number by typing it again, right under the first place where you typed it. Remember your new PIN number—this is the number you must type every time you want to access your bank account electronically.

Q&A ***Now that I've set up my electronic communication with my bank account, what can I do that I couldn't do before?***

You can pay bills electronically from your computer keyboard, you can check your bank balance on the computer, you can download information from your bank account (like which checks you've written and didn't record, or how many times your husband or wife has been withdrawing money from the electronic teller machine without writing it down) directly into your Quicken register.

TIP **A number of banking institutions have agreed to work with** Quicken to introduce this new online service. To view the names of the banks, read a bit about the services they offer, and get their phone numbers, select Financial <u>D</u>irectory from the Quicken Online menu. Then just click the name of the bank from which you want more information.

Chapter 25, "Doing Your Banking Online," gives much more detail about online banking, whereas this chapter is more concerned with online bill-paying. You don't have to bank online to pay bills online. If your bank doesn't offer this service, you can register with Quicken for Online bill-paying service.

Talking to my bank

If you're signed up to use Quicken's online banking service, you can access the service by selecting the Online menu in Quicken and choosing Online Banking. Make sure your modem is attached and your phone line is open!

Click the Get Online Data button. Quicken calls your bank and gets your bank account activity, which it then displays on your screen. Look over the information you see. You can make changes to any of this information, or delete items you've already entered into your register. When you're ready, select Update Register to instruct Quicken to download this information from your bank right into your register. Entries that already exist in your register will not be duplicated. (See Chapter 25 for more information about online banking.)

CAUTION **If you get online data from your bank and you haven't reconciled** your bank account in more than a few months, Quicken may not be able to determine whether an entry at the bank duplicates an entry on your register. Make sure your register has been recently reconciled before using online banking.

Now I want to set up electronic payees

Select Online Payees from Quicken's Lists menu to enable you to prepare to pay bills electronically, then follow these steps:

1 Click New in the Online Payee List window.

2 In the Set Up Online Payee window, begin typing the name of one of your payees (see fig. 11.5), or click the down arrow across from the Name category to see a list of your QuickFill payees. When you begin typing a name of one of your payees, Quicken fills in the rest of the name for you.

Fig. 11.5

Begin typing a payee's name and Quicken fills in the rest of the name for you.

3 Type the address, city, state, and ZIP code for your payee.

4 Fill in the account number—this is your personal account number with that payee. You should be able to find this on a copy of a bill from that payee. If you have no account number, you may leave this blank, or type your name in the space for account number.

5 Type the payee's telephone number. This is the number you call if you have a question about your bill.

I'm ready to pay a bill

The bills are approaching their due dates; it's time to try paying someone online. To set up a new online payment, follow these steps:

1 You can prepare a payment for the Online Bill Payment online service right from the Quicken register. In your register, type the date on which you want the payment made.

2 In the Num field, type **Send**.

3 Fill in the name of the payee—Quicken expects you to type the name of a payee from your Online Payee list. If the name you type is not on the Online Payee list, you can add it "on-the-fly," that is, as you enter it in the register Quicken gives you a chance to add the name to your Online Payee list.

4 Fill in the rest of the information about this payment (amount, category, memo).

5 Click Record to record the transaction. Quicken adds the payment to your Online Bill Payment list.

6 Choose Online Bill Payment from the Online menu.

7 Make sure your modem is hooked up and your phone line is free.

8 Click the Send button and your payment is dispatched, via your bank, to the payee.

Your bank finds out if this payee is able to receive an electronic funds transfer. If that is possible, the funds can be received by the payee within 24 hours. If the funds cannot be sent electronically, your bank will issue a check and mail it to the payee, using the mailing address you entered when you set up the payee as an online payee. Typically there is no additional charge for this mailing service.

Entering recurring transactions

You can create Scheduled Transactions to be paid through your online payment feature, just like you created Scheduled Transactions for entry into your register. To set up a Scheduled Transaction that will be paid online, follow these steps:

1 Choose Scheduled Transaction, from the Lists menu.

2 You can set up a new Scheduled Transaction by clicking the New button. The Scheduled Transaction Type window appears and at this time you can select Online Repeating Payments.

 TIP **You must be using an account that is registered as a member of** Quicken's online services in order to have the option to make online repeating payments. This registration process is described earlier in this chapter.

3 In the Create Online Repeating Payment window (see fig. 11.6), you should enter the payment date, payee, category, amount—just as you would for setting up any new Scheduled Transaction (as described in Chapter 10, "Scheduling Future Transactions").

Fig. 11.6
The Create Online Repeating Payment window opens when you select Online Repeating Payment from the Scheduled Transaction Type window.

4 If the payee you enter is not already set up as an online payee, Quicken gives you a message indicating the payee is "not found." To set up this payee for electronic payment, click the Set Up button and enter the address and account number information for this payee in the window provided; then click OK to add the payee to your online payee list

5 Select the payment frequency and duration. You can also set the "Prompt To Go Online x Days Before Due Date," filling in a number for the "x" and requesting that Quicken place this entry in your register and remind you a certain number of days in advance to order the bank to make the payment.

You can change an existing Scheduled Transaction to an online payment by clicking the Scheduled Transaction for which you wish to make online payments and click the Edit button. The Edit Scheduled Transaction window opens. In the Type box, change the type from whatever method was there previously to Online Pmt.

If you're planning a vacation and have bills you need to pay while you're away, set them up as online transactions. You can dispatch the online payments with Online Bill Payment but the payments won't actually be made by your bank until the designated due date (taking into account the requested lead time).

66 *Plain English, please!*

Lead time is the amount of time in advance of the due date of a payment that you want your bank to begin the transfer of funds. If you want to make sure a payment gets where it's going two days early, request a lead time of three days—two days of lead time plus one day of transferring the funds from your account to that of the payee. Quicken omits holidays and weekends when figuring lead time, only regular business days are counted. **99**

Help! I need to stop payment on a check

If a payment has been sent to your online banking service but the payment has not yet actually been made, you can transmit a stop payment order. To stop a single payment, follow these steps:

1 Click the transaction you want to stop in your register.

2 Make sure your modem is hooked up and your phone line is free.

3 Choose Stop Payment from the Edit menu.

4 Quicken calls in a stop payment request.

Hello, bank? Did my payment get made yet?

You can check the status of a payment at any time. When you send a payment request using Online Bill Payment, Quicken logs information about when that payment occurs. You can see this information at any time by clicking the payment you are concerned with in your register, and then choosing Edit, Payment Inquiry.

Quicken opens a window that tells you the date when you requested payment, the lead time for the payment, and the status of the payment.

12

Storing Addresses in Quicken

● **In this chapter:**

- **Open the Financial Address Books**

- **Where do these addresses come from?**

- **Add a new address**

- **Put addresses in groups**

- **Print addresses**

Look! Quicken's got an Address Book that I can easily access and update to keep all the addresses and phone numbers I need in one place! . . . . ●>

A new feature in Quicken 5 for Windows makes your life easier by keeping all your work, family, friends, and Quicken addresses and phone numbers at your fingertips. The new Financial Address Book is available to you while you're working in Quicken or any other program on your computer. Use it to look up addresses and phone numbers, or use it to print mailing labels. Updating address changes is easy in the Financial Address Book; no more messy looking address books with pencil scratches marking out old information with the new.

What is the Address Book and how does it work?

The Financial Address Book organizes and stores the addresses you need to pay bills or perform other financial activities for each of your Quicken files. It holds addresses and phone numbers of your business associates, family members, or friends.

I want to open the Address Book

You can open the Financial Address Book from Quicken or while you're working in another program. If you need to check an address or phone number, just open the Financial Address Book and look it up right on the spot.

I can open the Address Book from Quicken

If you're already in Quicken, open the Financial Address Book by selecting Activities, Financial Address Book. Quicken opens the Financial Address Book for the Quicken file you are working in. There's a separate Financial Address Book for each of your Quicken files. Look at the title bar at the top of the Address Book to see what book you're working in.

A closer look at the Address Book

Button Bar
Use the Address Book button bar to add, edit, delete, and find addresses. Also, print addresses, get help, and close the Address Book using the button bar

Menu
The Financial Address Book has its own menu that you use to perform tasks

Finding an address
Type a name here to quickly find an address

Displaying a group
Select the group that you want to show at one time in the Address Book

List view
This part of the Financial Address Book is the List view where you see each name and address on one line

Scroll arrows
Click the arrows at each end to see more information in the List view of the Address Book

Detail view
The Detail view of the Address Book displays all of the information for the address highlighted in the List view above. Here's where you add new addresses or update existing ones

Saving addresses
Save the new address or changes using this button

Adding notes
Add additional information for the highlighted name through Notes

Assigning a group
Assign a group to a name and address

Or, open the Address Book from the program folder

Even if you're not working in Quicken, you can still open, and work in, the Financial Address Book. In Windows 95, just select the Financial Address Book program from the Quicken program folder, and the Address Book opens. From Windows 3.1, click the Financial Address Book icon in the Quicken program group to open the Address Book. So, if you're writing a letter in Microsoft Word and need to look up an address, just open Quicken's Financial Address Book and find it there.

Where did these addresses come from?

So, you've opened the Financial Address Book for the first time and there are already some names and addresses there. How did they get there?

You know when you're working in Quicken and you enter an address for a payee? Quicken not only stores the address for you, but it also stores it in the Financial Address Book. Any payee names and addresses that you have set up in the Memorized Transaction List, the Scheduled Transaction List, or the Electronic Payee List are also copied into the Financial Address Book.

TIP **New Quicken users won't have anything in your Financial Address Book.** As you begin your work in Quicken, the information that you enter for payees will automatically be imported into the Address Book.

CAUTION **When the Financial Address Book imports personal names from Quicken, the first and last name is placed in the Last Name field.** That's because Quicken has no way of knowing whether the payee name is a personal name that should be divided into first and last name, or the name of an organization that shouldn't be divided.

If you want to sort the addresses in your Address Book, you'll want to edit personal names to correctly divide the first and last names. I'll show you how to edit entries in the Address Book a little later in this chapter.

I'd like to update the Address Book

Some of the names, addresses, and phone numbers of the people and organizations that I deal with have changed. Can I change them in my Address Book? Sure. You can add new entries in the Address Book, too.

Before you make any changes, here are some things to remember:

- In the Financial Address Book, if you change Leo Smith to Smith in the Last Name field and Leo in the First Name field, Quicken changes the payee name in, say, your Memorized Transaction List.

- If you change Bob Jones's address in the Address Book, it also gets changed in the Memorized Transaction List.

- If you change the address for one of your electronic payees in the Address Book, you'll have to go to the Electronic Payee List in Quicken and make the change there, too.

If you make changes to payee names and addresses from within Quicken, here's what happens in the Address Book:

- When you enter a transaction in Quicken for a new payee, the payee name and address automatically gets sent to the Financial Address Book.

- If you delete a payee name and address from the Memorized Transaction List, the Scheduled Transaction List, or the Electronic Payee List in Quicken, it's not automatically deleted from the Address Book. You'll have to open the Address Book, find the name and address, and then delete it from there.

How do I add a new address?

Open the Financial Address Book and then click the New button or double-click the New line in the List view of the Address Book. The cursor is moved to the first field in the Detail view of the Address Book so that you can begin entering a new name and address.

Entering information for a new address

Fill in the Detail view of the Address Book with as little or as much information as you want. For example, if you only want a name, street address, city, state, and ZIP, just fill in these fields and leave the others blank. Move forward from field to field by pressing the Tab key; to move back a field, press Shift+Tab.

Saving information in the Address Book

After you've entered the information for a new entry in the Address Book, save it by clicking the Record button. If you've selected to have the Address Book sorted by last name, the new entry is placed in the Address Book in alphabetical order by last name. If you've selected to sort by city, then the new entry is placed in the Address Book based on its city location.

 TIP   Click the **N**otes button to display a notepad where you can enter more data for a name in the Address Book. You can't sort the data that you enter in the notepad; it's for informational purposes only.

What if I want to change or delete an address?

You can easily change or delete an entry in your Address Book. Just select the entry first, and then select whether you want to edit it or delete it by clicking the Edit or Delete buttons in the button bar.

 TIP   Type a name in the F**i**nd box at the top of the List view to select an address to edit or delete. The element that Quicken looks for in the F**i**nd box depends on what's displayed after Find (like Last Name, First Name, and so forth).

I want the Address Book sorted another way

Usually, you'll sort your Address Book by last name and that's how the Address Book is set up when you first use it. But if you need it sorted another way, like by organization or by city, you can do that too.

First, you'll need to open the **S**ort menu from the Address Book (see fig. 12.1).

Fig. 12.1
The Sort menu shows
you the fields you can
use to sort the Address
Book.

Select one of the fields from the Sort menu to sort the list another way. If
there's a field that you don't see in the Sort menu, like maybe you want to
sort by ZIP code or phone number, select By from the menu. Quicken shows
you the other fields that you can sort by.

Using address groups

You can assign each of the entries in your Address Book to a group so that
they're all together. For example, you may want all of your family member
addresses together so that you can print mailing labels for birthday, gradua-
tion, or anniversary parties.

Your Address Book is already set up with five predefined groups: Quicken
(assigned to all addresses that come from Quicken lists), Family, Friends,
Works, and Unassigned. When you click the Group drop-down arrow in the
Address Book, you'll see these predefined groups. You can add your own
groups (up to 100) or modify the ones already there.

If you want to assign a group to an address that's already in your list, just
select the address, click the Assigned to Group drop-down arrow, and select
the group that you want from there.

TIP **You can add a new group by selecting Options, Set Up Groups to**
open the Set Up Groups window. From here, click New in the Available
Groups list and then type the new group name in the box below. Click the
Record button to add the new group to the list of Available Groups.

Searching for an address

If you need to search through your Address Book for an item in more than
one field or if you don't know which group an address is in, you can call an
all-out search with the Search button. When you click Search, Quicken
displays the Search window that you see in figure 12.2. Here, you can enter
an item to search for, and tell Quicken which fields and groups to look in.

Q&A *What's the difference between fields and columns?*

Absolutely nothing. You'll see the terms used synonomously in the Address Book. They both refer to the items of information you enter in the Address Book. For example, the Last Name field and the Last Name column are the same; the City field and the City column are also the same.

If you're not sure of the item that you're looking for, type something that sounds like it and click this option

Fig. 12.2
Call an all-out search for an address in your Address Book using the Search window.

Click OK to start the search

Type the item within the address entry that you're looking for

Then tell Quicken which groups to look in

Click the field that you want Quicken to search in. For multiple fields, press Ctrl or Shift first and then click

I want to print addresses

Take advantage of having all of your names and addresses in one place that can be quickly printed for whatever reason. Maybe you want to send invitations to a big birthday bash and need mailing labels for all your family members. Or, maybe you'd like to put together a call list of all your clients with their telephone numbers.

The Financial Address Book lets you print addresses in several different formats:

- Names with complete addresses
- Names and telephone numbers
- Mailing labels with names, organizations, and primary addresses

- Rolodex cards (Avery #4168 for continuous feed printers; Avery #5385 for laser printers)

- #10 Envelopes

If you're using mailing labels, here are the Avery label styles that are compatible with the Address Book:

Label #	Labels up	Label size	Description
4143	2	4" x 15/16"	Standard continuous
4144	3	2 1/2" x 15/16"	Standard continuous
4145	1	3 1/2" x 15/16"	Standard continuous
5160	3	2 5/8" x 1"	Standard laser
5161	2	4" x 1"	Standard laser

CAUTION **Before you start printing, you'll need to select the size and** orientation of the paper that you're printing on. To get Quicken ready to print from the Address Book, select File, Print Setup from the Address Book menu. Quicken opens the Print Setup window where you enter printer settings.

Selecting the addresses to print

Before you begin printing, you'll need to select the addresses you want to print. If you don't select an address, Quicken will print all addresses within the current group.

Select to print just one address by clicking it in the List view of the Address Book. To select more than one address from the current group, press and hold the Ctrl key as you click each address.

To select a number of consecutive addresses, click the first address and then press and hold the Shift key and then click the last address you want to include. All addresses will print between the first address you clicked and the last address.

Printing addresses

Now that you've entered your printer settings and selected which addresses you want to print, select File, Print. Quicken opens the Print window shown in figure 12.3.

Complete the Print window by specifying the print format, type of paper to print on, the print range, and the font. Click OK to begin printing addresses.

Tell Quicken the print format you want to use; complete addresses, a telephone list, addresses for mailing labels, addresses for rolodex cards, or addresses for envelopes

Fig. 12.3
Complete the Print window to print the selected addresses from the Address Book.

Select what you'll be printing on

If you're printing a single address, change this setting to Selected addresses

Click OK to begin printing addresses

To change the font, click this button

TIP **If you want to see an on-screen preview of what will print before** you actually print on paper, labels, envelopes, or rolodex forms, select File, Print Preview and then complete the Print Preview window (which is identical to the Print window in fig. 12.3).

Part III: Organizing Your Finances

13

Tracking Cash and other Assets

● **In this chapter:**

- ● Set up a cash account

- ● Track your cash expenditures

- ● Balance the cash in your pocket with your cash account

- ● Set up and use an asset account

If only I had a way to track how much I spend each month and how much I have. Wouldn't that make my life easier?

How did you pay for the things you bought today? Maybe you wrote a check to pay some bills, paid cash at the grocery store, and used a credit card at the shoe store. Quicken gives you a way to record all these expenditures so you can stay on top of your finances.

So what do you do with cash expenditures? They can't go in the checking account register because the cash isn't in your checking account when you spend it. Quicken lets you set up a cash account to record your cash expenses. There's also a credit card account in Quicken (discussed in Chapter 14, "Managing Your Credit Cards").

Now, while we're talking about cash, did you know that cash is an asset? You may have noticed that in Quicken there are asset accounts, too. Well, even though I just told you that cash is an asset, you don't use an asset account to keep track of your cash. Quicken's provided a special cash account for that. You'll use the asset accounts in Quicken to track the value of the things that you own, like your house, cars, boats, furniture, and so forth.

 Plain English, please!

An **asset** is any personal or business resource you own that has lasting value. The assets that you might own are your house, cars, furniture, and investments. Businesses' assets include money owed by customers (accounts receivable), inventory held for resale, and any fixtures or equipment used in the business. **99**

How do I set up a cash account?

Setting up any kind of account in Quicken is easy. If you remember from Chapter 3, Quicken guides you through the steps for setting up accounts with a series of windows that asks you for the information it needs. Cash accounts are no exception; they're easy to set up, too.

Here's what you'll need to do to set up a cash account:

- Assign a name to your cash account.

- Enter the amount of cash you have on hand to start your account and the date that you're starting the account.

- Tell Quicken some additional information about your account, however, this is probably not necessary with a cash account.

When you're ready to set up your cash account, click the Accts icon to display the Accounts List. Then, click the New button to display the Create New Account window (see fig. 13.1). From here, you can select the type of account you want to set up. Obviously, for a cash account, you'll select Cash.

Fig. 13.1
Click the Cash button from the Create New Account window to set up a cash account.

When you select Cash, Quicken opens the EasyStep Cash Account Setup window (see fig. 13.2) that puts you on your way to setting up a cash account.

Fig. 13.2
Quicken's EasyStep windows make it a snap to set up a cash account. Just follow the instructions in each window and you're there!

Click these tabs to proceed to the next step

Or, click the Next button to proceed

Earlier in this book, I explained how to set up bank accounts in Quicken. Setting up a cash account is very similar. Just follow the EasyStep Account Setup windows to name the cash account (remember, you can only use 15 characters, including spaces, but not :] [/ | ^), enter a start date and balance, and any other information you may want to add to your cash account.

When you're finished, Quicken displays the Summary window (see fig. 13.3) with the information you entered for your cash account. Look it over carefully to make sure it's all correct. If it's not, move to the box with the wrong information and change it.

Fig. 13.3
Review your information in the Summary tab for your new cash account. If there's anything that's wrong, correct it here.

TIP **In the Summary tab, you see a Tax button. When you select this button,** Quicken provides the Tax Schedule Information window so that you can assign a tax schedule to the transfers that occur from and to your cash account. Because you'll have many different types of transfers in a cash account, you won't want to assign a tax schedule to it.

When you're sure that the information in the Summary window is correct, click Done and Quicken adds your new cash account to the Account List.

I'm ready to use my cash account

Once you've set up your cash account, you can start using it to track those expenses that you pay cash for—like when you go to the movie theater and spend $14 for the movie and another $12 on popcorn and soft drinks. There's $26 that you've spent in cash that could go unaccounted for if you didn't enter it in your cash account.

When you're ready to enter a cash transaction, open your cash account register by selecting it from the Account List, or selecting it from the Account selection bar from any register.

When you open your cash account register, it looks like other registers you've already seen in Quicken (see fig. 13.4), except cash account registers have Spend and Receive columns instead of Payment and Deposit columns.

Fig. 13.4
Here's the register for my cash account. Notice that it looks just like other registers you've seen in Quicken.

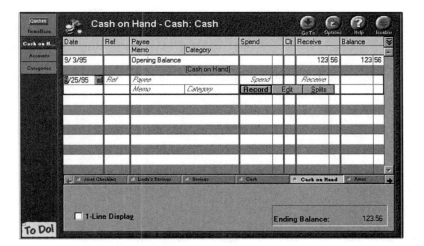

Once you've opened your cash account register, you're ready to do some cash transactions.

Enter only cash expenditures in your cash account

Now that you're working with more than one account type (bank accounts and cash accounts), you'll want to make sure that you enter only cash transactions in your cash account. If you make a mistake and enter a cash transaction in, say, your checking account, you'll not only mess up your cash account balance, but your checking account balance will be off as well.

 TIP **Did you know that each account type register is a different color?** Bank accounts are yellow, cash accounts are green, credit card accounts are blue, and so forth. Quicken color codes your registers so that you'll quickly recognize the type of account that you're using. You won't likely enter a cash transaction in a register that's blue because you'll know it's a bank account. Oh, and you can change the colors if you want a different color scheme. Just select the Options button in any register. You'll see a Color button as one of the register display options that when you click will show you a color palette for each account type you can choose from.

Enter a cash transaction in the cash account register just like you enter transactions in the checking account register. You'll enter the date of the cash expenditure, a description of the expense (if you want) in the Payee field, the amount you spent in the Spend field, and then assign a category. Click Record to record the transaction in your cash account register.

Figure 13.5 shows the cash transaction for the night out at the movies.

Keeping track of petty cash

If you're running a small business, I recommend setting up a cash account to track your petty cash fund. You'll benefit in two ways; one, you'll be accurately classifying each cash expenditure as to the type of expense, and two, you'll always know how much should be in your petty cash fund.

Petty cash is usually a tough one to track since more than one employee may have access to it. Tracking petty cash in a cash account will keep your employees honest because they'll have to account for any cash used from the fund.

Fig. 13.5

Entering a cash transaction *is just like* entering a transaction in your checking account register. Quicken updates your cash balance each time you enter a cash transaction.

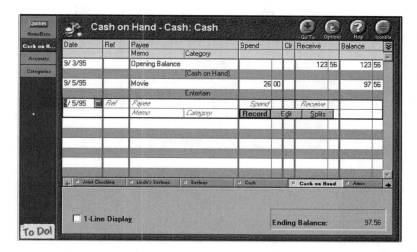

Adjust the balance in your cash account to match the cash you have

No matter how diligent you are in entering cash expenses in your cash account, there's probably going to be some small ones that you miss. You may forget to enter a transaction for your lunch or for the parking fees you paid yesterday. These expenses may be small by themselves, but in aggregate over an extended period, they add up.

Periodically, you'll want to adjust the balance in your Quicken cash account with the amount of cash you actually have on hand. If your cash account register says you have $97.56 and you only have $92.49, then you'll want to adjust your cash account for the difference.

Adjust your cash account balance by choosing Recon from the Activities menu. Quicken displays the Update Account Balance window like you see in figure 13.6. Complete this window and click OK to update your cash account balance.

Fig. 13.6
Update your cash
account balance in
Quicken to match the
cash that you actually
have on hand.

Here's where you enter the amount of cash that you actually have

This should be the date that you take an actual count of your cash

Assign a category to the transaction that Quicken enters to adjust for the difference in the cash you have on hand and the balance in your cash account

What do I track in asset accounts?

If you want to use Quicken to track all of your assets, you have to set up an asset account for each. It's important to set up asset accounts if you want to use Quicken to determine your net worth (remember back in Chapter 3, I explained that net worth is the difference between all your assets and all your liabilities). Quicken won't know what your total assets are unless you set up an account so that you can enter asset values for each. (Obviously, you'll need to set up liability accounts for each, but you won't learn about liability accounts until Chapter 15).

Here's some of the assets you might want to set up asset accounts for:

- **Your home.** This is probably your most valuable asset, so you'll want to include its worth in a Quicken asset account.

- **Furniture and personal belongings.** In aggregate, these will be a significant part of your net worth.

- **Jewelry.** If the value of your jewelry is high, set up an asset account to track it.

- **IRA account.** IRA accounts can be set up as asset accounts if you don't want to track the price of securities held in your IRA. If you do want to track security prices in an IRA, it's better to set it up as an investment account.

- **A 401k or other retirement account.** Asset accounts can be used to track the value in retirement accounts and you can even designate the earnings from these accounts to be tax free, if necessary.

- **Business property.** If you own a business, you'll want to set up an asset account for capital equipment and accounts receivable.

 Q&A ***What about my stock investments? They're certainly considered assets that I own.***

You're right. But you don't set up investments as asset accounts in Quicken. Quicken has special investment accounts that you use to track assets that you have invested in stocks and securities. The exception, here, is the IRA account. If you don't care to update prices for securities held in your IRA, you can set up your IRA as an asset account. See Chapter 17, however, to learn how to set up and use investment accounts.

Setting up an asset account

Setting up an asset account is pretty much like setting up a cash account like you did earlier in this chapter. If you refer to figure 13.1, you see the types of accounts that you can add in Quicken. When you set up a cash account, you selected the C<u>a</u>sh account type; to set up an asset account then, you'll select the Asse<u>t</u> account type.

When you select to set up an asset account, Quicken displays a series of EasyStep account setup windows (like you saw when setting up your cash account) that asks you for the information it needs. Here's what you'll need to enter:

- A name for your asset account and a brief description of the asset.

- The value of the asset and the date that you wish to start using the asset account.

- Tell Quicken whether you're going to use the asset account to track an IRA or tax-free investment. Tax-free investment accounts are those whose earnings are not taxable. The earnings from an IRA, for example, are not taxable at the current time.

- Assign a tax schedule to transfer in and out of the asset account, if you want.

- Any additional information that you may want to attach to the asset account, like a bank name, contact person, account number, and so forth.

In figure 13.7, I've set up an asset account to track the value of my house. After I click Next and then click Done at the last Summary window, my asset account is added. Quicken includes a register for the account that I can use to record any activity that affects the value of my house.

Fig. 13.7
Adding an asset account is similar to adding other types of accounts. Just name the account, enter the value and start date, and some tax informa-tion (if necessary), and you're done.

Recording activity in an asset account

Once you've set up an asset account to track an asset's value, you can enter transactions in the account's register. Transactions are entered in asset account registers just like any other Quicken register that you may have already used. You'll see one difference in an asset account register from other registers. Instead of the Payment and Deposit columns that you see in your checking account register, or the Spend and Receive columns in your cash account register, you'll see the Decrease and Increase columns. The Decrease and Increase columns let you adjust the value of your asset.

So, if you spend $5,000 to add a new patio to your house, you can enter a transaction in the asset account register for your house to increase its value by $5,000. Figure 13.8 shows the asset account register for My House with a transaction for the $5,000 patio addition.

Fig. 13.8
Activities that increase or decrease the value of an asset can be entered as transactions in your asset account. Here, the value of this asset has increased by $5,000.

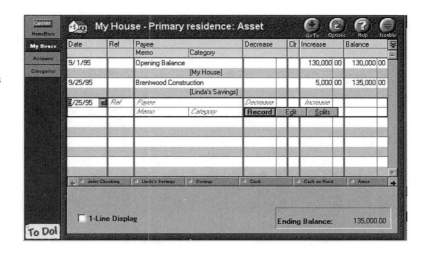

Working with transfer transactions

In Chapter 5, I told you a little about transactions between two accounts in Quicken, called transfer transactions. Now that we're working with asset accounts in Quicken, it might be a little easier to see how these kinds of transactions work.

 Plain English, please!

> **Transfer transactions** are transactions in Quicken that affect two different accounts. In a transfer transaction, another account is assigned to the transaction in the Category field. **99**

Look again at figure 13.8 with the transaction for the addition of a $5,000 patio to the My House asset account. Notice that in the Category field, I assigned another account (the Linda's Savings account) instead of a category. What actually happened here is that the patio addition was paid for from the Linda's Savings account. So, this transaction affected two different accounts; the My House account and the Linda's Savings account. The value of the My House account increased while the value (or balance) in the Linda's Savings account decreased.

In figure 13.9, you see what the other side of the transaction that you saw in figure 13.8 looks like. This transaction was entered by Quicken when I assigned the Linda's Savings account to the transaction in the My House account.

Fig. 13.9
Quicken enters a transaction in the register for the account that you assign in the Category field of a transfer transaction.

 TIP **A quick way to move between transactions in a transfer trans-** action is to highlight one side of the transaction and then press Ctrl+X.

14

Managing Your Credit Cards

● **In this chapter:**

- Set up a credit card account

- Enter credit card transactions

- Balance your credit card account

- Make a payment

Quicken can't pay those credit cards bills, but record-keeping will be a breeze . . . . ●

L et Quicken help you get a handle on those credit card bills you have stacking up. You can set up a credit card account for each credit card you have and enter purchases and payments in registers that you're already accustomed to using. This way, you're sure to include credit card purchases as expenses and will have an easy way to track each of them by category.

Even if you're diligent and always pay your credit card balances each month, you can still benefit by using a Quicken credit card account. You'll still want to enter each credit card purchase as a transaction in your credit card account so that you can assign it to a category.

If you use credit cards, setting up a credit card account is essential if you want to accurately track *all* of your expenses.

Why do I need to set up a credit card account?

So what kind of credit card user are you? Do you use your credit card instead of cash so that you have a record each month of what you spent? Do you use credit cards instead of writing checks because it's quicker when you're checking out? Or, do you use credit cards to finance your lifestyle (you know, buy something today and pay for it tomorrow).

Whatever the reason, you can use Quicken's credit card accounts to stay on top of those credit card bills so they don't get ahead of you. When you use a Quicken credit card account, you've got a place to record your credit card purchases so that you can assign a category to them. If you use credit cards, you won't have an accurate picture of your finances if you don't include credit card transactions in Quicken.

 TIP   **You don't have to set up a credit card account in Quicken if you** pay off your credit card bill each month. When you pay your bill each month, you can enter a split transaction in the register for the account that you pay bills from. Then, enter each credit card purchase as a separate line in the split transaction.

TIP　**If you carry credit card balances, the amounts outstanding are** considered liabilities. If you want to use Quicken to determine your net worth, you must set up credit card accounts so that these liabilities enter the net worth equation. Remember, net worth equals your total assets minus your total liabilities.

Setting up a credit card account

By this time, you've probably set up several accounts in Quicken. In previous chapters, we've talked about bank, cash, and asset accounts. So I know you know how to set up an account by now. There's really not much difference when setting up a credit card account. You'll start from the Create New Account window that you see in figure 14.1. Select the Credit Card button to set up a credit card account and display the first EasyStep Account Setup window. Here's what you'll need to enter to set up a credit card account:

- A name for the account and a brief account description.

- If you have your last credit card statement, the balance and statement date. (If you don't have your last statement, Quicken will use today's date and a $0.00 (zero) balance to start your credit card account).

- If the credit card account you're setting up is for a Quicken credit card or another account that you want to use with online banking to download your statements, enter:

     The financial institution

     Credit card number

     Your Social Security number

     Your bank's routing number

- Your credit limit.

- Any additional information, like the name of the financial institution associated with the card, your account number, a contact person, and so forth.

Fig. 14.1
Open the Create New Account window by clicking the New button in the Account List or selecting Activities, Create New Account.

Click the Credit Card button to set up a credit card account and display the first EasyStep Account Setup window

Now, proceed through Quicken's EasyStep Account Setup windows to enter a name for the credit card account and the balance shown on your last credit card statement with the statement date. Optionally, you can enter your credit card limit and additional information about your account.

If you're not setting up a Quicken Credit Card account or a credit card account that you'll use online banking for downloading statements, then you'll see the first Summary tab window (see fig. 14.2) when you're finished entering credit card information.

Fig. 14.2
In the Summary tab window, you see all of the information that you've entered for your credit card account. Review it carefully and make changes here if you need to.

Click Next to see each Summary tab window. After you're finished reviewing the information in the Summary tab windows, click Done to add the credit card account to your Account List.

Q&A   *I used to have an IntelliCharge credit card account that I used to receive my statements by disk or modem. What's different in this version of Quicken?*

The Quicken Credit Card replaces the IntelliCharge account; however, it's still used in the same way that you're used to. The Quicken Credit Card is now part of online banking and works like any other online bank account. Don't worry about what to do with your old IntelliCharge account. Quicken automatically updates your account to online banking during installation.

Okay, now I can use my credit card account

Now that you have a credit card account set up in Quicken, you can start entering your credit purchases. Credit card accounts have registers just like bank accounts, cash accounts, and asset accounts. Figure 14.3 shows you the register for Linda's Visa credit card account. Instead of the Payment and Deposit columns you see in bank accounts, though, credit card accounts have Charge and Payment columns.

Credit card transactions can be entered in your credit card register in one of two ways:

- Enter each credit card purchase as you make it. For example, when you come home from shopping, enter your credit card purchases. Even though you may have up to 30 days to pay for these purchases (dependent on your statement cut-off date), they will be reflected in the outstanding balance in your credit card account.

- Wait until you get your credit card statement and then, at one time, enter all of the transactions that appear on your statement. This is not ideal, however. The problem that arises when you enter transactions from your statement is that not all of your purchases are reflected. For example, you may have made major credit purchases after your statement cut-off date that now won't be in your credit card account. The outstanding balance, therefore, is somewhat distorted. It will be more than Quicken says it is.

So what about credit card payments? Well, they're entered in the account that you use to pay your credit card bills. If you use your Joint Checking account to write the check to the credit card company, the payment is entered in that account.

Other credit card transactions, like finance charges or credits from returned items, are entered directly into the credit card account register. Or, if you choose to balance your credit card account, you can enter these transactions when you reconcile the account. (I tell you how to balance your credit card account a little later in this chapter).

Fig. 14.3
Here's the register for a credit card account. Notice that it looks the same as other registers. You'll enter credit transactions just like you enter transactions in other registers.

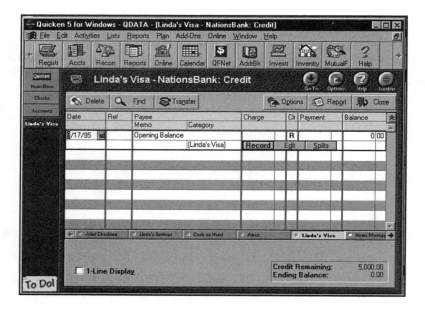

Avoid high interest costs

Many credit cards allow you to get a cash advance and treat it as a credit purchase where you don't pay it back until you receive your statement. But don't make the mistake of assuming that the cash you receive is interest-free for up to 30 days (like purchases). Unfortunately, cash advances start accruing interest from the day the money is advanced to you. Sometimes, banks charge an additional fee of as much as 1.5 percent on cash advances. So, if you're in a bind for cash, take the advance but pay it back as soon as possible to avoid high interest costs.

I'll enter each credit card purchase

Regardless of the method you choose to enter your credit card transactions, you'll enter them the same way. Here's what you'll need to enter for each transaction:

- The date that you made the credit purchase.

- In the Payee field, tell Quicken who you made the credit purchase with (if you made a credit card purchase at Sears, enter Sears in the Payee field).

- The amount of the credit purchase.

- A memo describing the purchase (if you want).

- The category that you want to assign to the purchase.

Figure 14.4 shows a few credit card purchases entered in a credit card account register.

Fig. 14.4
Credit card transactions are entered in the register just like transactions in other registers in Quicken. Be sure to assign a category to each of your credit card transactions.

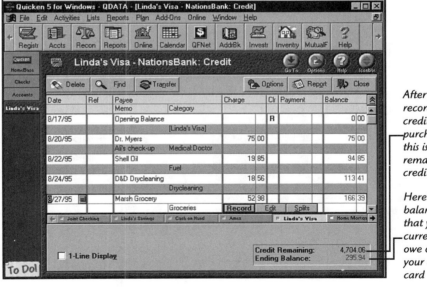

After your recorded credit card purchases, this is your remaining credit limit

Here's the balance that you currently owe on your credit card

TIP **You can edit and delete transactions in a credit card account** register the same way that you do in any other register. If you need some help working with transactions, go to Chapter 5 and read about editing and deleting transactions in the register.

I can balance my credit card account to make sure it's accurate

In Chapter 7 I told you all about how important it is to balance your checkbook. Well, it's just as important to balance your credit card account against your statement to make sure that all of the transactions that appear are accurate. Balancing your credit card helps you uncover unauthorized uses of your credit card, errors recorded in your account by the credit card company, or any mistakes you may have made when you entered credit transactions. The time to balance your credit card account is before you make a payment. That way, you can first make sure that the balance is correct and then decide how much of the balance you want to pay.

Balancing your credit card account each month is not only smart, but easy. If you've already balanced your checking account with Quicken, then you know most everything you need to know to balance your credit card account. The steps are almost identical.

Entering information from your credit card statement

Enter information from your credit card statement first (see fig. 14.5).

Fig. 14.5
Review the information from your credit card statement and enter it here.

If any finance charges appear on your statement, enter them here

When you're finished, click OK

Enter the total charges and cash advances as shown on your credit card statement

Enter payments and credits here

Enter the ending (or outstanding) balance as shown on your credit card statement

Put the statement closing date here

If you incurred a credit card finance charge, assign a category here

Marking transactions

Next, mark those transactions that appear on your statement (see fig. 14.6).

Fig. 14.6
Click a credit card transaction to mark it as cleared.

Mark the transactions that appear on your statement by clicking the transaction or highlighting it and clicking the Mark butto

If you're not quite finished balancing your credit card account but need to quit for now, click the Finish Later button and your work will be saved

When you're finished marking credit card transactions, click the Finished button

Use the New button to go to the register to enter an omitted transaction

Change or delete transactions using the Edit and Delete buttons

Go back to the Credit Card Statement Information window by clicking the Info button

This amount will be zero if your credit card account balances with your statement

When your credit card account balances, you're ready to pay your bill.

 Q&A **What if my credit card account doesn't balance?**

First, go through all of your credit card transactions and make sure that you marked the right ones. Then, make sure that the transaction amounts are the same as those shown on your credit card statement. If it still doesn't balance, you may need to make an adjustment to your credit card account. When you click Finished, Quicken recommends the amount of the adjustment transaction to make your credit card account balance.

Time to make a payment

When you've successfully balanced your credit card account, Quicken displays the Make Credit Card Payment window shown in figure 14.7. Here's where you tell Quicken whether you want to make a payment now or not. If you do want to make a payment, select the account to pay and how you will make the payment.

Fig. 14.7
Are you ready to pay your credit card bill? If so, click OK and Quicken enters the payment for you in the Write Checks window or the register for the bank account that you select.

Select the bank account from which you want to make the payment

How will you make the payment? By a Quicken check or a manual check?

Click OK to enter the payment transaction

If you don't want to pay your credit card bill right now, click Cancel

I like to pay the entire balance each month

If you don't want to incur any finance charges, you'll want to pay the entire credit card balance as shown on your statement. Click OK in the Make Credit Card Payment window that you saw in figure 14.7. If you selected the Printed Check method, Quicken writes the check for you and displays it next in the Write Checks window (see fig. 14.8). If you selected to write a handwritten check, Quicken enters the transaction in the register.

Fig. 14.8
Quicken writes a check to pay off the balance that your credit card statement says you owe. To pay the entire balance, just record the check as is.

To pay off the balance on your credit card, just record the check in the Write Checks window or the transaction in the register. If you wrote a check in Quicken, all you have to do now is print the check. If Quicken entered a transaction in the register, write your handwritten check for the credit card balance now.

What if I don't want to pay the whole thing?

If money's tight right now, you may not want to pay the entire balance on your credit card. With the exception of the American Express Card, you can make a minimum payment on credit cards. Beware though—if you only pay the minimum payment each month and continue to make credit purchases, you'll never get rid of your credit card debt!

So if you don't want to pay off your balance, decide how much you do want to pay and just edit the amount field in either the Write Checks window (see fig. 14.9) or the register. Then record the check or the transaction; it's that simple.

Fig. 14.9
If you don't want to pay your entire balance on your credit card, just change the amount that Quicken enters in the Amount field.

 TIP If you have a Quicken credit card, be sure to read Chapter 25 to learn how it works with online banking to download your data by modem.

15

Keeping Track of Your Loans

● **In this chapter:**

- **Set up your loans in Quicken**

- **See loan information in one place**

- **Time to make a loan payment**

- **Do some refinancing**

- **Calculating loans**

- **Set up and use other liability accounts**

I've got a car loan, student loan, and a mortgage! How can I keep track of them all? And more importantly, when am I ever going to get them paid off? . . . . ●

You've probably figured out by now that if you've got a financial task that needs to be done, Quicken can do it for you. Keeping track of your outstanding loans is no exception. With Quicken, you can set up a loan for all your amortized loans, like your mortgage, car loan, or student loan. Then, Quicken keeps all of your amortized loans in one place so that at any time you can view a loan and its amortization schedule.

 Plain English, please!

An **amortized loan** charges you a specified rate of interest on the part of the loan (or outstanding balance) that is unpaid. Each payment that you make on an amortized loan is divided into principal and interest; a certain portion reduces the principal balance of the loan and the remaining portion is the interest charge. When you set up an amortized loan, Quicken creates an **amortization schedule** that tracks the principal and interest portion of each loan payment. **" "**

If you have other types of liabilities that aren't amortized (like maybe a loan from a friend who isn't charging interest on the outstanding balance), you can set up a liability account to track the balance.

I want to set up a loan

Quicken's EasyStep Loan Setup windows make it easy for you to set up any amortized loan that you have. For each of your outstanding loans, you'll want to set up a separate loan in Quicken. Even though the EasyStep windows prompt you for the information Quicken needs to set up your loan, here's an overview of what you'll need to enter so that you can have this information ready:

- **Original amount that was borrowed.** This is the amount that you originally financed. If you borrowed $15,000 for a new car, for example, the original balance of the loan is $15,000.

 CAUTION **When EasyStep asks you for the original balance of your loan,** don't make the mistake of entering the amount that you currently owe. If you do, your loan payment schedule will be way off. The amount that you currently owe subtracts all of the payments that you've already made on the loan and will be less than the original loan amount.

- **Date the loan was created**. This is the date that you signed the loan documents and became liable for the loan amount.

- **Balloon payment amount**. Your loan may not have a balloon payment due at the end of the loan term. If the terms of your loan require that you pay the unpaid principal balance at the end of the payment period, then you'll need to enter the balloon payment amount when you set up your loan.

- **Original length of the loan**. This is the period of time over which you make payments on the loan in order to pay off the original balance. Most mortgages are paid over 15 or 30 years. Car loans are usually paid over periods from 3 to 5 years.

- **Payment period for the loan**. This relates to the intervals over which you make payments on your loan, like monthly, semi-monthly, and so forth.

- **Compounding period for the loan**. How is the interest calculated on your loan? This is the compounding period. Usually, interest is compounded monthly or semi-annually. Contact your lender if you don't know the compounding period.

- **Current balance of the loan and date**. This is the principal amount that you still owe after you've made payments and the date of that balance. For a new loan, the current balance will also be the original loan balance. But, if you've made some payments on a loan, then the current balance will be less. If you don't know the current balance, you don't have to enter it. Quicken can calculate the current balance after you've entered all other loan information.

- **Date of next payment**. When are you supposed to make your next loan payment?

- **Amount of the next payment**. What payment amount will you be making the next time you make one? If you don't know the payment amount, Quicken can calculate it for you.

- **Interest rate of the loan**. This is the rate of interest that's charged on the outstanding principal balance of your loan. If the loan is a fixed rate loan, the interest rate will be constant. If it's a variable rate loan, enter the current rate of interest that's being charged.

• **Escrow amounts**. Portions of your loan payment may be to pay for things like real estate taxes, insurance, and so forth. The bank **escrows**, or holds, these funds for you until these amounts are due and then pays them for you.

TIP **If you need to calculate a loan to find out what the payment** amount is or the current interest rate, you can use Quicken's Loan Planner. The Loan Planner is a handy on-screen financial calculator that computes the variables of a loan. Later in this chapter, I show you how to use the Loan Planner.

Setting up your loan

So let's get started setting up your first loan in Quicken. First, you'll need to open the View Loans window (see fig. 15.1) by selecting Activities, Loans.

As you can see in this View Loans window, there are currently no loans set up in Quicken

Fig. 15.1
In the View Loans window, you can set up a new loan, delete an existing loan, or view a loan that you've already set up.

You'll click the New button to open the first EasyStep Loan Setup window

Next, click the New button to open the first EasyStep Loan Setup window that you see in figure 15.2. Get on your way to setting up a loan in Quicken by clicking the Next button.

Fig. 15.2
Here's the first
EasyStep Loan Setup
window that will put
you on your way to
setting up a loan in
Quicken.

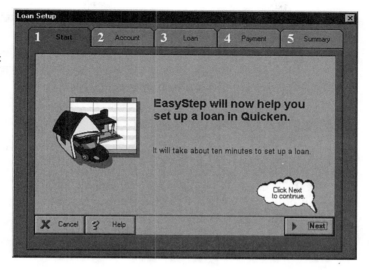

There is quite a bit of information that you'll need to enter to get your loan set up in Quicken. Basically, you'll need to:

- Tell Quicken whether you're setting up a loan for money you've borrowed or money you've lent to others.

- Set up a loan account that Quicken can use to track your loan. Select an existing liability account or, if there isn't an existing account in Quicken that represents this loan, type a name for the loan account using up to 15 characters, but not :] [/ | ^.

- Enter information for your loan, like the amount, loan period, and interest rate.

- Tell Quicken how you'll make payments on the loan.

As you complete each EasyStep Loan Setup window, click the Next button to continue.

TIP **As you know by now, an outstanding loan is a liability. And as I've** advised you in other chapters, you need an account for all of your assets and liabilities if you want Quicken to determine your net worth. When you set up a loan in Quicken, a liability account automatically gets set up for you. So, for each loan that you set up, Quicken sets up an associated liability account.

There will be some liability accounts, though, that you need to set up yourself. These are liabilities that aren't amortized, like an interest-free loan from a friend, income taxes payable, insurance premiums payable, accounts payable (for businesses), and so forth. Much later in this chapter, I show you how to set up liability accounts.

Reviewing your loan

Now that you've set up your loan account, entered loan information, and set up your loan payments, you can look through the next few Summary windows to review your loan. If there's some information that's not correct, change it now. When you see the last Summary window (see fig. 15.3), click Done to set up your loan payments in Quicken.

Fig. 15.3
This is the last Summary window that shows the balance and payment information for your loan. Click Done when you're sure all loan information is correct.

Setting up loan payments in Quicken

Quicken has all of your loan information, except payment information, which you provide in the Set Up Loan Payment window.

Click the Edit button to open a Splits window so that you can enter any escrow amounts included in your loan payment. If you add escrow amounts, Quicken adds them to your total payment amount

Click OK when you're finished setting up payments on your loan

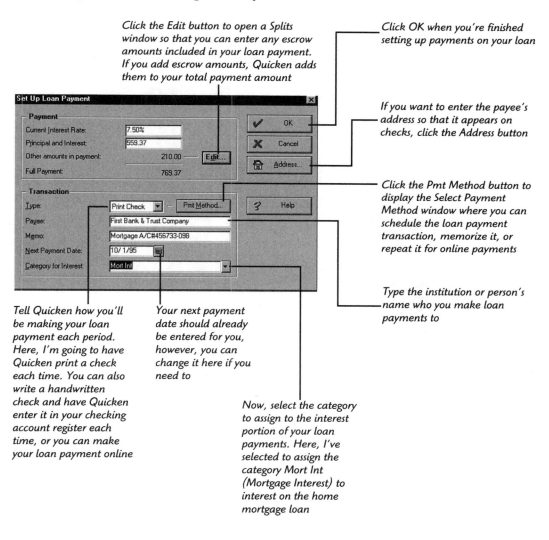

If you want to enter the payee's address so that it appears on checks, click the Address button

Click the Pmt Method button to display the Select Payment Method window where you can schedule the loan payment transaction, memorize it, or repeat it for online payments

Type the institution or person's name who you make loan payments to

Tell Quicken how you'll be making your loan payment each period. Here, I'm going to have Quicken print a check each time. You can also write a handwritten check and have Quicken enter it in your checking account register each time, or you can make your loan payment online

Your next payment date should already be entered for you, however, you can change it here if you need to

Now, select the category to assign to the interest portion of your loan payments. Here, I've selected to assign the category Mort Int (Mortgage Interest) to interest on the home mortgage loan

Adding your loan to Quicken

Now that you've entered all the loan and payment information, your loan is added to Quicken and appears in the View Loans window that you see in figure 15.4.

Click here to see a list of all the loans you've set up in Quicken

Click on these tabs to see different information for the current loan

Fig. 15.4
After you set up a loan in Quicken, you'll see it in the View Loans window.

What if I need to change a loan?

Just like most things in Quicken, you can change them after they're entered or set up. So what if you need to change the name of the lender, the interest rate, the payment method, or delete a loan altogether? You can change any of these things from the View Loans window that you saw in figure 15.4.

To change a loan, it first needs to be the current loan in the View Loans window. To make a loan the current loan, just select it from the Loan drop-down list. In figure 15.4, the current loan is the Home Mortgage loan.

Editing a loan

To change loan information, such as the original loan amount, the date the loan was opened, the length of the loan, and so forth, click the Edit Loan button in the View Loans window (refer to fig. 15.4). When you click this button, Quicken displays one of two Summary windows with the existing loan information. Just move to the appropriate box to change the information that you need to.

Changing the interest rate

If the loan that you set up in Quicken has a variable interest rate, then at some point the rate will change. So how do you deal with this? Simple. Just click the Rate Changes button in the View Loans window (refer to fig. 15.4) and Quicken displays the Loan Rate Changes window shown in figure 15.5. Here, you'll see all of the interest rates charged on your loan.

Fig. 15.5
Quicken keeps track of interest rate changes in the Loan Rate Changes window.

To enter a new interest rate, click the New button to see the Insert an Interest Rate Change dialog box in figure 15.6. Enter the date that the new interest rate is in effect and the new rate. Quicken automatically calculates your new payment based on the changed rate.

Fig. 15.6
Enter a new interest rate on your variable rate loan and the date the new rate is in effect. Click OK to change the interest rate on the current loan.

Changing loan payments

Need to change the payee on a loan, the payment method or type, or the category you've assigned to the interest portion of your payments? From the View Loans window (refer to fig. 15.4), click the Edit Payment button. Quicken displays the Edit Loan Payment window with the same information that you saw in the Set Up Loan Payment window. Make your changes here.

Q&A *What if I want to make a payment on a loan before I've scheduled it in Quicken?*

You can make a payment at any time, regardless of when it's scheduled in Quicken. From the Edit Loan Payment window, there's a Pay Now button that lets you make an early payment. Or, from the View Loans window, you can select the Make Payment button to make a regular payment on your loan now.

Deleting a loan

When do you think you'd delete a loan? Certainly, you'd delete a loan you inadvertently set up (maybe it isn't an amortized loan and should be set up as a liability account—we get to this later). But the time you'll be most happy to delete a loan is when it's paid off!

When you delete a loan, Quicken permanently removes all of the loan and payment information from the View Loans window. If your loan payment was set up as a scheduled transaction, it gets deleted from the Scheduled Transaction List; if it's a memorized payment, it gets removed from the Memorized Transaction List, too. You can select, however, whether or not Quicken deletes the associated liability account for the loan.

To delete a loan, first make the loan that you want to delete the current loan in the View Loans window (refer to fig. 15.4), and then click the Delete button. But not so fast—Quicken doesn't let you make a hasty decision here. You'll first see a confirmation message that tells you you're about to delete an amortized loan. Quicken also asks if you want to save the associated liability account or delete it.

If you want to delete the loan from the View Loans window and also delete the liability account, select Yes. If you want to delete the loan *and* delete the associated liability account in Quicken, select No. If you really don't want to delete the loan at all, select Cancel.

Time to make a loan payment

Undoubtedly, you'll have to make payments on the loans that you've set up in Quicken. So what happens when it's time to make a payment? Well, remember when you set up loan payments as you were setting up your loan? You selected how payments would be made; by a scheduled transaction, a memorized transaction, or online bill payment.

If you selected a scheduled transaction or to make loan payments online, then your payments are entered automatically by Quicken. Each time a payment is due, Quicken automatically writes a check or enters the transaction in the register for the account that you use to pay bills.

If you're using a memorized transaction to make loan payments, you'll have to recall the transaction each time a payment is due. I showed you how to recall memorized transactions in Chapter 9.

Regardless of how the loan payment is entered, Quicken divides the principal and interest portion of each payment. If part of your payment goes to other charges, like insurance or real estate taxes, Quicken also enters these and assigns the appropriate category to each. And as if Quicken didn't have enough to do when you make a loan payment, the program also updates your loan balance each time. So, you know at any given point how much you still owe on a loan.

You can make regular loan payments when they're due, make extra payments so that you reduce your loan faster, or pay off the entire balance of your loan.

Making a regular loan payment

When it's time to make a loan payment, Quicken will remind you if you've set up the payment as a schedule transaction or an online payment. For this reason, I strongly urge you to use one of these payment methods so that you never forget to make that all-important loan payment. Lending institutions almost always charge significant late fees for payments that aren't made on time.

When Quicken reminds you to make a payment, it's pretty easy. When you start Quicken, you'll see a Scheduled Transaction Due window, like the one in figure 15.7, that tells you which payments are due. To select to make the payment now, click Re**c**ord and Quicken enters the payment for you.

Fig. 15.7
When you start Quicken, you'll see a list of scheduled transactions that are due now. If you've set up payments on your loan as scheduled transactions, you'll see the loan payment in this list.

 TIP **If you want to make a loan payment before Quicken thinks it's** due, just select the loan in the View Loans window and click the Ma**k**e Payment button. This is helpful if you need to get all of your bills paid ahead of time (like when you go on vacation).

Making extra loan payments

In an amortized loan, payments are scheduled to be made at regular intervals, like very month, week, etc. Part of a loan payment reduces the principal balance of the loan and the other part is an interest charge (you also may have other charges or fees included in your payment).

If you want to make some extra principal payments, though, so that you can payoff your loan sooner, Quicken provides a way for you to do that. Just select the Ma<u>k</u>e Payment button in the View Loans window to see the Loan Payment dialog box (see fig. 15.8). Click the Extra button to tell Quicken that you're not making the usual loan payment, but an extra one.

Fig. 15.8
Click Extra to prepay some of the principal balance on a loan.

Quicken then shows you the Make Extra Payment window where you can specify how much of the principal you want to pay now (see fig. 15.9). Most of the information in this window is entered for you based on regular loan payments. You'll have to tell Quicken, however, the amount of the extra payment you'd like to make now. Enter this amount in the Amount field and click OK to have Quicken enter the payment for you.

Fig. 15.9
Tell Quicken how much the extra payment is and click OK.

Paying off a loan

It's sure a happy day when you finally get a loan paid off. Especially that 30-year mortgage.

If you're making the last payment on a loan, just make it as usual. It will reduce your loan balance to zero. If you're paying off a loan early, get the payoff amount from your lending institution first. Then select the Ma<u>k</u>e Payment button in the View Loans window and change the payment to the payoff amount. When you record the edited payment, the loan balance should be reduced to zero.

After you've paid off a loan, you can delete it from the View Loans window if you want. If you delete the loan account, you can also select to delete the associated liability account, too.

Undoing a loan payment

What if you enter a loan payment inadvertently? Maybe you didn't really make last month's payment. If this happens, just delete the loan payment from the register for the account that you use to make loan payments (probably your checking account).

When you undo, or delete, a loan payment, Quicken removes the payment from the loan's payment schedule in the View Loans window and also deletes the payment from the associated liability account register. The outstanding loan balance will now be correct.

What happens when I refinance a loan?

With fluctuating interest rates, you may want to refinance a loan to take advantage of a lower interest rate. Refinancing home mortgages is very common because interest rates are otherwise locked in for long periods of time, like 15 or 30 years. If you took out a mortgage in the early to mid 1980s, the interest rate may be twice the going rate today. If you refinance, your mortgage payments can be reduced significantly.

Before you jump into refinancing a loan, you should carefully evaluate the cost benefits. Many mortgage lenders charge closing costs and points when

Pay off your loan early!

You'd be surprised what a difference a few days makes on your outstanding loan balance. If you're contemplating paying off a loan early, check with your lending institution first to get the exact payoff amount as of the date that you're going to make the payment. Make sure that you are specific about the date that you'll be paying off the loan. So if you're paying the loan off today, get today's balance. If you're paying it off ten days from now, get the balance for that date. Just one or two days makes a difference in the amount of interest that has accrued on your loan.

you refinance. When you take these extra costs into consideration, a lower interest rate may still not save you money in the long run.

TIP **Don't be fooled into thinking that refinancing is the answer just** because you can secure a lower interest rate. With added closing costs and points to refinance a mortgage, you may not come out ahead at all. If your existing mortgage isn't very old and you incurred closing costs at the time you took out the mortgage, refinancing may not be prudent unless the new interest rate is significantly less than your current rate.

Evaluating refinancing options

Quicken can help you determine whether refinancing your current loan makes sense with the Refinance Planner. Open the Refinance Planner (see fig. 15.10) by selecting Plan, Financial Planners, Refinance. Then fill in your old payment and any escrow amounts, the amount you'll refinance, the new interest rate, and any closing costs. The Refinance Planner instantly shows you the cost savings and how many months it will take to break even if you pay closing costs.

Fig. 15.10
The Refinance Planner calculated the payment difference on a $100,000 loan at 8%, refinanced at 6.75% with $2,500 in closing costs. You can see that it will take 29.36 months to break even because of the closing costs involved in refinancing.

TIP **If you want to print out the data that the Refinance Calculator** just computed for you, click the Print button.

Refinancing a loan

So, you've decided that it makes economic sense to refinance a loan. If this is a loan you've set up in Quicken, you'll have to make some changes to reflect the new interest rate on the loan. Basically, you'll set up a new loan and then pay off—or delete—the old loan.

Set up the new loan first with a name like Refinance or a name other than the name you used for the old loan. Since you're setting up the new loan first and the old loan still exists in Quicken, you can't use the same name.

 TIP   **If you want to use the same name for your refinanced loan as you** used for your old loan, just edit the new loan to change its name after you've deleted the old loan.

Your new loan should reflect the amount you're refinancing as the Original Balance and the date that you refinance the loan. After you've set up your new loan, Quicken creates a liability account for it.

Now you're ready to pay off the old loan. Remember, you just set up a loan for the amount that you refinanced. This amount should be the same as the outstanding balance of the old loan, right? For example, if your old loan started out at $100,000 but after a few years of payments is now $94,958.81, then the amount you refinance is also $94,958.91.

To pay off the old loan, first go to the register for your new liability account. So, if you called it Refinance, go to the Refinance account register. You should see only one transaction—the Opening Balance transaction. Move to this transaction and replace the words Opening Balance with the name of the lender who refinanced your loan.

Then, in the Category field, select the old account. What happens here, is that you're decreasing the old loan account by the outstanding balance. Figures 15.11 and 15.12 show you the transactions in the new and the old accounts that pay off the old loan with the amount of the new loan.

 TIP   **If your refinanced loan includes closing costs, enter those in the** Splits window when you're editing the new account register transaction.

Fig. 15.11
In the new account, change the entry in the Payee field to the name of the new lender. Then select the old account in the Category field.

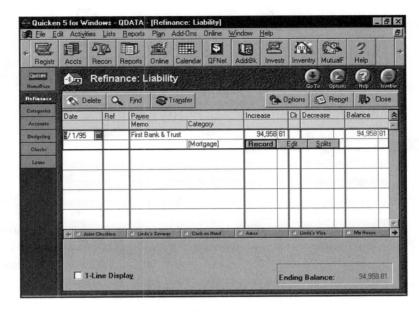

Fig. 15.12
As you can see in the old account, the outstanding balance is paid off with the transaction from the new account.

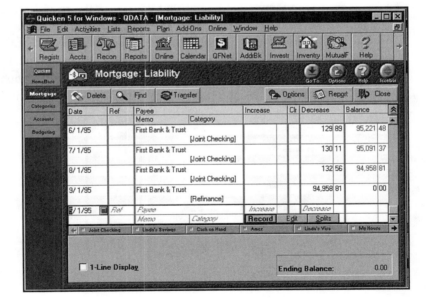

Now that the old account has a balance of zero, you can delete the loan account from the View Loans window. When you delete the old account, you can choose whether you want to also delete it's associated liability account. If you select to keep the liability account, it will show a zero balance with a complete record of all of your payments.

Calculating loans

If you're contemplating the purchase of a new home, car, or whatever, and want to see what the payments will be if you finance your purchase, use Quicken's Loan Planner. With the Loan Planner, you can enter a loan amount, interest rate, and loan period and instantly see your payments. Or, enter the payment that you can afford, the going interest rate, and a loan period, and the Loan Planner will tell you what purchase price you can afford based on those payments.

To use the Financial Planner, select Plan, Financial Planners, Loan. Quicken opens the Financial Planner that you see in figure 15.13. Fill in the Financial Planner and tell it what you want to compute; the loan amount or the payment amount. Calculations are made instantly as you enter data in the Financial Planner. If you want to see a payment schedule for the loan scenario that you entered, click the Schedule button and Quicken shows you each payment, broken out into principal and interest until the loan's paid off.

Fig. 15.13
Using the Financial Planner to calculate the payment on a $15,000 loan, at 7.5%, for five years.

What about other liabilities I have?

Up to now, you've been working with loans that are amortized. For amortized loans, you set up a loan in Quicken that's added to the View Loans window (and then Quicken sets up an associated liability account for you). But you won't set up a loan for other kinds of loans that aren't amortized, like an interest-free loan, income taxes payable, and so forth.

For loans that aren't amortized, you'll set up a liability account only. Liability accounts have registers just like other accounts in Quicken that track the activity in the account. So, if you make a payment on a loan that you've set up a liability account for, you can enter a transaction for the payment that decreases the outstanding balance.

 Q&A   *Let me get this straight. If I have a loan, like my home mortgage, that charges interest on the unpaid balance, then I set up a loan account for it in Quicken. Right? But if I want to track the amount that I owe for income taxes this year, even though my taxes aren't due until next April 15th, I set up a liability account for this liability.*

You're absolutely right. Just remember, if you have a loan that charges interest at regular intervals, then you'll track this loan in Quicken in a loan account and set it up in the View Loans window. If you have other types of liabilities that you want to track, like your example of the income taxes payable, you'll set up a liability account for them.

Setting up a liability account

You've probably set up several different types of accounts in Quicken by now. I know that you set up a checking account when you first started using Quicken. Setting up a liability account is very similar. If you need some detailed explanation to the steps for setting up accounts, go back and read Chapter 2.

When you're ready to set up a liability account, start from the Account List (click the Accts icon) and then click the New button. Quicken then displays the Create New Account window. Click the Liability button to open the first EasyStep Liability Account Setup window. Then just follow the EasyStep instructions for setting up your liability account. You'll enter a name for the account, the starting date and balance, and other information that you might want to add about the account.

TIP **When you set up a liability account, Quicken asks if you want to** set up an associated loan account. If you're setting up a liability account for an unamortized loan, don't have Quicken set up a loan account for you. In the first part of this chapter you learned how to set up a loan account for those amortized loans that you have.

Working in the liability account register

After you've set up a liability account, you can begin using its register to track your liability. Figure 15.14 shows the Taxes Payable liability account register with some transactions that affect the outstanding balance in the account. Enter transactions in a liability account the same way that you enter transactions in other Quicken accounts.

Fig. 15.14
Here's a liability account set up to track income taxes that are estimated through the year and then paid on April 15th.

16

Creating Your Budget

● **In this chapter:**

● **Putting together a budget**

● **Save as many budgets as you'd like**

● **Simplify your budget with supercategories**

● **Look at how I'm doing with my budget**

Tired of not being able to eat lunch out at the end of the month? Did you miss that movie last month because you were out of money? Quicken's budget feature could solve these problems and more . . . . ●

Most of us know we need a budget but don't want to take the time to sit down and put it on paper. We may have an idea in our minds about how much we *should* be spending, but really don't have an easy way to monitor it. The thought of a budget to many is unpleasant. So budgeting gets an undeserved bad reputation.

Most think of a budget as financial handcuffs, an obstacle to enjoyment, and just a plain drag on their financial freedom. Nothing is farther from the truth. Actually, with a realistic, well-planned budget, you'll feel more comfortable buying that new suit, taking a vacation, or making an investment in the stock market. When you know that you can afford something because it's provided for in your budget, it makes spending money less stressful. Just think of a budget as a game plan for how you're going to make and spend money. You can be as creative as you want, but most importantly, be realistic. With Quicken, budgeting is painless. There's lots of helpful features that make setting up a budget quick and easy. And when you're ready to see how well you're sticking to your budget, Quicken provides some handy tools to take a look.

Do I really need a budget?

If you make and spend money, then you do need a budget to make sure that you don't spend more than you make. And even if you're very financially responsible and would never dream of spending money you don't have, you still need a budget to help you allocate and prioritize your spending.

So I guess the answer to the question on budgeting here, is that everyone can benefit by setting up, and living within, a budget. And now that you're using Quicken, setting up a budget couldn't be easier.

Okay, I need a budget. How do I set one up?

You're about to find out how easy creating a budget is in Quicken. Here's an overview of the simple steps you'll go through to set up your budget:

1   Open the Budget window.

2   Change the layout of the Budget window, if necessary.

3   Enter your budget amounts.

4   Save your budget.

First, I need to open the budget window

Budgeting starts in (where else?) the Budget window. The Budget window is like a spreadsheet with rows for each category that you use and columns for each period that you want to budget.

When you're ready to set up your budget, open the Budget window by selecting Plan, Budgeting.

Changing the layout in the Budget window

Notice that the Budget window is set up to budget on a monthly basis. Each column in the Budget window represents a month in the year. But what if you don't want to budget monthly? Maybe you want to budget on a quarterly or annual basis instead. Or, maybe you want to budget for transfers from one account to another.

You may need to change the layout of the Budget window so that it meets your needs before you start entering budget amounts. Just click the Layout button in the button bar to see your options in the Layout Budgets dialog box (see fig. 16.1). Select what you want shown in columns and in rows and click OK to change the Budget window. In figure 16.2, you see that I changed the Budget window to budget on a quarterly basis and to include rows for transfers.

A close look at the Budget window

All your budget information is entered in the Budget window.

Budgets button
Lets you manage more than one budget. Use this button to select the budget that you want to work with.

Edit button
Is used to enter data in the Budget window.

Layout button
If you want to change what appears in the Budget window, click this button.

Print button
When you're ready to print your budget, click this button.

Save button
To save the data entered in the current Budget window, click Save.

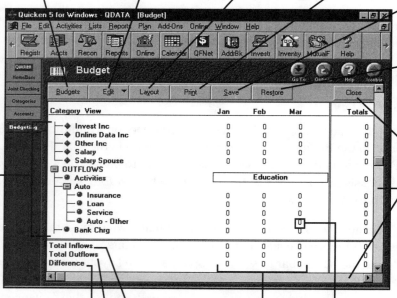

Restore button
Click Restore to change the current budget back to the way it was the last time you saved it.

Close button
The Close button closes the current Budget window.

Scroll bars
Use the scroll bars to move up and down or right and left in the Budget window. As you move through the Budget window with the scroll bar, Quicken shows you where you are in the window by displaying the category name in a box to the left of the scroll bar.

Categories
Each of these rows represent the categories that you use in Quicken.

Difference
This section totals your inflows and outflows and computes the difference between the two for each period in your budget.

Inflows
Your income categories are listed first, in the INFLOWS section.

Outflows
Expense categories are listed next, in the OUTFLOWS section.

Columns
The Budget window includes a column for each period that you want to budget. Here, we can budget for each month.

Cells
The intersection of a column and a row is called a cell. Budget amounts are entered into cells in the Budget window.

Fig. 16.1
You can change what Quicken shows in columns and in rows in the Budget window.

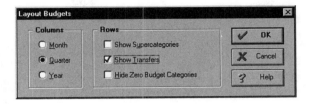

Fig. 16.2
In this Budget window, I can budget on a quarterly basis and enter budget amounts for transfers.

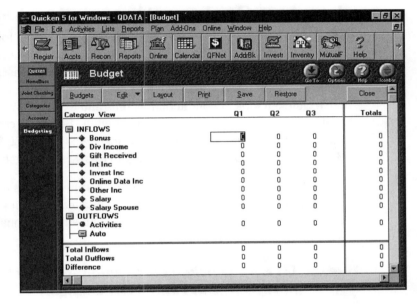

Once the Budget window is laid out the way you want it, you're ready to enter budget amounts.

Q&A *I see from figure 16.1 that I can select to show supercategories in the Budget window. What are supercategories and how are they used?*

Supercategories group categories into broad levels for budgeting purposes. When you have several categories that are similar, you can group them together so that you don't have to enter a separate budget amount for each. For example, you may have several entertainment categories that you use, like Movies, Sporting Events, Videos, and Theater. Instead of setting up budget amounts for each category, you can set up a supercategory called Entertainment and set up one budget amount for all entertainment expenses. Later in this chapter, I show you how to set up supercategories and assign categories to them.

Entering budget amounts

So now you're ready to start entering budget amounts in the Budget window. You can enter budget amounts in one of two ways—automatically with previous Quicken data, or by entering amounts yourself in each cell within the Budget window.

I can have Quicken enter amounts automatically

When you enter budget amounts automatically, Quicken looks at data from a prior period and copies those amounts in the appropriate column and row in the Budget window. For example, if you used Quicken last year you'll have a year's worth of income and expenses entered in account registers. You can have Quicken look at your actual income and expenses from the prior year and base this year's budget on those amounts. So, if you earned $50 per month in interest income last year, Quicken will enter $50 for each month in the Int Inc (Interest Income) category in this year's budget.

You can select to have Quicken enter the actual amounts from the prior period into the same month in this year's budget. Or, Quicken can average the actual amounts from the prior period and enter an equal amount into each month that you're budgeting.

Q&A   *If I have Quicken enter amounts in my budget automatically, can I make any changes?*

Yes. No matter how budget amounts are entered in the Budget window, you can change any of the amounts at any time. Just move to the cell with the budget amount that you want to change and type in the new amount. You can change just one amount or all budget amounts.

To enter budget amounts automatically, click the Edit button in the Budget window button bar to open the Edit menu. From here, you can select Autocreate to have Quicken enter budget amounts automatically from previous data.

Select the Autocreate option to open the Automatically Create Budget dialog box (see fig. 16.3). Give Quicken some instructions for creating your budget and click OK.

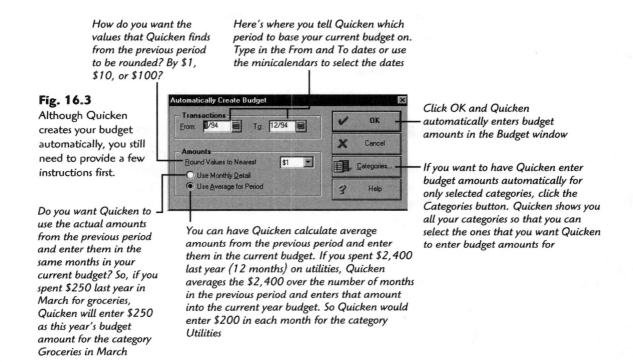

How do you want the values that Quicken finds from the previous period to be rounded? By $1, $10, or $100?

Here's where you tell Quicken which period to base your current budget on. Type in the From and To dates or use the minicalendars to select the dates

Fig. 16.3
Although Quicken creates your budget automatically, you still need to provide a few instructions first.

Click OK and Quicken automatically enters budget amounts in the Budget window

If you want to have Quicken enter budget amounts automatically for only selected categories, click the Categories button. Quicken shows you all your categories so that you can select the ones that you want Quicken to enter budget amounts for

Do you want Quicken to use the actual amounts from the previous period and enter them in the same months in your current budget? So, if you spent $250 last year in March for groceries, Quicken will enter $250 as this year's budget amount for the category Groceries in March

You can have Quicken calculate average amounts from the previous period and enter them in the current budget. If you spent $2,400 last year (12 months) on utilities, Quicken averages the $2,400 over the number of months in the previous period and enters that amount into the current year budget. So Quicken would enter $200 in each month for the category Utilities

Or, I can enter amounts manually

If you just started using Quicken, then you won't have any previous data that Quicken can look at to automatically enter your budget amounts this year. In this case, you'll need to enter your budget amounts yourself. This is not as difficult as it may sound. Just think of the Budget window as a spreadsheet with columns and rows for you to enter data. Enter amounts just as you would in a spreadsheet, like Excel or 1-2-3.

To enter a budget amount for a category, first move to the row for that category; then, decide which period you want to enter the amount in. If you're budgeting monthly, you probably want to enter a budget amount for January first, then February, and so forth. Use the Tab key or your mouse to move to the right one column at a time. After you enter a budget amount, press Enter to move down one row at a time.

TIP **You don't have to enter budget amounts for expenses as a nega-**
tive number. When you type an amount in an expense category cell,
Quicken automatically converts the amount to a negative when you press
Enter.

Quicken gives me lots of budget shortcuts

If you have a lot of categories that you use in Quicken, entering your budget
amounts may become tedious and time-consuming. Quicken provides several
shortcuts for entering budget amounts quickly and easily. These shortcuts
are all found in the Edit menu that you see in figure 16.4. Here, I'll point out
how these handy time-savers work:

Fig. 16.4
Click the Edit button
in the Budget window
button bar to open the
Edit menu.

- **2-Week**. Select 2-Week to budget for items that you receive or pay on a
  biweekly basis. Use this to budget your paycheck if you receive it every
  two weeks.

- **Copy All**. This option is really not used for entering budget amounts in
  the Budget window. Use the Copy All option to copy the current budget
  amounts to the Windows Clipboard. You can then paste your budget
  into a spreadsheet program.

- **Clear Row**. The Clear Row option erases all of the budget amounts in
  the current row. This saves you time if there are amounts entered for a
  category and you later decide the budget amounts should be zero.

- **Clear All**. If you need to erase the current Budget window so that you
  can start, select the Clear All option.

- **Fill Row Right**. If there's an amount that you want to copy to every
  cell in the current row, select Fill Row Right. Quicken copies the
  amount from the current cell to each cell to the right in the entire row.
  To fill in $100 in each month for the category Charity, enter $100 in the
  January cell and then select Edit, Fill Row Right, and then select Yes.

- **Fill <u>C</u>olumns**. To fill in columns to the right with the same budget amounts from the current column, select E<u>d</u>it, Fill <u>C</u>olumns and then select <u>Y</u>es.

Saving your budget

Well, you've done all that work on your budget, you'd better save it now. Just click the <u>S</u>ave button in the button bar and Quicken saves your current budget. The next time that you open the Budget window, the budget you just saved will appear.

If you forget to save your budget and try to close the Budget window or even exit Quicken, you'll be reminded that you've just made some changes that need to be saved. If you want to save them, click <u>Y</u>es. If you don't want the budget to remain the way it was before you made changes, select not to save the budget by clicking <u>N</u>o.

 Q&A *I just made some changes to my budget that I don't want to keep. Is there a way to get back to my original budget?*

Yes. Click the Res<u>t</u>ore button in the Budget window button bar and you'll see the budget as it was the last time that you saved it. If you made your changes, however, and then saved them, you won't be able to get back to your original budget. When you select the Res<u>t</u>ore button, Quicken restores your budget amounts from the last time that you saved your budget.

 With Quicken 5, you can save multiple budgets. You may want to create more than one budget based on different scenarios. Maybe one budget if you stay in your current job, and another if you decide to take that new job with the 20 percent pay increase. Later in this chapter, I show you how to create more than one budget.

What are these supercategories all about?

In a Q & A earlier in this chapter, I told you a little about supercategories. Supercategories are used to group similar categories together to make budgeting less burdensome. When the categories in your Budget window are grouped into supercategories, your budget becomes much easier to set up and work with.

You don't have to micro-manage those smaller categories because they'll be lumped into a larger supercategory. You'll find four supercategories already set up in Quicken: Discretionary, Non-Discretionary, Other Income, and Salary Income. These are very common supercategories that probably everyone can use.

66 *Plain English, please!*

Some of your income and expenses is considered **discretionary** and some is considered **non-discretionary**. Discretionary items are those that you can make choices about or control the amounts of. Examples of discretionary items are entertainment, clothing, dining, and so forth. These are discretionary because you can make a conscious choice about how much you'll spend in these areas. Non-discretionary items, however, are those that you have little control over, like your mortgage payment, rent payment, child care fees, insurance premiums, and so forth. 99

You can set up other supercategories, if you'd like. Then, you can assign categories to each supercategory that you set up. After you've set up the supercategories that you want to use in your budget, you can change the Budget window to show categories grouped by supercategory so that you can enter budget amounts for each supercategory.

Setting up supercategories

Before you set up supercategories, review your category list and maybe even your actual amounts for last year. This review will help you decide which categories should be grouped into supercategories.

When you're ready to set up a supercategory, select Edit, Supercategories to open the Manage Supercategories window shown in figure 16.5. Set up a new supercategory by clicking the New button. Then give your supercategory a name using up to 22 characters.

Here's the list of all the categories that you currently use

Quicken has already assigned one of the predefined supercategories to each of your categories

All of the supercategories that have been set up are in this list

Fig. 16.5
Set up a new supercategory or assign categories to supercategories in the Manage Supercategories window.

Assign a category to a supercategory by highlighting the category and also highlighting the supercategory and clicking the Assign button

Remove a supercategory assignment from a category by highlighting the category and clicking the Clear button

Click OK to save your supercategories

Click the New button to add a new supercategory; edit or delete supercategories with the Edit and Del buttons

After you've set up a supercategory, assign categories to it by highlighting the supercategory and the category that you want to assign and clicking the Assign button. Figure 16.5 shows the category Bonus is assigned to the Other Income supercategory.

Showing supercategories in the Budget window

After your supercategories are set up and you've assigned the appropriate categories to them, you'll want to change the Budget window to show a row for supercategories. Do this by selecting Layout, clicking the Show Supercategories checkbox, and then clicking OK.

Figure 16.6 shows the Budget window after the layout has been changed to include a row for supercategories. Notice that the Budget window is in Supercategory View. When you saw the Budget window earlier in this chapter, it was shown in Category View.

Fig. 16.6
Showing the Budget window in Supercategory View.

There's a row for each supercategory. You can enter a single amount for each supercategory

Click the + button for a supercategory to show each category assigned to it

I want to create more than one budget

Even though there's only one Budget window, you can create more than one budget in Quicken. This is a brand new feature in Quicken 5 and works great if you'd like to create multiple budgets to take into consideration different scenarios, like a job change, college expenses for your son, retirement, or whatever.

To create another budget, select <u>B</u>udgets to open the Manage Budgets window that you see in figure 16.7.

Fig. 16.7
Click the Create
button if you want to
set up another budget.
If you want to work
with a budget that
you've already set up,
highlight the budget in
the Manage Budgets
window and click
Done.

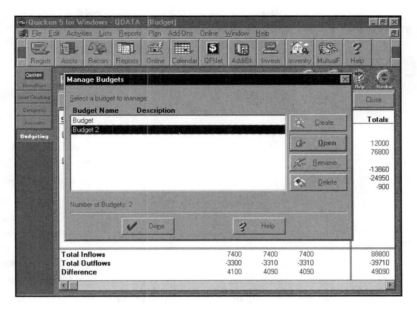

From the Manage Budgets window you can either create a new budget or, if you've already set up more than one budget, select the budget that you want to work in.

If you've already created another budget, you'll see it in the Manage Budgets window. To work in that budget, highlight it and click Done.

If you're creating a new budget, click the Create button to see the Create Budget window shown in figure 16.8. Here, you assign a name to your budget, a description (if you want), and tell Quicken how to create the budget. Click OK to open a new Budget window to work in.

Enter a name for your new budget

If you want to add a description of the new budget, enter it here

Fig. 16.8
Assign a name to your
new budget and tell
Quicken how to
create it.

*Copy the budget amounts
from the Budget window
that you're currently
working in*

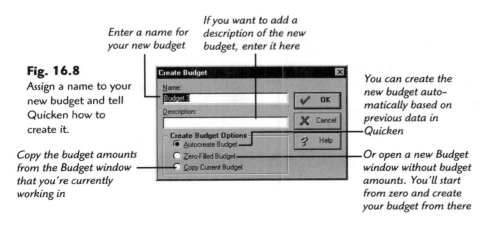

You can create the new budget auto- matically based on previous data in Quicken

Or open a new Budget window without budget amounts. You'll start from zero and create your budget from there

I want to see how well I'm sticking to my budget

You set up a budget in Quicken and have been diligent about entering all of your financial activity. It's only been a few months since you started using Quicken and set up your budget, but you're anxious to see how well (or not so well) you're doing. Or, maybe you're not anxious at all. Assessing your budget can be like stepping on the scale in the morning. It's tough to do when you know you just had that caramel torte the night before; it also may not be pleasant looking at your budget after a recent splurge at the shopping mall. In either case, you know it ain't gonna look good! But you have to face up to it so that you can get back on track (with your eating *and* your spending).

Quicken provides a few tools that you can use to quickly assess the progress you're making with your budget. You can create a Monthly Budget Report that shows your budgeted amounts right alongside your actual amounts. Then there's the Budget Variance Graph that charts budget variances in a bar graph. And finally, you can monitor your budget using the Progress Bar that shows your actual income or expenses for a single category compared to budgeted amounts through the current month, quarter, or year.

 Plain English, please!

A variance, when talking about budgets, is the difference between actual amounts and budgeted amounts. There are positive and negative variances. A positive variance occurs when actual income exceeds budgeted income or actual expenses are less than budgeted expenses. You have a negative variance when actual income is less than budgeted income and actual expenses exceed budgeted expenses.

Creating a budget report

You're going to learn the ins and outs of Quicken's reports in Chapter 19, but for now, I'd like to show you how you can quickly create a Budget Report so that you can see how well you're doing with your budget.

Create a Budget Report by clicking the Reports icon from the iconbar to open the Create Reports window. From here, click the EasyAnswers tab to see the reports that you can create to answer some basic personal finance questions. See the one that says "Did I meet my budget"? This is the one you'll want to select. Decide which period you want to assess, like Did I meet my budget last month, last quarter, last year, and so forth, by making a selection from the drop-down list. Then click the Create button to see the report on your screen (see fig. 16.9).

Fig. 16.9
Here's a Budget Report for the month of August as shown on your screen. As you can see, Quicken lists each category, its actual amount, budgeted amount, and the difference between actual and budget.

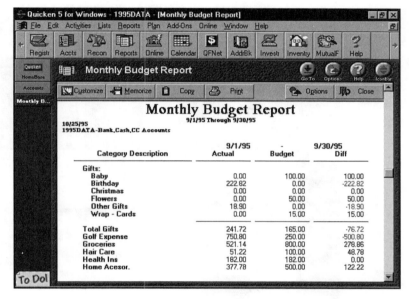

Use the scroll bar to move up and down the report to see all categories. If you want to print your Budget Report, click the Print button while the report is displayed on your screen. To remove the Budget Report from your screen, click the Close button.

Looking at a budget graph

Quicken has some really neat graphing features that help you assess your financial situation, but more specifically, the progress you're making with your budget. You're not going to learn everything you need to know about graphing in Quicken from this chapter (read Chapter 20 for the unabridged discussion of graphs). Like with the Budget Report, I want to show you how you can create a graph that shows you how you're doing with your budget.

Here's how you can create a graph that compares your actual and budgeted data. Choose Graphs from the Activities menu to open the Create Graph window. Next, enter the time period that you want to look at in the From and To text boxes. If you don't enter dates, Quicken will create a graph from January to the current month. Then click the Budget Variance Graph option and click Create to see the graph on your screen (see fig. 16.10).

Fig. 16.10
The Budget Variance Graph compares actual and budgeted amounts in two bar graphs—one for income and one for expenses.

You can print the Budget Variance Graph by clicking the Print button or remove it from your screen by clicking Close.

Monitoring your budget with the Progress Bar

Quicken's Progress Bar is one more handy tool that you can use to monitor your budget. The Progress Bar (when you select to use it) is displayed at the bottom of your screen and monitors two categories or supercategories for you. Let's say that you're really worried about how much you've been spending on dining out and entertainment, both of which are discretionary expenses that you could easily cut back on. You can select to have your Dining category and your Entertain category monitored by the Progress Bar so that you can see your actual dining and entertainment expenses as compared to your budgeted expenses for the current month, quarter, or year.

Here's how you get the Progress Bar to appear on your screen. Select Plan, Progress Bar. In figure 16.11, you see the Progress Bar at the bottom of the screen. You're doing pretty well here; your dining expenses are under budget and your entertainment expenses are only $3.32 over budget.

Fig. 16.11
Here, the Progress Bar is monitoring dining and entertainment expenses against budget.

The amount that you have actually spent is shown inside the gauge and the budget amount is shown to the right of the gauge

The Cust (customize) button is used to select the categories that you want to monitor and also to determine how the Progress Bar appears on your screen

Now you're probably wondering how I selected the two categories that I wanted to monitor with the Progress Bar. See the Cust button on the right end of the Progress Bar? Click this button to see the Customize Progress Bar window. From here, you can select the category for the left gauge by clicking the Choose Category button; click the other Choose Category button to select the category for the right gauge. Notice that you can also select which time period is monitored by selecting one from the <u>D</u>ate Range drop-down list. When you've made your selections in the Choose Category window, click OK to begin monitoring the category that you selected.

TIP **Want a quick peek at the budget amount for a monitored** category? Just point to the gauge in the Progress Bar (the mouse pointer changes to a magnifying glass) and double-click. Quicken opens the Budget window and highlights the budget amount for the category being monitored.

Q&A *I like using the Progress Bar to monitor my budget, but it's just so darned big that it gets in my way. Is there any way to make it smaller?*

Yes. You can choose to not show the labels (like Dining Budget in fig. 16.11) above the gauges. Do this by clicking the Cust button and then clicking the Show Labels option to turn it off. The absence of labels reduces the size of the Progress Bar by about half.

Part IV: Analyzing Your Finances

17

Staying on Top of Your Investments

● **In this chapter:**

- Use up your investments in Quicken

- Use Quicken to track your investments

- Use mutual fund investment accounts

- You can enter purchases and sales of stocks

- Use your investment activity with reports

- Using online services to update investments

- One-click access to the Quicken Web site on the Internet

Keep track of that stock certificate your grandfather gave you when you were born, or manage a diverse portfolio. Either way you can use Quicken to monitor your investments and to keep you informed of changes and trends . . . . ❯

One of the main reasons people purchase programs like Quicken is to monitor their investments. Keep your investment records all in one place with Quicken and you can always be assured of getting a complete, up-to-the-minute summary of all your investment activities.

What types of investment accounts can I set up?

Quicken lets you choose between two types of investment accounts:

- Regular investment accounts keep track of the market value of multiple securities, the number of shares you own, and the cash balance

- Mutual fund investment accounts keep track of the number of shares you own and the market value of individual mutual funds

Create a separate account for each mutual fund you own, and set up one regular investment account to track all your other investments. If you prefer, you can create more than one regular investment account to group investments. For example, you may want all the investments held by one broker in one account. Or you may want to track one investment in an account by itself.

How do I set up a regular investment account?

Keep track of one or more securities in a regular investment account. Much like your check register, the register for your regular investment account keeps track of increases and decreases in the value of your investment and presents a balance showing the amount in the account.

To set up a regular investment account, choose Create New Account from the Activities menu. Select Investment, click Next, enter your account name, click Next again to proceed. Make sure No is selected in order to make this a regular investment account as opposed to a mutual fund account.

If your investment account works like a checking account—in other words if you get to write checks and withdraw cash from your investment account just like in your checking account—click the Yes button.

You are asked whether this is an IRA or other Tax-Free Account. Whether you choose Yes or No, the next screen asks if you want to assign tax schedules to this account. You can designate with which part of your tax return the income from this account is associated. You then have the capability to merge your information from Quicken with a tax software program such as TurboTax.

You may enter some additional information about this account such as the name and telephone number of your broker or other comments. Whether you choose Yes or No for entering additional information, click Next to continue. On the Summary screens make sure the information entered agrees with your expectations for this account. Click Next to finish the account set up.

 TIP **Notice at the bottom of the Create New Account window there is** a little button that reads, "Start With Summary Information." Rather than going through all these steps, you can enter all the information at the Summary screens and save yourself some time.

How do I enter my securities?

You can enter securities in Quicken in two ways:

- Enter securities right into the register. As you enter a new security, one you haven't had before, Quicken pops up a Set Up Security window (see fig. 17.1) in which you can enter information about the stock, including the Symbol.

- Select Security from the Lists menu. Quicken brings up a Security List window which lists all the securities you've entered into Quicken so far. Click the New button and you'll see the Set Up Security window.

Fig. 17.1

Use this window to tell Quicken about your security investment.

Enter the ticker symbol for the stock here

The Set Up Security window requests several pieces of information from you:

- In the Name box enter the full name (as many as 18 characters including spaces) of the security.

- In the Symbol box enter the ticker symbol. This is the symbol used in the stock exchange columns of a newspaper.

- In the Type drop-down list box choose from Bond, CD, Mutual Fund, and Stock to identify the type of security you are setting up.

- Optional: Use the Goal box to describe your long-range goal for the investment. Options include: College Fund, Growth, High Risk, Income, Low Risk.

- Check the Add to Watch List box if you are entering a stock in which you don't personally have an investment, just a curiosity. You can chart the progress of the stock through Quicken by checking this box.

- Enter the income per share you anticipate earning from this stock in the Est. Annual Income, per Share ($) box.

- Check the Tax-Free box if this is a tax-exempt investment.

- Choose OK to add the security to your Security List.

Repeat these steps for as many securities as you want to enter.

I need to tell Quicken how many shares I own

In the register for your investment account you can add your securities (the names of all the securities you entered in the last section will appear when you click on the drop-down menu in the box where you enter the name of your security) and enter additional information about your investments.

Move to a new record at the bottom of the register (Ctrl+End takes you to the bottom of the register) to add securities. Or, you can click the Action button at the top of the window, choose Add Shares to Acct, and then continue to enter information about your security.

For the Date field, enter the date you purchased your security, not the date on which you are making the entry.

The Action field should contain information about how you acquired the security: Buy, Stock Dividend, or other choices.

Enter the number of shares you acquired when you received the stock and the cost per share—not the total cost for all the shares—Quicken calculates the total for you.

What's different about the mutual fund investment account?

With a mutual fund account, you record your starting balance in the fund, then you periodically record changes in your fund balance based on the purchase of additional shares or the redemption of shares. When you get a statement in the mail from your mutual fund, you can update your Quicken account register as well.

Set up a mutual fund investment account in much the same way you set up a regular investment account, clicking Yes when asked if this is a mutual fund account. Quicken gives you an opportunity to enter the number of shares you own in the mutual fund, and the price per share in the Create Opening Share Balance (see fig. 17.2). Enter this information, then click OK. Your new money market account register is displayed.

Fig. 17.2
Enter the number of
shares and cost per
share of your mutual
fund in this window.

Can Quicken help me choose a mutual fund?

Are you considering investing in a mutual fund? Quicken's new Mutual Fund Finder can help you select from many mutual funds based on the performance of the funds and your tolerance for risk.

You won't find the Mutual Fund Finder on your Quicken menus. You have to open the Mutual Fund Finder as a separate program. In Windows 95, go to the Start button and select Programs from the pop-up menu. Then select Quicken (or Quicken Deluxe) from the list of programs, then select the Mutual Fund Finder.

TIP **To open the Mutual Fund Finder, if you are using Windows 3.1,** use the task list (Ctrl+Esc) to return to the Program Manager, find the Quicken 5 for Windows Group window, and double-click on the Mutual Fund Finder program icon.

Click the Next button to get past the Mutual Fund Finder introductory material. If you want to import your own list of mutual funds, funds that you have entered into Quicken, click the Import button in the Mutual Fund Finder, otherwise click the Next button.

On the next screen, the Criteria tab, you select from various criteria options in an effort to streamline your information request to funds that appeal specifically to you and your personal financial situation.

TIP **When selecting criteria in the Mutual Fund Finder, you can select** more than one criteria option by holding down the Ctrl key while you click on the options.

When you have finished considering the criteria that seems appropriate for your needs (and you can always go back and make changes in the criteria), the Mutual Fund Finder presents a summary screen that shows the criteria you have selected (see fig. 17.3).

View and sort the list of mutual funds that meet your needs in a variety of ways by clicking on the Sort By and View selections

Fig. 17.3
You are presented with a list of funds that currently meet your criteria.

Switch to the Next Steps tab for guidance from Quicken in evaluating the funds on your list

See the details of any of the funds on the summary screen, including the minimum investment fee, and the phone number and address where you can contact the fund for further information, by clicking on the Details button

Print a copy of the summary screen by clicking on the Print button

Choose Exit from the Mutual Fund Finder File menu to close the Mutual Fund Finder program.

The Quicken investment register looks familiar

The Investment Register for tracking Quicken investments looks like the check register you are familiar with (see fig. 17.4). Entries in the Investment Register are made in much the same way as they are in the check register.

The price of the security goes here

Enter the number of shares in this column

Fig. 17.4
The Quicken Investment Register looks a lot like the Check Register.

The date gets entered in this column

Enter the type of activity (buy, sell, and so on) here

Enter the name of the security here

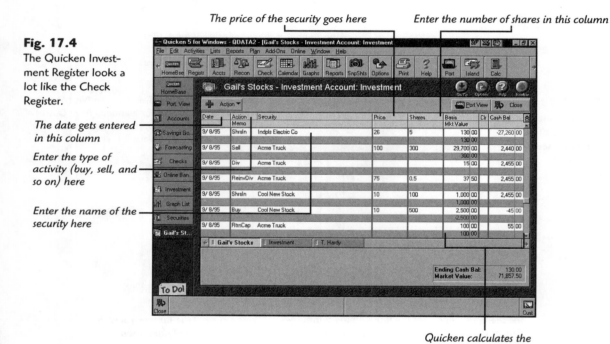

Quicken calculates the amounts in these columns

I need to enter my investment transactions now

Select the investment account into which you want to enter transactions, then click on the Register button at the top of the account list. This opens the Investment Register.

I bought a security

When you open the Investment Register, your cursor should be blinking on the first free line in the register, right under the last transaction that you entered. Today's date is already entered for you. Follow these directions to enter a new transaction:

1 Using the tools you learned in the "Never Type a Date Again" section of Chapter 9, change the date (if necessary) to the date on which your transaction occurred. Press Tab to advance to the next field.

2 Enter "B" for "Buy" in the Action field and Quicken will fill in the rest of the word. Press Tab to advance to the next field.

3 Enter the name of the security using the QuickFill feature—either drop down a list of securities currently in the system or begin typing and Quicken fills in the name.

4 Enter the price of the security and the number of shares you purchased. Quicken fills in the calculated amount. Press Tab.

5 Enter the broker's commission if you paid one. Click Record.

You can change any transaction by clicking in any field of that transaction, typing your change, and clicking on Record.

I sold a security

To record the sale of a security, follow the steps in "I Bought a Security," changing step two to type in "S" for "Sell" in the Action field.

When you click Record for the transaction, Quicken asks you if you want to identify specific lots. What this means is, if you purchased the shares of stock you are now selling on different dates (not all on the same date), do you want to specify which shares you are selling today.

If you click Yes on the specific identification question, Quicken opens the Specify Lots For (your investment) window (see fig. 17.5) which shows all the purchases you made on the stock you are now selling. You can click on one of the purchases, then choose Use All to specify that all shares you sold are from this lot, or Use Part to indicate that some shares are from this lot and some are from another lot.

Fig. 17.5
Use this window to
identify from which
lot(s) your stock sale
occurred.

Click on the lot from which you are selling

*Click here to sell all
your stock from the
selected lot*

*Click here to clear the Total Selected
from above and start over*

*Click here to sell part of your
stock from the selected lot*

I received income from my investments

Your investment account should reflect all the activity of your investments,
not just purchases and sales. So whenever there is a stock split, whenever
you receive a dividend, when you reinvest a dividend, whenever anything
transpires that affects your investments, make an entry in the account
register. That way you will always have the most up-to-date image of your
portfolio.

To enter income into your investment account, open the account, choose the
correct date, and choose the appropriate activity: Div (Dividend Income) or
ReinvDiv (Reinvest Dividend Income). Select the name of the security, then
enter the amount. Enter cash dividends at actual cash value. If you are
entering a reinvested dividend, you must know the price per share of the
stock and the number of shares you acquired on reinvestment. This information should be available on your statement. If you don't have a statement,
contact your broker.

How do I handle stock splits and stock dividends?

Sometimes, instead of paying cash dividends, companies pay their sharehold-
ers in additional shares of stock, known as stock dividends. If you receive a
stock dividend, record it by following these steps:

1 Open the investment register for the account.

2 Enter the date of the transaction in the Date field.

3 In the Action field, click on the Action button at the top of the Investment Register window. Choose Advanced from the list of actions. Choose Stock Dividend from the list of advanced transactions. Quicken opens up a Stock Dividend window like the one in figure 17.6.

Fig. 17.6
In this example, the shareholder received a stock dividend of .2 new shares for every share he owned previously.

Quicken fills in the quantity of shares you received and updates your stock records.

If you receive a stock split, in the Action field enter StkSplit. Quicken will prompt you to enter both the old number of shares you owned and the new number you now own.

Can I memorize an investment transaction?

Some people repeat their investments transactions regularly. If you have a stock purchase plan at your job, for example, and with each paycheck you purchase a share of your company's stock, you would like to be able to enter this purchase quickly from a memorized transaction list rather than having to enter all the details every time you get paid.

Quicken provides you with the opportunity to create a memorized transaction in the investment journal. Memorized transactions in your investment register work in the same way as they do in a regular register.

I'd like Quicken to remind me about my investments

You can rely on Quicken to remind you of forthcoming investment events and considerations. For example, you may want a reminder of the maturity date of a CD, or you may want to remind yourself to make a deposit to your IRA account before the tax return deadline.

Make notes in the Investment Register that will appear in the Quicken Billminder and Reminder features. To enter an investment reminder:

1 In the Investment Register, press Ctrl+End to move to the next empty transaction line.

2 Rather than today's date, enter the date on which you want to be reminded.

3 Type **Reminder** in the Action field. Quicken fills in the rest of the word.

4 Type the text of your reminder in the Description field.

5 Click Record when you are finished entering the reminder.

You can keep the reminder in the Investment Register, even after you're finished being reminded, in case you want to use it again. Click two times in the Clr (Cleared) field to place an "**R**" in that field. That has the effect of turning off the reminder without deleting it.

Summarize your investments in the portfolio view

Switch to Portfolio view by clicking on the Port View button at the top of your investment register. Portfolio View (see fig. 17.7) gives you a summary of your investments, each security listed alphabetically, with general information such as number of shares owned, current price, and current market value.

Record transactions by clicking on a security, then clicking on this Action button. An appropriate window opens based on the action you choose

Click on a security then click on this Report button (or click twice on the security name) for a report of all the transactions involving that security

Fig. 17.7
You can see all your investments at a glance in Portfolio View.

Click the Graph button to see a visual rendition of the price history of the selected security

Change the way in which the portfolio items are sorted in the screen display by clicking on the column heading that you want to use in your sort

Click the Prices button to see a window detailing the price history of the selected security

I want to update my stock prices

You can read the stock section of the daily newspaper and get the closing stock prices for the previous day. Quicken lets you update the market value of your securities in the Portfolio View window by following these steps:

1 Click the Port View button if you're not already in Portfolio View.

2 Click the View box at the top right corner of the Portfolio View window and choose Price Update from the drop-down list.

3 Select the security you want to update.

4 Enter the latest market price in the Mkt Price column.

Alternatively, you can let Quicken update your stock prices for you online. There is a fee for this service. Call Intuit Online Services Customer Service at (800) 245-2164 to ask about signing up for the Portfolio Price Update service. Fees are billed monthly to your credit card (which you could track in your credit card register with a Repeating Memorized Transaction!).

To use the online stock price update service, follow these steps:

1 Click the Update button at the top of the Portfolio View window.

2 Enter your Portfolio Price Update account number (assigned to you when you register for this service), then click OK.

3 Make sure your modem is hooked up and your telephone line is free. Quicken connects you via modem to the Portfolio Price Update service. Sit back and watch as Quicken updates all your stock prices to the current market value.

4 Click OK when Quicken lets you know the price update has been completed.

Hey, can I really visit the Internet from Quicken?

With this latest version of Quicken, you can click one button and get immediate access to the Quicken Financial Service located at the Quicken Web site on the Internet. This is a free service to all Quicken users; however, you must have a modem connected to a phone line in order to access this service. Once connected, browse through information offered by the many financial institutions that are working with Quicken to provide on-line banking services. You can also read personal finance tips and place orders for Intuit software. Ultimately, Quicken plans to offer access to stock quotations, mutual fund information, and other services through this Internet site.

18

Getting Ready for Tax Time

● In this chapter:

● Match a tax form to a category

● Get help from the Tax Link Assistant to assign tax form lines to categories

● Put together some tax reports

● It's tax time again!

● Don't let Uncle Sam catch you with your pants down—estimate your tax liability ahead of time

Now that you're using Quicken, tax time's going to be a breeze. There will be no more worrying when the April 15th deadline nears . . . . ●

You've been entering transactions in Quicken all year to stay on top of your finances. So why not take it one step further and use those same transactions to get ready for taxes? As April 15th approaches, Quicken can summarize all of your tax-related transactions and put them in one place. With Quicken, you can even export your data to a tax preparation software program so that you don't have to reenter anything.

Also use Quicken to estimate your taxes so that you don't have any big surprises at tax time. With Quicken's Tax Planner, you can forecast your income tax liability at any time.

I first need to designate tax categories

As you know, when you enter a transaction in Quicken, you assign a category to it so that you can track your income and expenses by type. You can go one step further by designating some of your categories as tax-related.

 Plain English, please!

A category is **tax-related** if the transactions that are going to be assigned to it are associated with taxable income or tax-deductible expenses. For example, the category Salary is tax-related because your salary is considered taxable income. The category Charity is also tax-related because charitable contributions are tax-deductible. **99**

Designating categories as tax-related can be done while you're adding a new category or by editing an existing one. Whether you're adding a new tax-related category or editing an existing category, start from the Category & Transfer List. Click the New button to add a new category, or edit a category by highlighting it and clicking the Edit button. You'll see the Set Up Category (see fig. 18.1) or Edit Category window next (depending on which button you click). The same information is included in each window.

Move to the Tax-related check box and click to select. This tells Quicken that this category is tax-related and all transactions that have this category assigned to them should be summarized and included in tax reports. Those categories that you've designated as tax-related are shown in the Category & Transfer List (see fig. 18.2).

Fig. 18.1
When you add a new category, you can designate it as tax-related by selecting the Tax-related check box. Then select the tax form or schedule where transactions for this category should be reported.

Fig. 18.2
The categories that you designate as tax-related appear with the word *Tax* in the Tax column of the Category & Transfer List.

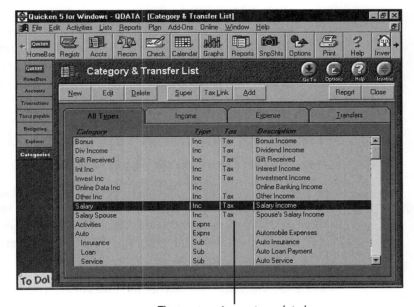

These categories are tax-related

Now, if you want, you can assign a tax form or schedule to the category.

TIP **If you are using one of Quicken's predefined category lists,** tax-related categories are already designated for you. If you add another category, however, you'll have to select whether it's tax-related. Or, you can edit one of Quicken's categories to change its tax-related status.

Assigning tax forms to categories

After you've designated a category as tax-related, you can assign a tax form or schedule where transactions for the category should be reported. Just click the drop-down list and select the form or schedule. The Salary category, for example, is reported on the W-2 Salary schedule. The Investment Fee category that is shown in figure 18.1 is reported on Schedule A.

Q&A ***What if there's not a drop-down list to select the tax form or schedule in the Set Up Category or Edit Category windows on my screen?***

If you don't see the Form drop-down list box in either of these windows, then you don't have the tax schedule option in Quicken turned on. To turn on this option, click the Options button and then select General. In the General Options window, select the Use Tax Schedules with Categories option. Chapter 24 explains in more detail how to set general options in Quicken.

Assigning tax form lines with the Quicken Tax Link Assistant

Now you've got your categories set up as tax-related and selected the forms or schedules where they should be reported. Track your tax-related transactions even closer by designating the line on the form or schedule where they should be reported. With Quicken's new Tax Link Assistant, you can select tax form lines all from one place.

Clicking the Tax Link button from the Category & Transfer List (refer to fig. 18.2) opens the Tax Link Assistant window that you see in figure 18.3. Use the scroll bar and click in the Category list to highlight the category to which you want to assign a tax form line. Then highlight the line that you want to assign and click the Assign Line Item to Category button. Continue assigning lines to categories and then click OK when you're finished.

Fig. 18.3
Assign specific tax form lines to categories in the Tax Link Assistant window.

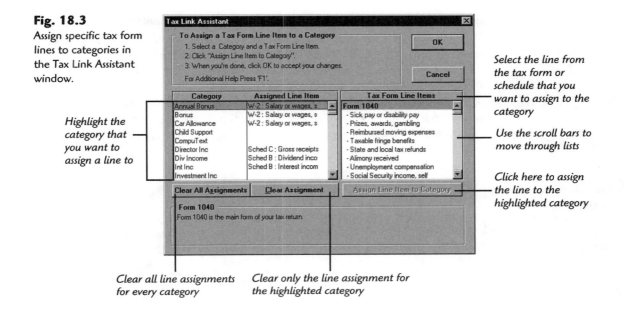

Highlight the category that you want to assign a line to

Select the line from the tax form or schedule that you want to assign to the category

Use the scroll bars to move through lists

Click here to assign the line to the highlighted category

Clear all line assignments for every category

Clear only the line assignment for the highlighted category

Quicken summarizes my tax data in reports

During the year, as you've assigned tax-related categories to transactions, your tax data is being accumulated by Quicken. At any time, you can generate tax reports that extract the information that you need to complete your tax return (either manually or using tax preparation software).

There are two reports that you can generate to summarize your tax data:

- *Tax Summary Report.* Groups and subtotals your tax-related transactions by category, starting with taxable income categories first, and then tax-deductible expense categories.

- *Tax Schedule Report.* Groups and subtotals your tax-related transactions by tax form or schedule line.

I need a Tax Summary Report to prepare my return manually

If you're preparing your income tax return yourself, or you need to accumulate your tax data to give to a paid preparer, the Tax Summary Report provides all the information you'll need. This report groups all tax-related transactions by category. For instance, it will total all Salary income, all Dividend income, and all Charity donations. With this information, you can easily transfer the totals to the tax forms and schedules in your return.

Here's how to generate a Tax Summary Report. First, click the Reports icon to open the Create Report window. Click the <u>H</u>ome tab to display the list of reports for home use. Then select the Tax Summary option and click the <u>C</u>reate button. Figure 18.4 shows you what the Tax Summary Report looks like when it's displayed on your screen.

Fig. 18.4
This report groups and subtotals transactions assigned to your tax-related categories.

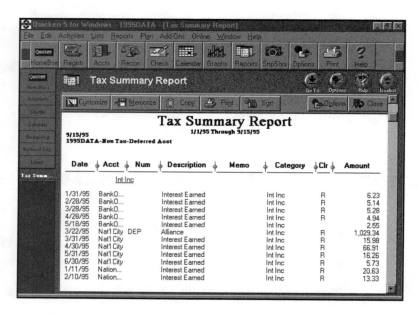

Click the Pri<u>n</u>t button and change options as needed in the Print Report window. Then click OK to get a printed copy of the Tax Summary Report.

TIP **If you want to change the dates that the Tax Summary Report** covers or exclude some of the accounts included in the report, click the Customize button and make your changes. Chapter 19 tells you all about customizing reports so that they give you the information you need in the format that you want.

I need a Tax Schedule Report because I use tax preparation software

If you're using tax preparation software to prepare your income tax return, then you'll need to create a Tax Schedule Report. This report not only subtotals your tax-related transactions by income and expense, but groups and subtotals them by form or schedule and then again by line. After you've created a Tax Schedule Report, you can then transfer the data in the report to a tax program.

Create a Tax Schedule Report by clicking the Reports icon to open the Create Report window, where you click the Home tab to see the list of home reports that you can create. Then select the Tax Schedule option and click the Create button. Figure 18.5 shows you what the Tax Schedule Report looks like.

Fig. 18.5
This report groups and subtotals transactions assigned to your tax-related categories by tax form or schedule line.

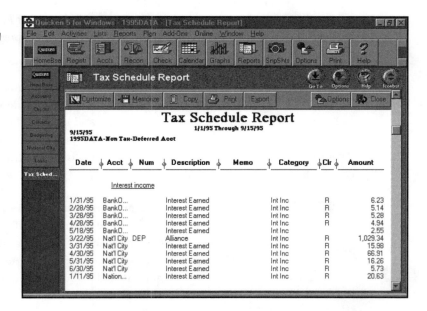

You can choose to print a copy of your Tax Schedule Report to your printer (click the Print button) or export it to a file that can be transferred to a tax preparation program. (You'll learn about exporting files in the next section.)

It's time to prepare my return

When you're ready to prepare your income tax return, create the appropriate report. You just learned how to create a Tax Summary report that groups your tax-related transactions by category and then how to create the Tax Schedule Report that groups transactions by tax form line.

Just print a copy of either report to use in preparing your return manually or give the report to your CPA as part of your tax information.

If you're using a tax program, however, you'll export the Tax Schedule Report to a TXF file for transfer.

 Plain English, please!

TXF (Tax Exchange Format) refers to the extension that's given to the file for the tax report that you're exporting. Files must be saved in the tax exchange format to be exported and read by tax preparation programs.

Create the Tax Schedule Report as explained in the previous section. Then click the Export button to open the Create Tax Export File window. Here is where you'll give a name to your report file and include the TXF as the extension. So, provide a file name (using DOS naming rules) and the location where you want the file stored. Then click OK to export the data in the Tax Schedule Report to a TXF file.

 TIP **If you're using TurboTax to prepare your income tax return, you** won't need to create the Tax Schedule Report. TurboTax can read and import your tax data directly from Quicken. You can start TurboTax while you're using Quicken by selecting TurboTax from the Add-Ons menu. (Of course, you must have already installed TurboTax on your hard drive).

Because all tax preparation programs are different, I'll refer you to the documentation for the program that you're using to learn how to import the TXF file into the program.

CAUTION **Make sure that the dates covered by the Tax Schedule Report are** appropriate for your return. If you're preparing your tax return for 1995, the dates should include 1/1/95 to 12/31/95. To change the date range in the report, click the Customize button and then change the Report Dates in the Customize Tax Schedule Report window.

I want to estimate my taxes for next year

Want to know how much tax you're going to owe for this year? Or what about next year? And how much will your tax liability go up if you take that new job with the nice pay increase? These are all questions you can get answers to with Quicken's Tax Planner. The Tax Planner lets you estimate the amount of tax you'll owe on that dreaded day (April 15th) so you're not caught by surprise.

To use the Tax Planner to estimate your taxes, first gather your tax information together. You'll need tax items, like paycheck stubs, medical and dental receipts, tax receipts, interest payment records, child care receipts, charitable contributions, and perhaps your prior year's tax return. Then, open the Tax Planner by selecting Plan, Tax Planner (see fig. 18.6). From here, you'll change the tax rate (if necessary), enter data, and then analyze the results.

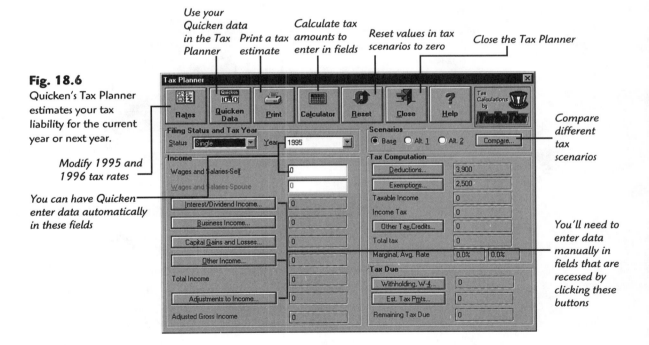

Use your Quicken data in the Tax Planner

Print a tax estimate

Calculate tax amounts to enter in fields

Reset values in tax scenarios to zero

Close the Tax Planner

Fig. 18.6
Quicken's Tax Planner estimates your tax liability for the current year or next year.

Modify 1995 and 1996 tax rates

You can have Quicken enter data automatically in these fields

Compare different tax scenarios

You'll need to enter data manually in fields that are recessed by clicking these buttons

What if the tax rates change?

You know how Congress is—continually changing the tax code and rates, especially around election time. Quicken's Tax Planner incorporates the tax rates based on the most recent tax legislation. However, if these rates increase or decrease, you can easily change them in the Tax Planner so that your tax calculations are up-to-date.

Before you change the tax rate, be sure that the appropriate filing status and year are shown in the Tax Planner. In figure 18.6, the rates in effect are for Single filing status in 1995. If you want to change the rates for next year, select 1996 in the Year drop-down list box. Now you can click the Rates button at the top of the Tax Planner to open the Tax Rates window shown in figure 18.7. Type over any of the existing rates with the new rates, or modify the AMT exemptions or the inflation rate and click OK.

Fig. 18.7
If Congress decides to change the income tax rates, you can modify the rates that the Tax Planner uses to make its calculations so that you can get an up-to-date tax estimate.

Entering data in the Tax Planner

The Tax Planner needs a little information before it can estimate your taxes, like how much your income will be and the amount of your tax-deductible expenses. You can use your Quicken data in the Tax Planner, or you can manually enter data. You might use a combination of both, however, if you're estimating taxes for the current year (Quicken for year-to-date data and manual entries for the remainder of the year). Quicken can, however, annualize any year-to-date information so that you don't have to enter anything manually.

If you want to use the tax-related information that you already have in Quicken, click the Quicken Data button in the Tax Planner to open the Preview Quicken Tax Data window (see fig. 18.8). Quicken summarizes all of your transactions through the end of the last full month completed. If the period that Quicken uses is not a full year, you can select to have Quicken annualize any or all of the amounts in the Preview Quicken Tax Data window. Click OK to use the data in the Tax Planner.

Fig. 18.8
Here's all of your tax-related items summarized by tax form or schedule. If you want, you can annualize any or all of these amounts.

Double-click an item to annualize it

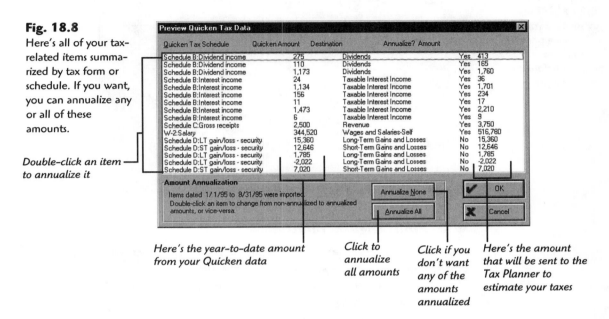

Here's the year-to-date amount from your Quicken data

Click to annualize all amounts

Click if you don't want any of the amounts annualized

Here's the amount that will be sent to the Tax Planner to estimate your taxes

If you want to enter information directly into the Tax Planner, click the appropriate button to display its related dialog box for you to enter data. For example, to enter interest or dividend income, click the Interest/Dividend Income button; to enter tax deductions, click the Deductions button.

Analyzing my tax estimate

The Tax Planner makes instant tax calculations as you enter data. So, you'll see what your taxable income is, the total tax, marginal and average tax rates, and how much tax you still owe. Figure 18.9 shows a completed tax estimate in the Tax Planner window.

Fig. 18.9
Here's your tax estimate for 1996. Looks like you'll be cutting a check to the IRS for $3,277 unless you increase your withholding or make an estimated tax payment before the end of the year.

> ❝ *Plain English, please!*
>
> Your **marginal tax rate** is the rate of tax on the highest range of your taxable income. If you are married, filing jointly, with a taxable income of $40,000 in 1995, for example, your marginal tax rate on the last dollar of income is 28%. Your marginal tax rate is determined by the specified tax rates set forth by the Internal Revenue Code. In 1995, this rate was 28% for taxable income between $39,000 and $94,250 for joint filers.
>
> The **average tax rate** that the Tax Planner computes is the overall rate of tax on your adjusted gross income. If your adjusted gross income is $50,000 and your tax liability is $10,000, for example, your average tax rate is 20% ($10,000/$50,000). ❞

If you want a printed copy of your tax estimate, click the Print button. Then complete the Print window and click OK to print your tax estimate.

Can I see different tax scenarios at the same time?

The Tax Planner not only estimates your current tax liability, but can also compare two more tax scenarios and show the results side by side. Let's say that you're contemplating selling a stock at a gain and you want to see what the tax effect will be. Or, you're paying off the mortgage on your house this year and you want to see what how your tax liability will be affected when you no longer have the mortgage interest deduction. You can compare all of these scenarios without affecting any of the data in Quicken.

Your current scenario is the Base scenario and uses the data from the Tax Planner window. You can create two other scenarios: Alt. 1 and Alt. 2. To create and compare scenarios, click one of these buttons in the Tax Planner window. Quicken asks whether you want to copy the current scenario. If you're comparing similar scenarios, it's probably easiest to copy the current one and then make one or two changes to it. After you've made changes to either Alt. 1 or Alt. 2, or entered new data, click the Compare button in the Tax Planner window to see a side-by-side comparison as shown in figure 18.10.

Fig. 18.10
Here's how your tax scenarios compare. The Tax Scenario Comparisons window shows you the total tax and marginal and average tax rates for each scenario so that you can make an apples-to-apples comparison.

Tax Scenario Comparisons				
	Base Case	Alternate Case 1	Alternate Case 2	
Filing Status	Married-Joint	Married-Joint	Married-Joint	✔ OK
Tax Year	1996	1996	1996	
Adjusted Gross Income	136,730	145,150	130,150	? Help
Deductions and Exemptions	37,501	36,945	37,845	
Taxable Income	99,229	108,205	92,305	
Total Tax	23,837	26,039	22,139	
Marginal, Avg. Tax Rates	26.0% 17.4%	26.0% 17.9%	26.0% 17.0%	

19

Printing Reports

- ### In this chapter:

- **Create many different types of reports in Quicken**

- **The ins and outs of creating a report**

- **How to print reports**

The world has come a long way from scratching with rocks on cave walls to printing spiffy-looking reports on computers! . . . . **>**

When I began working as an accountant, I had to write up reports on wide sheets of ledger paper. Column after column of numbers, adding down and adding across, making sure everything was accurate. If a number was to change on the report, all the columns had to be re-added and the totals double-checked for accuracy. And if someone wanted the report presented in a different way, maybe organizing numbers by month instead of by week, or sorting accounts alphabetically instead of by dollar amount, I'd have to start over, get a clean sheet of ledger paper, and begin the process again. I logged many hours over those big sheets of paper filled with columns of numbers, my trusty 10-key calculator by my side.

Now computer programs and printers have made all that work I used to do obsolete. Click a button with the mouse to display a report on-screen, click a few more buttons to change the order of the display, one more click and the report is sent to my printer, and there's never any question at all about the accuracy of the totals.

What kind of reports can I create with Quicken?

You can create many different types of reports from the numbers in your Quicken registers. Among Quicken's standard reports are those for cash flow, budget, net worth, transaction summary, tax, investment performance, profit and loss statement, and income and expense comparison.

This is just a partial list of the standard reports from which you can choose, reports that are already designed for you and ready to be displayed when you request them. Each of these standard reports can be customized in many different ways, so that you can retrieve just about any information you may want from the amounts you have entered into your registers.

I sure like Quicken's EasyAnswers reports

If accounting terms like Cash Flow and Net Worth throw you for a loop, then you'll enjoy working with Quicken's EasyAnswers reports—reports geared to answer the questions that you may have regarding the amounts you've entered in your registers. EasyAnswers reports provide answers to the following questions:

- Where did I spend my money?

- How much did I spend on (fill in the category)?

- How much did I save in a particular time period compared to a prior time period?

- What am I worth?

- Did I meet my budget?

- What taxable events occured during a particular time period?

- How did my investment do?

- What are my investments worth?

To display the EasyAnswers reports, click the Reports button in the Quicken iconbar, or choose Easy Answers from the Reports menu. Click the EasyAnswers tab in the Create Report window as shown in figure 19.1.

Fig. 19.1
Select the time period and category that fits your needs, then click the Report button to display the EasyAnswer report.

You can choose a time period for these reports by clicking the down arrow and selecting from the drop-down list. For example, the first report is "Where did I spend my money?" You can select Last Year, Last Month, Year to Date, Current Month, or any number of other choices. When you've selected the time period for the report, click the button just to the left of the report question to view the report on-screen. Click Close to remove the report from your screen, or see the section "Okay, let's print!" later in this chapter for printing options.

Can I see a "snapshot" of my finances?

Snapshots are miniature reports that give you different perspectives on your financial position. A page of snapshots can contain as many as six reports and can include a graph, a budget-to-actual comparison, a cash flow report, a monthly income statement, calendar notes, and more.

To display snapshots on your screen, click the SnpShts button on your Quicken iconbar or choose Snapshots from the Reports menu.

Choose how many snapshots you want to display and what type of information you would like to see summarized by clicking the Custom button in the Snapshots window. When snapshots are displayed on your screen, you can click with your left mouse button on the graph images to see the actual number represented in the graph. Also, you can double-click many of the snapshot images and numbers to see the detail that makes up the amount in the snapshot.

Click the Close button when you are finished displaying snapshots.

What are QuickReports?

Throughout your Quicken screens you will often see a Report button (see fig. 19.2) that signifies Quicken's QuickReport feature. QuickReport provides you with an instant summary of the information you are currently viewing. For example, if your checking account register is displayed on-screen, clicking the Report button at the top of the register gives you a report that summarizes all the transactions in your register, arranged chronologically by date.

There are quick reports available from the following locations in Quicken:

- *Category & Transfer List.* When the Category and Transfer list is displayed (choose Lists, Category and Transfer from), you can click a particular category, then click the Report button to see a detail of all the transactions from all your registers in that category.

- *Class List.* If you are using classes in Quicken, you can display the Class List and click the Report button to see a list of transactions from a selected class.

- *Memorized Transaction List.* While displaying the Memorized Transaction list, you can click a particular transaction, and then click Report to see a detail of all the occurrences of that transaction.

- *Register Window.* While displaying your register, click a particular transaction, then click the Rep**o**rt button to display all the transactions in your register with that same payee.

- *Portfolio View Window.* Click one of your securities in the Portfolio View window, then click the Report button to see all the transactions that have occurred with that security.

From any QuickReport you can double-click a transaction line in the report to see the detail of that transaction.

Fig. 19.2
Display a QuickReport
by clicking the Reports
button.

Reports button ———

I'm ready to create a report

Quicken has so many standard reports available, it's sometimes hard to know which one to choose. With time, you'll get used to the reports that come with the program and you'll learn to customize your own reports as well. This section discusses the steps for creating standard reports in Quicken. Later you'll learn how to adapt those reports to meet specific needs.

Let's see which report I want

Click the Reports icon on the iconbar to display the available standard reports.

TIP **If the iconbar is not currently displayed on your Quicken screen,** you can click the iconbar button in any window to display the bar.

From the standard reports screen, click the tab for the category you want to choose:

- EasyAnswers
- Home
- Investment
- Business
- Other
- Memorized

Within each report category there are several choices of reports. Notice that on some of the tabs you can't see all the report choices—there is a scrollbar at the right side of the screen that you can use to advance the report list.

Click the title of the report to select that report and to place the date options at the top of the report window. You can choose a date range for some of the reports, while for other reports you will select a specific date (the value of your investments as of today, for example). After the date at the top of the window is correct, click Create or click the Reports button, located to the left of the report's name, to display the report on your screen.

What's all this in the Report screen?

The report you display on-screen is just a starting point. You can take the standard report that you chose and massage it until it more appropriately meets your needs. Use the buttons at the top of the report window (see fig. 19.3) to change your report.

Fig. 19.3
One of Quicken's
many standard reports.

Click here to change
your report settings

Click here to memorize the
report if you have changed
the settings and want to
use the report again

Click here to copy your
report to the Windows
clipboard, making it
accessible to other
Windows programs

Double-click any transaction
in the report to see the source
of the transaction

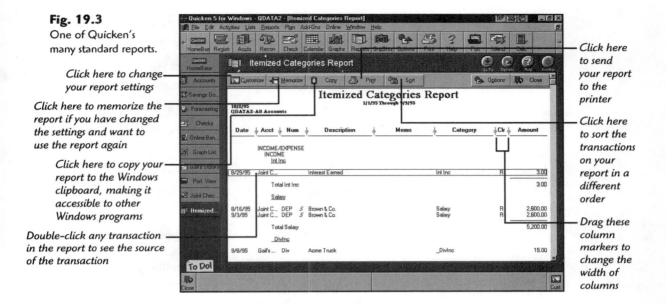

Click here
to send
your report
to the
printer

Click here
to sort the
transactions
on your
report in a
different
order

Drag these
column
markers to
change the
width of
columns

Okay, let's print!

There are separate print settings in Quicken for printing reports and for
printing checks. Before you attempt to print, be sure the settings for your
printer are correct.

Tell Quicken about your printer

To set up your printer for printing reports, follow these steps:

1 Choose File, Printer Setup, then click Report/Graph Printer Setup. The
Report Printer Setup window opens (see fig. 19.4). Check to see that
your printer is named in the Printer box. If it isn't, click the drop-down
arrow and select your printer.

Fig. 19.4
Adjust your printer
settings in this window.

2 Click the Settings button to select particular printer options such as orientation and paper size. Click OK to accept your settings.

3 On the Report Printer Setup window you can select Head Font and/or Body Font to customize the typeface of the header and the body text of your reports.

4 You can change the default margins by typing in new measurements in the Left, Right, Top, and Bottom boxes.

5 If you have a color printer, you can request that graphs and negative numbers be printed in color by checking the Print Reports and Graphs in Color check box.

6 Click OK to save your print settings for all future reports.

The settings you make in this window become your defaults. You can still select individual print options on your specific reports, overriding the defaults. For information on setting up your printer for printing graphs, see Chapter 20, "Looking at Data Through Graphs."

Ready to print

Click the Print button from your report window, or choose File, Print Report. The Print Report window is displayed (see fig. 19.5). You can also press Ctrl+P.

Fig. 19.5
Last chance to pick your printer settings!

Select the print options you want for your report from this window. The options are:

- Print to the Printer or select a file format for printing your report to a file on disk for use in another program.

- Choose P̲ortrait or L̲andscape orientation.

- Print A̲ll pages of your report, or select a range of pages by filling in the F̲rom and T̲o boxes.

- Select a typeface and size for your report heading with the H̲ead Font button, or choose a typeface and size for the body of your report with the Bo̲dy Font button.

You can preview your report from this Print Report window, to make sure it's going to look the way you want it to before you actually print it. Click the Prev̲iew button to examine your report on-screen.

I want to save a report to a disk file

You can retrieve your Quicken files in other programs by saving your reports to disk files. For example, you may want to pull your register summary into a spreadsheet program like Lotus, Excel, or Quattro Pro to perform some what-if projections or some more advanced calculations.

To save a report for use in a different program, choose one of the following print options from the Print Report window:

- *ASCII D̲isk File*. Use this choice if you want to import your Quicken report to a word-processing program.

- *Ta̲b-delimited Disk File*. A file saved in this format can be read by most word-processing and spreadsheet programs.

- *1̲23 (.PRN) Disk File*. This format can be read by most spreadsheet programs.

Neat! I can memorize reports

Don't work hard at creating a report that looks the way you want it to and provides the information you need, just to print it once, click the Close button, and have to do it all over again next month. You've got better things to do with your time than re-create the same report over and over again.

Let Quicken save your report, just as it saves transactions that you perform repeatedly. While your report is displayed on the screen, press Ctrl+M, just like you would if you were memorizing a transaction, or you can click the Memorize button at the top of the report window. The Memorize Report window appears (see fig. 19.6).

Fig. 19.6
Don't look now, but you're about to save yourself lots of time by memorizing a report.

Select the date for your report

Give your report a name here

Type an optional description for your report that will appear in the Memorized tab of the Create Report window

Choose an icon for your report

Your memorized report gets saved to the Memorized tab in the Create Report window (see fig. 19.7). Just click the Reports icon in the iconbar to open the Create Report window. Click the Memorized tab, then click the Report button for the memorized report you want to use.

Fig. 19.7
Your memorized report is added to the Memorized tab in the Create Report window.

20

Looking at Data through Graphs

● **In this chapter:**

● **You can create lots of different kinds of graphs in Quicken**

● **Before you print, display a graph on-screen**

● **What makes up this graph?**

● **Don't be satisfied with defaults; customize your graphs!**

● **Once you've designed a graph, memorize it so you don't have to create it all over again**

● **How do I print graphs?**

Why not take your reports one step further? Produce full-color, three-dimensional graphs and let your numbers tell their story visually. . . . . ▶

When I first learned to draw graphs, it was a process of joining a vertical line (the Y-axis) and a horizontal line (the X-axis), plotting points in the space around the lines, then connecting my points like a dot-to-dot picture. If I wanted to get fancy, I'd used a different colored pencil for connecting the dots, but that's about as innovative as I got.

With Quicken I can create graphs that are as eye-appealing as they are informative—graphs that tell a visual story of my finances, that make trends easy to spot, and that constantly remind me of just one more reason why I spent my money on a computer instead of, well, whatever else I might have spent my money on.

What types of graphs can Quicken display?

There are four basic types of graphs that you can display in Quicken, and then there are lots of variations on these four main types. The Quicken graph types are:

- **Income and Expense.** These graphs help you understand where your money is going. They help you determine trends in spending, compare the amount of cash coming in (income) to that going out (expense), and compare current income and spending with earlier periods.

- **Budget Variance.** These graphs provide a comparison between what you thought you would earn and spend and what you actually earned and spent. You can use these graphs to help you keep tabs on how close you are to meeting your budget goals.

- **Net Worth.** These graphs compare account balances from one period to the next. Is the month-end balance in your investment register decreasing every month? It may be time to reconsider how your money is invested.

- **Investment.** These graphs plot the trends in individual investments and show you how you are progressing toward meeting your investment goals such as retirement and college planning.

I want to display a graph

So, I got your attention, huh? Displaying graphs in Quicken is only a few mouse-clicks away. In fact, you already got a glimpse of some graphs in Chapter 19 when you looked at Quicken's Snapshot feature.

To create a graph in Quicken, choose Reports, Graphs and select any graph type from the drop-down list. The Create Graph window you see in figure 20.1 opens. From this window you can choose the type of graph you want to display, select the time period that the graph should cover, and choose specific accounts or categories to include in or exclude from the graph.

Fig. 20.1
Creating a graph starts right here.

Choose the time period you want your graph to cover

Select the type of graph you want to display

Include or exclude specific accounts and/or categories

When you have chosen the type of graph you want to display, you've picked the time period the graph should cover, and you've determined which accounts or categories belong in the graph, then you can click the Create icon and your graph appears on-screen. The graph in figure 20.2 is an Income and Expense graph.

Fig. 20.2
This graph compares
income and expenses.

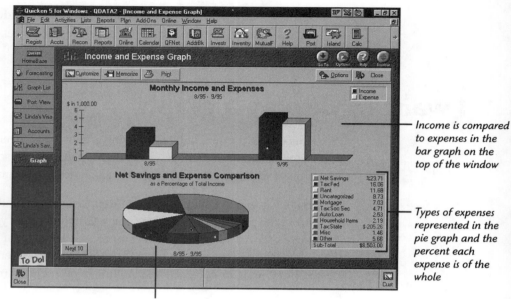

*This button reads either
"Next 10" or "First
10." Clicking the
button advances the
expenses that are being
graphed from the ten
highest expenses to the
next ten, and so on,
through all the expenses
that are in use in your
register*

*Income is compared
to expenses in the
bar graph on the
top of the window*

*Types of expenses
represented in the
pie graph and the
percent each
expense is of the
whole*

Expenses are shown as pieces of a pie on the bottom of the window

Can I see more detail behind an item on my graph?

All of the bars, lines, and pie pieces on your graphs represent numbers from
your account registers. You don't have to go back to the register or produce
reports to see what the actual amounts are behind the graphs. Just place your
mouse pointer over an area of the graph you want to investigate and hold
down the left mouse button. You'll see the amount that makes up the piece of
the graph displayed on the screen.

For even more detail, place your mouse over any bar or pie piece on the
graph and double-click. A new graph appears, breaking out the pieces that
make up the item on which you double-clicked. For example, if you

double-click on one of the bars representing income in the top graph, a new graph appears showing what is included in that first income bar (see fig. 20.3).

Fig. 20.3
Double-click on a piece of your graph and you get a QuickZoom graph like this one, giving you a close-up of the original piece.

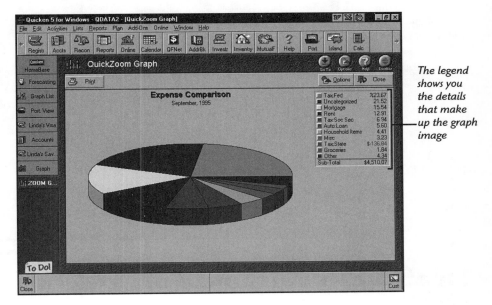

The legend shows you the details that make up the graph image

If that's not enough details for you, when you display a QuickZoom graph on-screen, you can put your mouse at any piece of the graph and your mouse pointer changes to a "Z" with a circle around it. With this symbol showing you can double-click on a portion of the QuickZoom graph and see exactly which transactions make up the piece of the graph on which you clicked. Figure 20.4 shows an Expense Comparison report that gives you the detail of a piece of the pie from figure 20.3.

Click the Close button on the Income Comparison report to return to the QuickZoom graph. Click the Close button of the QuickZoom graph and you're back at the original Income and Expense graph.

Fig. 20.4
This report shows you the detail after I double-clicked the piece of the QuickZoom graph.

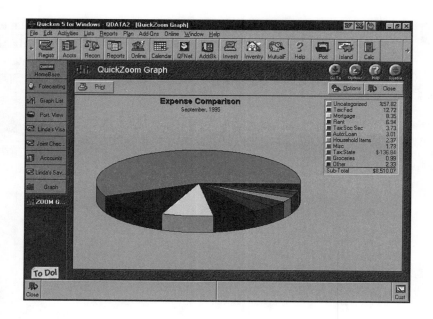

Neat! I can customize my graphs

You don't have to settle for the graph settings Quicken has chosen for you. You can set the dates to be covered in your graph, pick and choose what accounts you want to include, and select which transactions will appear in your graph.

When you first create the graph you have the options for customizing graph settings, but sometimes you don't know what you want to change until you actually see the graph. Unless you know exactly what you want to see, go ahead and create a graph, select the type of graph you want, and click Create. This will put a graph on your screen which you can examine and then decide how you want to change it.

I don't want this item in my graph

After your graph is displayed on-screen you can decide what you do and don't want included in the graph. Say, for example, in an Income and Expense graph, you only want to include amounts from your checking account and not any other accounts. Click on the Customize button at the top of the graph window, click on the Accounts button in the Customize Graph window that appears, and click on the accounts you don't want to include, unchecking them in the process.

Click OK and when you return to the Customize Graph window you will notice that there is a check mark in the Accounts button. This tells you that a particular selection of accounts has been made and your graph will not include every account.

I want to select the specific transactions included in my graph

Perhaps you don't want to show tax expenses on your graph. Click on the Categories button and you see a list of all the categories of expenses that are included in your register. Scroll down until you find the tax expenses. You can click on each expense that you want to exclude from your graph, unchecking each one as you click on it.

 TIP   **When unchecking items in the account and/or category list for** purposes of customizing your graphs, you can drag your mouse through several items, unchecking them all at once instead of clicking individually on each one.

A graph can be memorized too!

After you've figured out exactly how you want your graph to appear, you don't have to worry about remembering all the steps you went through to create that graph so that you can re-create again in the future. Just click on the Memorize button at the top of the graph screen.

When you click on Memorize, Quicken displays a Memorize Graph window in which you can name your graph. Give your memorized graph a meaningful name so that when you search for it in the future the name will lead you to the graph you want.

To access a memorized graph, choose Reports, Memorized Graphs. The Memorized Graph window appears on your screen (see fig. 20.5). Here you can choose one of your memorized graphs to display.

Fig. 20.5
Give your graph
a name before
memorizing it.

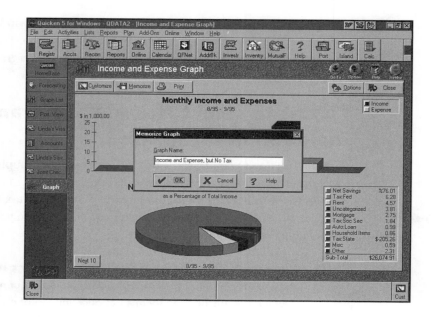

To use a memorized graph, choose Memorized Graphs from the Reports menu. In the Memorized Graphs window that appears (see fig. 20.6), click on the graph you want, then click Use to access that graph.

Fig. 20.6
Choose a memorized
graph from this
window—click the Use
button to display your
graph.

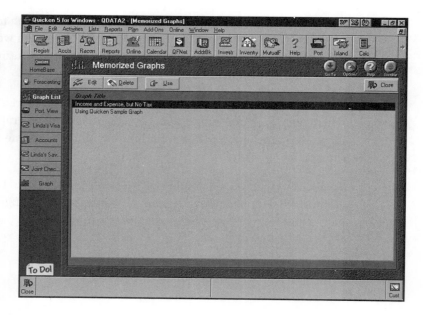

I want to change the way graphs appear

Your graphs appear in 3-D with color display by default, but you can change that appearance.

With a graph on your screen, click the Options button at the top of the graph window to open the Graph Options window displayed in figure 20.7. In the Graph Options window you can select any of the following options:

- **Display Patterns on Screen.** Instead of color bars, you can choose to display black and white patterns. Sometimes this makes the different pieces of the graph easier to discern, especially when printing the graph on a black-and-white printer.

- **Create All Graphs in Separate Windows.** Your graphs are really two graphs, one above the other. By checking this box you can display your graphs in separate windows and, therefore, have the option to print only one and not both.

- **Draw in 2D (faster).** Your three-dimensional graph looks nice, but two-dimensions may do the job and both the screen display and the printing will be faster.

Fig. 20.7
Click any of these options to change the appearance of your graph.

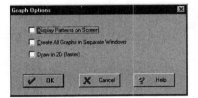

Let's print this graph

If your graph appears on the screen the way you want it to look you're just about ready to print. Before you print your graph, you should check the printer settings by choosing File, Printer Setup, then select Report/Graph Printer Setup. For information about the particular printer setup options, see Chapter 19, "Printing Reports." The printer options for reports and graphs are the same.

TIP   **Remember, you can customize the typeface for your graph** headings by selecting Head Font in the Printer Setup feature.

When you know your print settings are correct, choose File, Print Graph (or press Ctrl+P or click the Print button). Quicken sends your graph to the printer.

Part V: Planning for the Future

21

Forecasting Your Cash Flow

● **In this chapter:**

- **What's a cash forecast and how do I get one?**

- **Customizing your cash forecast**

- **Creating multiple forecasts**

- **Comparing forecasts**

Look into your financial future with Quicken's
crystal ball . . . .

Nobody really knows what the future holds, but we frequently have the opportunity to make intelligent guesses. Quicken's cash forecasting feature gives you one of these opportunities to make intelligent guesses about the future. Using financial information from your registers, working with the actual numbers you've entered, Quicken estimates your future income and expenses for a future period of up to two years.

Quicken creates a cash forecast out of existing numbers in your registers, but you can fine-tune that forecast, making changes in the estimates based on your knowledge of your financial situation. For example, if you anticipate receiving a raise next year at your job, or if you're about to start paying college tuition for your child, you can anticipate the changes that will occur in your cash flow, and make adjustments accordingly in your forecast for those changes.

I want to see my cash forecast

When creating a forecast, Quicken works with the numbers it knows—the amounts in your registers, and any future amounts you may have scheduled in your financial calendar, like future loan payments, tax payments, and so on (see Chapter 10, "Scheduling Future Transactions," for information about scheduling transactions on the Financial Calendar). Quicken then extends your numbers into the future, similar to the way in which you might design a budget, except that instead of the wishful thinking that sometimes goes into a budget, the forecast is based on real expectations.

The forecast is kind of like a financial timeline on which Quicken places the financial transactions of which it is aware. For example, if you get paid semi-monthly at your job, Quicken assumes this trend will continue and plots out semi-monthly payroll deposits in your forecast. Quicken also takes the bills you pay regularly and assumes that those payments will continue.

Quicken looks for trends when searching through your registers. For example, if your utility bills have increased by 10 percent for each of the past eight months, Quicken assumes that that type of increase will continue as it forecasts your utility expenses for the future. If you have a loan payment that is the same every month, Quicken keeps that payment stable in your forecast.

In addition, you can tell Quicken to consider additional amounts that aren't in your register or your financial calendar in its forecast. You can experiment with the forecast, changing projections to see what your forecast might look like if you get a raise in your salary or you make that last mortgage payment.

Use the forecast to help you plan for future expenditures and figure out your savings options.

To create a forecast, follow these steps:

1 Choose Forecasting from the Plan menu. The Automatically Create Forecast window appears (see fig. 21.1). (This window will only open the first time you create a forecast. From that point forward, the dates you set in the next step will enable Quicken to bypass opening this window.)

Fig. 21.1
Quicken will consider financial transactions from the time period you designate when determining your forecast.

2 Set the range of dates for Quicken to examine in determining your forecast.

Designate a range of dates that contains illustrative deposits and expenditures. For example, say it's October 1, 1995, and you've entered income, expenses, and investments into your Quicken registers since January 1, 1994.

Furthermore, say you feel the transactions from the current year (1995) closely resemble those you anticipate having in the future. Your range of dates would be January 1, 1995, to the present. Quicken would then consider only your 1995 transactions when making its estimates about your future financial activity.

3 Click OK to present your forecast graph on the screen (see fig. 21.2).

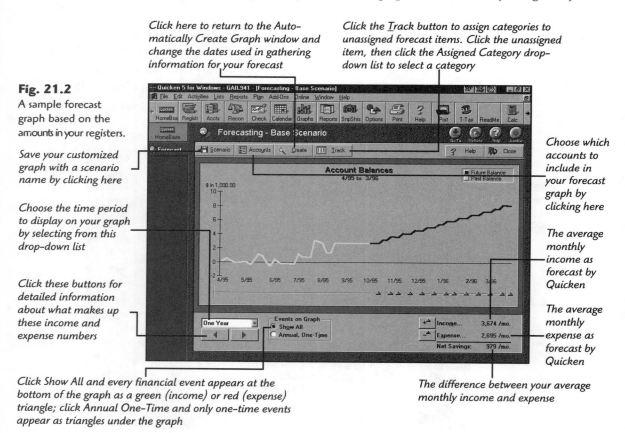

Click here to return to the Automatically Create Graph window and change the dates used in gathering information for your forecast

Click the Track button to assign categories to unassigned forecast items. Click the unassigned item, then click the Assigned Category drop-down list to select a category

Fig. 21.2
A sample forecast graph based on the amounts in your registers.

Save your customized graph with a scenario name by clicking here

Choose the time period to display on your graph by selecting from this drop-down list

Click these buttons for detailed information about what makes up these income and expense numbers

Choose which accounts to include in your forecast graph by clicking here

The average monthly income as forecast by Quicken

The average monthly expense as forecast by Quicken

Click Show All and every financial event appears at the bottom of the graph as a green (income) or red (expense) triangle; click Annual One-Time and only one-time events appear as triangles under the graph

The difference between your average monthly income and expense

What you see is a projection of your account balances—all your accounts combined. At the bottom of the screen on the right you can see the monthly projected average income and expense and the net increase (or decrease) to savings (Net Savings). You can advance the graph forward or backward six months at a time by clicking the arrows in the bottom left corner of the graph.

Print the graph if you want a hard copy by selecting Print Forecast from the File menu. Click anywhere on the graph line and hold down your mouse button to see the projected balance in your accounts at the date where you click.

My cash forecast can be fine-tuned

The graph you get the first time you click OK in the Automatically Create Forecast window is really just a starting point. There are several ways you can customize your forecast so it provides you with useful information.

- Click either the Show All button to include all the transactions and estimates in the graph, or the Annual, One-Time button to include just yearly figures in the graph.

- Click the Scenario button to choose or create a new forecast scenario.

- Click the Create button to open the Automatically Create Forecast window and change the dates used in analyzing data for your forecast. You can also click the Advanced button in this window and designate whether you want to draw information from your Register data or your Budget data.

I only want certain accounts included in my forecast

The forecast graph, by default, includes all your accounts—check register, investment accounts, savings accounts, credit card accounts, and so on. To exclude certain accounts and build your forecast just on the projections of particular accounts, click the Accounts button at the top of the graph window. The Select Accounts to Include window opens. From this window you can click the accounts you want to exclude, removing the check mark from alongside the account name. Alternatively, if accounts that you want to include in your forecast are unchecked, just click them to include those accounts in the forecast.

I want to change a forecast amount

On the main forecast graph window, you can change projected income and expenses by clicking on either the Income or Expense button at the bottom right side of the graph screen. Clicking either one opens a box in which you can, first of all, see what amounts make up those numbers, and second, you can add to the list of projected items (click <u>N</u>ew) or edit the existing numbers (click <u>E</u>dit). A sample Forecast Expense Items window is shown in figure 21.3.

Fig. 21.3
Look at all these expenses—both actual and estimated—that go into my expense forecast!

Once in this window you can easily switch among income and expense forecast items by clicking here

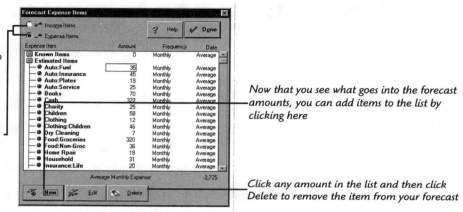

Now that you see what goes into the forecast amounts, you can add items to the list by clicking here

Click any amount in the list and then click Delete to remove the item from your forecast

Can I create more than one forecast?

Create as many forecasts as you like. To create a new forecast (called a Forecast Scenario), click the <u>S</u>cenario button on the top of the forecast graph screen. Creating a Forecast Scenario is a lot like creating a Memorized Transaction. You choose the settings you want to save, then give it a name. Then in the future you can recall those same forecast settings without having to re-create them.

When you click the <u>S</u>cenario button, the Manage Forecast Scenario window opens (see fig. 21.4). To save the changes you have made in your forecast graph into a new, named, recallable scenario, click <u>N</u>ew, type the name of your new scenario, and then click OK.

TIP   **Once you've saved a scenario by name, you can change the name** of the scenario by clicking the <u>S</u>cenario button on the forecast screen, and then clicking Edit. Also, you can delete an existing scenario if you don't think you'll ever use it again, by clicking Delete in the Manage Forecast Scenarios window.

Fig. 21.4
Creating a new
Forecast Scenario is
similar to memorizing
Transactions.

Click <u>N</u>ew to give your Forecast
Scenario a unique name.

Select the type of
display you prefer

Choose the display option you prefer for your scenario:

- **<u>C</u>urrent Scenario Only** displays just your newly named scenario.

- **<u>S</u>how How Forecast Looked on** (date) lets you display your scenario as of a particular date as opposed to the current date which is the default.

- **C<u>o</u>mpare Current Scenario with** (fill in name of another scenario) lets you display two forecasts on the same graph and compare them.

When you have selected the options you want, click Done to save the scenario.

Compare two forecasts

As previously mentioned, once you've created more than one forecast scenario, you can compare two forecasts on the same graph. To pull up a forecast and compare it with another, follow these steps:

1 Choose <u>F</u>orecasting from the Pl<u>a</u>n menu.

2 Click the <u>S</u>cenario button on the Forecasting graph window.

3 In the Manage Forecast Scenarios window that appears, choose C<u>o</u>mpare Current Scenario with, and choose the scenario you want to compare with in the drop-down box at the right.

4 Click the Done button to bring both scenarios onto the graph at once.

22

Saving for College, Retirement, and Everything Else

● **In this chapter:**

● Looking college, weddings, and other big expenses in the eye

● Help make retirement a reality with Quicken

● Watching your investment (garden) grow

● How can I use Quicken to track my savings?

How much do you need to save to reach your goals? Quicken to the rescue! . . . . **>**

I f your daughter came up to you tomorrow and said, "Dad, I need
$25,000. Will you write me a check?" would you say, "Sure,
honey!?" Or are you more likely to come back with, "In your dreams!?"

Usually, when big expenses are coming due, we like to know a little bit in
advance, so we can do some *planning* for those events. Not many people can
write a check on the spur of the moment for $25,000 (at least not a *good*
check), and even if you could, you wouldn't want to do it if you weren't
prepared.

Quicken's special planning features help you save for college and retirement,
and help you track your savings and investments.

I don't want college to sneak up on me

Unfortunately, no one is going to take you aside and tell you exactly how
much you need to project for your child's college education and how you
should save in order to meet that goal. It's all up to you, and the last thing you
want to do is come up short. So start saving today.

Start saving now even if your child is an infant and it seems like you'll have
forever to put aside money. Start now, even if your child is in high school and
it seems like it's too late to put aside money. No matter which end of the
college planning spectrum you're at (or even if you have both young and old
children that put you at both ends of the spectrum), every step you take
toward saving will benefit you and your children when college time comes.

 TIP **It doesn't just have to be college that you start saving for early.**
There are cars, weddings, vacations, homes, trips, home additions—whatever
your needs or dreams are.

Estimate your needs

In order to start planning for college, or any major expenditure, you first
need to have a handle on how much you'll need. For college costs, investigate
today's tuition costs at several colleges of varying size, both in state and out
of state, both state-funded and private. Figure out a range of potential costs.
Don't forget to include housing, food, books, pizza money, trips home, bus
passes, fraternal organizations, football tickets (or basketball, if the school is

in Indiana)—all the things that can make the tuition alone pale into insignificance.

Next, you need to get a feel for how much those costs are going to rise between now and the time little Judy and Bobby are ready for college. Do a little research. There are published reports on the projected rise in college costs. Also, talk to the financial aid offices at some colleges. The people who advise parents about paying for college can give you some guidance on planning for future college costs.

Okay, let's say you've arrived at a projected dollar amount for how much you think four years of college is going to cost. The next step is to estimate how much of that you expect to pay yourself. I'm not talking about scholarships, financial aid, or bank loans that you may have to rely on for part of the cost. I'm talking about how much is going to come out of your pocket.

For purposes of this example, I'm going to use $12,000 per year as the estimated cost of college for your student who is going to start college in the fall, five years from now. In five years, you're going to need $12,000 per year for four years and you haven't yet begun to save.

Figure out how much to save

Start planning for college with Quicken's College Planner. To use the College Planner, follow these steps:

1 From the Plan menu, choose Financial Planners, and then College. The College Planner window appears on-screen (see fig. 22.1).

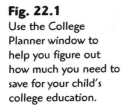

Fig. 22.1
Use the College Planner window to help you figure out how much you need to save for your child's college education.

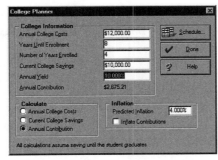

2 In the Calculate section of the College Planner window, choose the calculation that you want Quicken to perform:

- **Annual College Costs.** If you know how much you can afford to contribute regularly to a college savings fund, choose this option and Quicken calculates how much you will be able to afford to spend on college.

- **Current College Savings.** If you know the amount you plan to spend on college and the amount you can afford to contribute regularly to a college savings fund, choose this option and Quicken tells you how much you will have to add from your current savings to reach your goal.

- **Annual Contribution.** Tell Quicken how much college is going to cost and Quicken calculates how much you need to contribute regularly to a college savings fund.

3 Fill in the amounts in the College Information section to provide Quicken with the information it needs to make its calculations:

- **Annual College Costs.** Enter the total amount you expect to spend each year for college. Include in this amount not just tuition, but room and board, books, fees, and all other related college costs.

- **Years Until Enrollment.** How many years is it from right now until your child begins the first year of college?

- **Number of Years Enrolled.** For how many years will your child be a college student? Typically, this number will be four, but if you are planning on paying tuition for the next Dr. Kildare, this number will increase.

One of the following three items will be left blank, depending on which one you expect Quicken to calculate for you.

- **Current College Savings.** If you've already got a head start on saving for college, enter the amount of your college savings here.

- **Annual Yield.** Enter the annual rate of interest you expect to earn on your savings as they accumulate.

- **Annual Contribution.** Enter the amount you are able to contribute for college savings. Quicken assumes that the amount you enter is for the entire year's contribution.

4 In the inflation section of the College Planner, enter the current rate of inflation (by default, Quicken uses four percent) and check the Inflate Contributions check box if you want to have Quicken increase your required annual contribution by the expected rate of inflation.

5 Click the Schedule button and Quicken provides you with a yearly schedule of the amount of contribution you need to make. You can print this schedule by clicking the Print button in the Deposit Schedule window (see fig. 22.2). Notice that you are still expected to make contributions in the four years while your child is in college.

Fig. 22.2
You can print this deposit schedule and refer to it each year as you make college fund deposits. Notice the withdrawals for actual college costs in the last four years have been increased from your original estimate due to inflation.

Year	Deposit	Tuition	Balance
1996	2,675.21	0.00	17,715.10
1997	2,675.21	0.00	22,161.82
1998	2,675.21	0.00	27,053.21
1999	2,675.21	0.00	32,433.74
2000	2,675.21	0.00	38,352.32
2001	2,675.21	0.00	44,862.77
2002	2,675.21	0.00	52,024.25
2003	2,675.21	16,421.46	41,838.28
2004	2,675.21	17,078.32	29,911.17
2005	2,675.21	17,761.45	16,033.90
2006	2,432.01	18,471.91	0.00

TIP **Use the annual contribution amount calculated by the College** Planner in your Quicken budget (see Chapter 16, "Creating Your Budget," for more information). In your budget you can separate your contributions into monthly or quarterly deposits to spread the cost out through the year.

6 Click the Close button to close the Deposit Schedule window; then click the Done button to close the College Planner window.

I want to make sure I can afford to retire

Dreams of retirement seem farther and farther out of reach these days as our society gets older and stays healthy longer. But most people like to think that someday they will be able to stop working, rest, and enjoy their later years without worrying about having to earn a living.

Getting ready for retirement takes planning, just like any other long-term goal. If you wait until you're ready to retire to start thinking about how you're going to support yourself, you'd better hope you have lots of good friends and children who will care for you, because you won't be able to do it yourself. Start now—plan for the future as if it were a necessity, not just something that you'll deal with "later."

Quicken's Retirement Planner can help you figure out how much your current savings will earn and how you can add to those savings so that you will be able to retire in comfort. Work for your retirement now so that you can enjoy it later.

The Retirement Planner is one of Quicken's Financial Planners. To use the Retirement Planner, follow these steps:

1 Choose Financial Planners from Quicken's Plan menu, and then choose Retirement. Quicken displays the Retirement Planner window, as shown in figure 22.3.

Fig. 22.3
Make a financial plan for your retirement using Quicken's Retirement Planner.

2 First, determine what kind of information you want Quicken to calculate for you. In the Calculate section of the Retirement Planner window you can choose between the following options:

  • **Current Savings.** If you know how much you can contribute each year and you know how much you want to withdraw annually when you retire, let Quicken calculate how much of your current savings should be designated as retirement savings.

- **Annual Contribution.** If you know how much you would like to withdraw annually from your retirement account and you know how much you can designate as retirement savings from your current savings, let Quicken calculate how much you must contribute each year to meet your goals.

- **Annual Retirement Income.** If you know how much you can contribute each year and how much you can designate as retirement savings from your current savings, Quicken will tell you how much you are going to be able to withdraw from your retirement account when you retire.

TIP **Take advantage of Quicken's ability to quickly calculate several** scenarios for you. Experiment with the numbers, trying different combinations while you try to work out the plan that best fits your financial needs and your ability to meet the annual contribution amount.

3 Filling in the amounts in the Retirement Information section will provide Quicken with the information it needs to make its calculations. (One of the three, Current Savings, Annual Contribution, and Annual Income After Taxes, will be left blank, depending on which amount you want Quicken to calculate for you.)

- **Current Savings.** Enter the amount of your savings you have designated as being set aside for retirement.

- **Annual Yield.** Enter the annual amount of interest or dividends your retirement savings can earn.

- **Annual Contribution.** Enter the amount you plan to contribute annually toward your retirement.

- **Current Age.** How old are you today?

- **Retirement Age.** At what age do you plan to retire?

- **Withdraw Until Age.** This is the toughest one. You have to guess how old you're going to be when you stop withdrawing money from your retirement fund. I know—it's a shot in the dark. Just give it your best guess. You can always experiment with these numbers and try different ages.

- **Other Income.** What other sources of retirement income do you expect to have besides the amount you're putting away yourself—Social Security? retirement fund from your job? inheritance? Enter the annual amount you expect to receive beyond your retirement savings.

- **Annual Income After Taxes.** How much do you want to be able to withdraw from your retirement account each year?

As you fill in the answers to these questions, Quicken fills in the amount you requested it to calculate.

4 In the Tax Information section of the Retirement Information window, check whether your retirement fund is tax-sheltered. In other words, if your retirement fund is currently tax-deferred, like an Individual Retirement Account (IRA) but you'll have to pay tax on the amounts from the fund when you withdraw the funds, check Tax Sheltered Investment. If you pay tax currently on the money you put in your retirement fund, check Non-Sheltered Investment.

5 In the inflation section of the Retirement Planner, enter the current rate of inflation (by default, Quicken uses 4%) and check the Inflate Contributions check box if you want to have Quicken increase your required annual contribution by the expected rate of inflation. Check the Annual Income in Today's $ check box if you want Quicken to incorporate the effects of inflation into your retirement income. If you leave this box blank, Quicken will not adjust your retirement income for inflation.

6 Click the Schedule button and Quicken provides you with a yearly schedule of the amount of contribution you need to make and the annual increase in the balance of your retirement fund. The contribution schedule starts with your retirement savings already in place in the first year. You can print this schedule by clicking the Print button in the Deposit Schedule window.

 TIP **Use the annual contribution amount calculated by the Retirement** Planner in your Quicken budget (see Chapter 16, "Creating Your Budget," for more information). In your budget you can separate your contributions into monthly or quarterly deposits to spread the cost out through the year.

7 Click the Close button to close the Deposit Schedule window, and click Done to close the Retirement Planner window.

How fast will my investments grow?

Using the same concepts applied in the College Planner and the Retirement Planner, you can track the savings in any account or fund with Quicken's Investment Savings Planner. Indicate your opening balance and regular contributions and Quicken will calculate how those savings will grow. Alternatively, tell Quicken how much you want to have saved after a certain period of time has passed and Quicken will let you know what you have to do to reach that goal.

To use the Investment Savings Planner, follow these steps:

1 Select Financial Planners from Quicken's Plan menu, and then choose Savings. Quicken displays the Investments Savings Planner window, as shown in figure 22.4.

Fig. 22.4
Use the Investment Savings Planner to track your savings in any account.

2 First, determine what kind of information you want Quicken to calculate for you. In the Calculate section of the Investment Savings Planner window you can choose between the following options:

- **Opening Savings Balance.** If you know how much you can contribute each month (or quarter or year) and you know how much you eventually want to accrue, let Quicken tell you how much you need to start with to meet your goal.

- **Regular Contribution.** You know how much you're starting with and you know how much you plan on ending with; Quicken will calculate how much you need to contribute regularly to achieve your goal.

- **Ending Savings Balance.** If you know how much you're starting with and you know how much you can contribute regularly, Quicken will calculate the amount you will have in the end.

3 Filling in the amounts in the Savings Information section will provide Quicken with the information it needs to make its calculations:

- **Opening Savings Balance.** Enter the amount in your investment account at the start of this investment program, unless this is the amount you plan to have Quicken calculate.

- **Annual Yield.** Enter the annual amount of interest or dividends your investment savings can earn.

- **Number of (fill in a choice of a time interval—Weeks, Months, Quarters, Years).** Enter the time interval during which you plan to make contributions and then enter how many contributions you plan to make in this investment account.

- **Contribution Each (time interval).** The entry of a time interval here is automatic based on the entry at the line above. Unless you are letting Quicken calculate your periodic contribution, fill in the amount you plan to contribute regularly to your investment.

- **Ending Savings Balance.** Enter the desired ending balance of your investment account, unless this is the amount you plan to have Quicken calculate.

4 In the inflation section of the Investment Savings Planner, enter the current rate of inflation (by default, Quicken uses 4%) and check the Inflate Contributions check box if you want to have Quicken increase your required annual contribution by the expected rate of inflation. Check the Ending Balance in Today's $ check box if you want Quicken to incorporate the effects of inflation into your investment income. If you leave this box blank, Quicken will not adjust your investment income for inflation.

5 Click the Schedule button and Quicken provides you with a periodic schedule of the amount of contribution you need to make and the periodic increase in the balance of your investment savings account. The contribution schedule starts with any investment savings you may already have in place in the first year. You can print this schedule by clicking on the print button in the Deposit Schedule window.

6 Click the Close button to close the Deposit Schedule window, and click Done to close the Investment Savings Planner window.

Can Quicken help me track my savings?

Quicken offers a nifty little feature called the Savings Goal Account. A Savings Goal Account is like having a savings account without the trouble of setting up a separate account. For example, say you want to put aside $50 from every paycheck to save for your next vacation.

You wouldn't go to the bank and open a new savings account just to hold your savings for your trip. With Quicken you don't have to open a new account register either. Instead, Quicken lets you pretend you're withdrawing $50 from your check register each pay period, hide the money away so it will seem like that much has been removed from your checkbook, even though the money really hasn't left your checkbook at all. You can then peek to see how your secret savings are doing and keep track of how close you are to meeting your vacation goal.

CAUTION   **Once you set up a savings goal, your checking account balance in** your on-screen register will no longer match your real balance. Since you really have more than the register shows, you don't run the risk of writing a check you can't cover. You may feel uncomfortable, however, knowing the balance isn't right. Consider displaying your savings goals on-screen (see the section "How do I monitor my progress?" below for instructions) so that you'll know how much you've really got in your account.

I need a savings goal account!

To set up a Savings Goal Account, follow these steps:

1 Select Savings Goals from Quicken's Plan menu. Quicken displays the Savings Goals window, as shown in figure 22.5.

Fig. 22.5
You can track your
savings progress in this
Savings Goals window.

2 To begin a new savings goal, click the <u>N</u>ew button. The Create New
Savings Goal window opens (see fig. 22.6).

3 In the Create New Savings Goal window, enter the name of your savings
goal, the amount you want to save, and the date by which you want to
have accomplished your goal. Click OK when this information has been
entered.

Fig. 22.6
Pack your bags! We're
going on vacation!

The setup is finished. Now you're ready to start saving for your goal.

I want to enter a savings contribution

Setting up your savings goal is a good start, but now for the hard part. You
have to actually put the money aside. Here's how:

1 To make a contribution to your savings goal, display the Savings Goals
window on your screen. If you have more than one savings goal listed,
click the one to which you want to contribute.

2 Click the Contribute button at the bottom of the window. The Contribute to Goal window opens (see fig. 22.7). Today's date and the amount of contribution appear, but you can change either of these if you want to.

Fig. 22.7
Click the Contribute button and up pops the piggy bank.

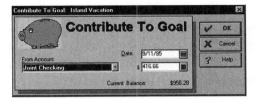

3 Select the account from which you want to make your imaginary withdrawal.

4 Click the OK button to execute the withdrawal from your account.

Quicken deducts the savings goal transaction from your account (but not really—the money is just being set aside with the hope that you won't spend it between now and your planned goal date—but if an emergency arises, or if you change your mind about your goal, you can always have access to your money). The contribution to the savings goal is shown in figure 22.8.

Fig. 22.8
Quicken entered your savings goal contribution just like a normal check.

This is the savings goal transaction

Click here if you want to see the account activity without the savings goal contributions

If you need some of the money you have put aside for your savings goal, you can "withdraw" funds from the savings goal by opening the savings goal screen and clicking withdraw. In the Withdraw from Goal window that appears on the screen, type in the amount you want to withdraw. That amount gets added back into your register as a deposit.

TIP **Use the skills you learned in Chapter 10, "Scheduling Future** Transactions," to schedule your savings goal contributions. That way you don't have to think about it at all—just let that money pile up until you're ready to cash it in and achieve your goal.

How do I monitor my progress?

There are two ways in which you can monitor your savings goal progress.

First, you can return to the Savings Goal screen at any time (choose Savings Goal from the Plan menu) and see a large bar that indicates how much you have saved and how far along you are toward meeting your goal.

Also, you can display a feature called the Progress Bar on the bottom of your screen. The Progress Bar monitors your savings goal amount for the time period that you specify. Display the Progress Bar by following these steps:

1 Choose Progress Bar from the Plan menu. The Progress Bar appears on the bottom of the screen. You can monitor two items in the Progress Bar and you get to choose what those items are.

2 Click the Cust button on the right side of the Progress Bar to display the Customize progress Bar window. This is where you can tell Quicken what you want to monitor in the Progress Bar.

3 Click the drop-down list in the Left Gauge Type or the Right Gauge Type to select the item on which you want to monitor progress. Select Savings Goal from the list of available items.

4 Click the Choose Goal button to select the savings goal that you want to monitor.

5 Click OK to display the Progress Bar at the bottom of your screen (see fig. 22.9).

Fig. 22.9
The Progress Bar is
displayed at the
bottom of your screen.

Part VI: Managing Quicken and Banking Online

23

Doing Some General Housekeeping in Quicken

In this chapter:

- **Create a new Quicken file**

- **Open and close files**

- **Copy and rename a file**

- **Delete a file**

- **Play it safe and back up your Quicken data**

- **Restore a file**

- **What's your secret password?**

Here are some helpful housekeeping tips that keep your Quicken data files in order and keep you from losing important data (and subsequently pulling your hair out!) . . . . . ⊗

You may have only worked with one file in Quicken, the one you established when you installed the program. But did you know that you can create multiple Quicken files to track related accounts together? I'll show you how to create new files, open existing files, and do some other neat things with your Quicken files.

By now, you've entered a lot of information in Quicken, so you want your data to be safe. I'm going to show you how to safeguard your data from power shortages or hard disk crashes and also how to keep those unauthorized eyes from looking at your Quicken files.

What's a Quicken file?

You've been working in a Quicken file all along and probably didn't know it. When you install Quicken, a file named QDATA.QDB is automatically set up for you to store your accounts, categories, and all transactions. Each Quicken file consists of several data files with the same file name, but different extensions. You really don't even need to concern yourself with files other than the QDATA.QDB file.

Most likely, you won't need more than one Quicken file. A separate Quicken file is needed only to store related accounts together. For example, if you and your spouse keep your finances separate, you'll want to create a different Quicken file for each of you. Or, if you want to use Quicken to handle the finances from your small business, you can create a business file that's separate from your personal file.

CAUTION **If you create separate Quicken files to store data, you cannot** make transfers between two files. For example, if you have one file for your personal finances and one for your business finances, you cannot make a transfer from one of your business accounts in your business file to a personal account in your personal file. If you need to record these kinds of transfers, you can keep both your personal and business finances in the same Quicken file. Just select both the home and business category lists so that your file can handle both types of transactions.

Creating a new file

If you decide that you do need another Quicken file, here's how you add one. Select File, New to open the Creating new file: Are you sure? dialog box (which may seem a little strange to you). Quicken wants to make sure that you really want to create a new file, and not a new account. Remember from Chapter 3 that accounts are used to store your transactions; files, on the other hand, are used to store accounts. So, select the New Quicken File option and then click OK.

What you see next is the Create Quicken File window (see fig. 23.1) where you assign a name to your new file, tell Quicken where to store it, and select the categories that you want to use. Fill in the Create Quicken File window and click OK to create the new file. Quicken closes the last file that you were working in and opens the new file for you. Remember that to work in a Quicken file, you have to have at least one account set up. So, Quicken displays the Create New Account window so that you can set up an account to use.

Even though you may be using Windows 95, you still must enter a valid DOS file name for your new Quicken file, which means any combination of up to eight characters; but no spaces, please

Click OK to create your new file

Fig. 23.1
Assign a name to the new file that you're creating and tell Quicken where to store it. Also, select the categories that you want to use in your new file.

Selecting the categories that you want to use in your new file is important. You can select just one predefined category list (Home or Business), or select them both to combine the lists together in your new file

Don't bother with the directory, file type, or drive unless you want to change where Quicken stores your new file. If so, select a different directory and drive

Q&A *Can I use my Quicken data in other programs?*

Yes. You can export your Quicken data into database programs, spreadsheet programs, word processing programs, and so forth. When you export data from a Quicken file, an ASCII text file is copied to another file that another program can read. You can also import data from another program into your Quicken file. Both the Export and Import commands are found in the File menu.

Show me how to open and close a file

If you have more than one Quicken file, you'll need to know how to open the one you want to work in. When you open another Quicken file, the file that you're currently working in is closed automatically. So you really don't ever have to close a Quicken file.

When you're ready to switch to another Quicken file, select File, Open to display the Open Quicken File window (see fig. 23.2). All of the Quicken files that are stored in the current directory are listed for you. In the File Name list box, double-click the file that you want to open.

Fig. 23.2
Select the file that you want to open from the Open Quicken File window. When you open another Quicken file, the current file that you were working in is automatically closed.

TIP **Want to see which Quicken files you've worked in recently?**
Quicken shows you the last four files that you opened in the File menu (select File to open).

What if I need to copy a file?

You can copy the data in your Quicken file to a new file. This may be helpful if you need to give your accountant a copy of your file at the end of the year or at tax time.

When you copy a file, Quicken copies the current file to another file. So, make sure that the file that you want to copy is the current file. If it's not, open it now.

Then, select File, File Operations, Copy to open the Copy File window (see fig. 23.3). Assign a name for the new file to copy your data to (remember those DOS naming rules) and tell Quicken which transactions to copy. Then, click OK to copy your file. After Quicken has copied your file, you can select to return to the original file or go directly to the new file.

Fig. 23.3
Quicken copies all or selected transactions from the current file to a new file. Then, you can choose whether to keep the current file open or open the new file.

TIP **If the power went out while you were working in Quicken, you** may experience some difficulties when you restart your computer and Quicken again. To check the integrity of your Quicken file, select File, File Operations, Validate and then select the file that you want to check.

I don't like this file's name

Want to change a file's name? Go ahead—Quicken lets you rename a file without changing any of the data in it. Rename a file by selecting File, File Operations, Rename. In the Rename Quicken File window that follows (see fig. 23.4), select the file that you want to rename and then enter the new file name. Click OK and the file's got a new name.

Fig. 23.4
Select the file that you want to rename and then enter the new name using DOS naming rules (up to eight characters without spaces).

TIP **I like to rename my Quicken files for each year that they** represent. For example, for my 1995 financial activity, I name the file 1995DATA. For the next year, I create a file and call it 1996DATA.

Let's get rid of this file

If you want to get rid of an old file that you no longer need, you can delete it. Delete files with caution because when you delete a file, all accounts and transactions in the file are permanently removed.

CAUTION **Since Quicken permanently removes your file when you choose to** delete it, take a little precaution first by backing up the file. Even if you're sure that you don't need the file anymore, it can't hurt to make a backup copy before you delete it.

Delete an unneeded file by selecting File, File Operations, Delete. Quicken opens the Delete File window that looks just like the Open Quicken File window you saw in figure 23.2. Select the file that you want to delete and click OK. You know by now that Quicken won't let you make any rash decisions, so a confirmation dialog box is displayed so that you can affirm the deletion. Type **YES** in the confirmation dialog box and click OK to delete the selected file.

Q&A *Is there any way to get a file back that I've deleted?*
If you made a backup copy of your file before you deleted it, you can get your file back by restoring it. I'll show you how to restore Quicken files a little later.

I don't want to lose any of my Quicken data

No matter how careful you are, inevitably you're going to lose some of your data. Reduce this possibility by faithfully and diligently backing up your Quicken data. It only takes a few seconds (or minutes, if you have a large data file) to back up your file, and the time it saves you in the long run if you lose data makes backing up well worth it.

If you've made backups of your Quicken files, losing data isn't that catastrophic. You can easily restore your file using the back-up copies.

TIP **Quicken won't let you forget to back up your files. When you exit** the program or open another file, Quicken reminds you that you haven't backed up your current file in a while. You can then choose to back up before you leave the current file; just follow the on-screen instructions.

Backing up is critical!

You know how important it is to back up your Quicken files, and you're ready to do it. First, you'll need at least one formatted disk. If your Quicken file is large, you may need more than one disk to back up to, so have more than one ready.

Next, select File, Backup to open the Select Backup Drive window (see fig. 23.5). Select the drive where you've inserted your backup disk and then tell Quicken whether to back up the current file or another file that you'd like to select. Usually, you'll back up the current file.

Fig. 23.5
You can back up the current file or select another Quicken file to back up.

Click OK to begin backing up your Quicken file

Insert a blank disk to back up to and tell Quicken which drive it's in

Do you want to back up the file that you're currently working in?

Or, do you want to select another file to back up? If so, Quicken displays the list of files so that you can select one

You can choose to back up to your hard disk drive, but you should always back up to a floppy disk to avoid the risk of losing your original data and your backup data in the case of a hard disk crash.

Click OK to begin the backup procedure, which takes only a few moments.

CAUTION **Store the backup copies of your Quicken files in a safe place.** Don't keep all your backup copies in the same place in case of fire or burglary. Store at least one copy at a location other than your home or business.

Restoring your files

I really hope that you never have to restore a Quicken file because you've lost the original one. Even though you know you have a backup copy, losing data can still make your heart stop for a moment.

If you do need to restore a file from a backup copy, here's what you do. First, open the file that you want to restore. Even though you may have lost data from the file, it should still be in your list of Quicken files. After you've opened the file, select File, Restore to open the Restore File window (see fig. 23.6). Then select the drive where your backup copy is stored and the backup file name. Click OK. Quicken cautions you that restoring the backup file to the current file will overwrite any existing data. Select Yes to tell Quicken to go ahead. When Quicken's finished restoring the data, you'll see a message that the file was restored successfully.

Fig. 23.6
Tell Quicken where your backup copy is (which drive) and the name of the backup file. Then click OK to restore the backup data to the current file.

CAUTION **If disaster befalls a Quicken file that you didn't back up recently,** you may have to reenter transactions that you transpired from the time you backed up to the day you lost your data. Hopefully, you have an up-to-date printed copy of your registers that you can use to enter these transactions. If you don't, however, you'll have to go back to the original source documents—checks, deposit slips, receipts, and so on—to recreate the lost transactions.

Do I need to do anything with my files at the end of the year?

If you've got more than one year's worth of transactions in your Quicken file, you may want to archive the transactions from prior years for safekeeping. When you archive a file, Quicken makes a copy of transactions from previous years and stores them in a separate file. Your current file isn't changed; it still includes transactions from the current year and previous years.

Did you know that you can store up to 65,534 transactions in a single Quicken file? But even though you have the space to store all of these transactions, you probably don't want to work with that many transactions in your Quicken registers. At the beginning of a new year, you can start a new file that contains only the new year's data. Starting a new year's file helps to curtail the growth of your Quicken file.

I can archive my file data

Archiving the data in your file simply means that you copy old transactions (those from previous years) into a separate file. This file becomes your archive file.

Select File, Year-End Copy when you're ready to archive your data. Quicken displays the Year-End Copy window as shown in figure 23.7. Select the Archive option and click OK to display the Archive File window that you see in figure 23.8. By default, Quicken assigns the archive file the current file name followed by the preceding year and stores the file in the directory where the program files are stored. The transactions that Quicken includes in the archive file are any that precede the current year. Change any or all of this information, if you want, and click OK to begin archiving old data.

Fig. 23.7
If you want to copy (archive) old transactions to a separate file, select the Archive option.

Fig. 23.8
Fill in the Archive File window and click OK to begin archiving old data to a separate file.

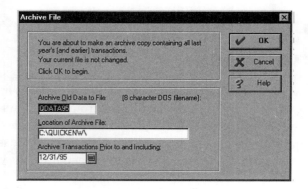

Or, I can start a new file

The best time to start a new file is not necessarily on January 1. It's better to wait until after you've completed your income tax return and any end-of-year reports. When you start a new file, Quicken copies the current file and then creates a new file with only those transactions from the current year.

Start a new year's file by selecting File, Year-End Copy to open the Year-End Copy window (refer to fig. 23.7). Then, select the Start New Year option and click OK. What you see next is the Start New Year window shown in figure 23.9. Enter a name for your new year's file and make sure the right transactions (based on the date) are going to be deleted. Then, tell Quicken where to store your new file and click OK.

Fig. 23.9
Just assign a name to the file for your new year's transactions and Quicken sets up the new file for you.

What's the password?

I don't have to tell you how confidential your financial data is. So what you've got stored in Quicken right now is information that you don't want just anyone to access or modify. Using passwords in Quicken helps to maintain the integrity of your data and keep unauthorized users out.

Assigning passwords

There are two kinds of passwords that you can use: **file** and **transaction** passwords. A file password prevents unauthorized users from accessing your Quicken file. Quicken requires the password before opening a file. A transaction password restricts users from adding, changing, or deleting transactions before the date that you specify. So without a transaction password, a user cannot modify your data.

Setting up a file password

To keep unauthorized users out of your Quicken files, set up a file password. Select File, Passwords, File to open the Set Up Password window (see fig. 23.10). In the Password text box, type the combination of letters and numbers you want to use as a password (using up to 16 characters). Quicken doesn't distinguish between the use of upper- and lowercase letters in your password, so the password **ABC** is also recognized if you enter **abc**.

As you type your password, you won't see the characters on your screen. Instead Quicken displays asterisks (*) so that others can't see your password. Press Tab to confirm your password. Type the same characters again and click OK to save your password.

Fig. 23.10
Set up a file password so that unauthorized users can't get into your Quicken files.

Quicken won't activate your file password until you close the file or exit the program. When you try to open the file the next time, though, you'll have to enter the correct password first.

Setting up a transaction password

To keep others from modifying your transactions, set up a transaction password. Select File, Passwords, File to open the Password to Modify Existing Transactions window (see fig. 23.11). In the Password text box, type the combination of letters and numbers you want to use as a password (using up to 16 characters) and press Tab. Then confirm your password by typing it again in the Confirm Password text box.

Next, select the date before which a password will be required to change a transaction. For example, if you don't want anyone to touch transactions dated prior to 9/11/95, select this date. Now, click OK to save the transaction password and immediately activate it.

Fig. 23.11
If you don't want users to modify your transactions, set up a transaction password and specify which transactions are restricted.

You can always change or do away with passwords

If you know the password, you can change it or eliminate it altogether. Select File, Passwords and either File or Transaction (dependent on which password you're changing). Quicken displays the Change Password window like the one you see in figure 23.12. Regardless of whether you're changing or eliminating a password, enter the old password first.

If you're changing the password, type the new password and then confirm it. (For transaction passwords, you can also change the date for transactions that require a password). If you're eliminating a password, leave both the New Password and Confirm Password text boxes blank. Click OK to save your password changes.

Fig. 23.12

If you're eliminating a password, leave the New Password and Confirm Password text boxes blank.

Making Quicken Work the Way You Want It To

● **In this chapter:**

- **The types of things you can customize in Quicken**

- **How to customize your Quicken program**

- **Changing the iconbar**

Who's the master here, you or your computer? Teach Quicken to behave the way you want it to! . . . . **>**

I n the early days of computer programs (oh, maybe seven or eight years ago), the thought of being able to change the appearance or the performance of a program to fit the needs of the user was ludicrous. Now, a program that can't be customized in some way doesn't seem to have a chance of lasting in the marketplace. My how times have changed.

When you start using Quicken, certain assumptions have already been made for you. For example, you see your registers displayed with two lines for every transaction, and the transactions appear in a particular typeface that has been chosen for you. Also, certain icons have been placed on the Quicken iconbar—these may or may not be icons you need. These assumptions, called **defaults** in some computer programs, are referred to as **options** in Quicken. You have the right to change the options in your own program.

Where do I go to change Quicken?

You can gain access to Quicken's options, the changeable, customizable features in Quicken, by choosing Edit, Options. The Options window (see fig. 24.1) appears on-screen, showing six choices for customization. You can customize features in the following areas:

Fig. 24.1
Pick your area of customization from the Options window.

- **General.** Controls the general appearance of dialog boxes, screen colors, and other screen options. General options are covered in this chapter.

- **Checks.** Control the information that prints on checks, warn if a check number is being re-used. Check options are covered in Chapter 6, "Writing Checks."

- **Register.** Control the way in which information is entered in the registers, how the registers are displayed, and how QuickFill works. Register options are covered in Chapter 5, "Introducing the Quicken Register."

- **Reports.**   Controls the way in which items are displayed in reports and the way in which reports are created. Report options are covered in Chapter 19, "Printing Reports."

- **Reminder.**   Turns on the Reminder and Billminder features and sets the number of days in advance of events that Quicken sends you its reminders. Reminder options are covered in Chapter 10, "Scheduling Future Transactions."

- **Iconbar.**   Picks the icons you want to see displayed on the iconbar. Iconbar options are covered in this chapter.

Click any of the buttons in the Options window to open an additional window, giving you access to the particular type of options you have selected.

Changing general options in Quicken

General options control the way dialog boxes look, the colors on your screen, and other on-screen features. To change the general options, click the General button in the Options window (see fig. 24.2). You can then customize the following features:

Fig. 24.2
You can customize Quicken by choosing from several General Options.

- **Use Quicken's Custom Colors.**   By default this feature is turned on. Click the box to turn Custom Colors off and you change the color of Quicken's dialog boxes from gray to white, losing some of the three-dimensional appearance of the boxes. Turning the Custom Colors off will save you a little bit of computer memory.

- **Confirm Investment Transactions from Forms.**   If this option is turned on when you enter an investment transaction on an investment form, Quicken will ask you if you're sure you want to enter that investment before putting it in the investment register. (Entering investments is covered in Chapter 17, "Staying on Top of Your Investments.")

- **Use Tax Schedules with Categories.**   When this feature is turned on, you have an opportunity to assign a tax schedule to new categories that you set up. (The setup of new categories is covered in Chapter 4, "Tracking Income and Expenses with Categories.")

- **Use Bold Text in Dialogs.**   Normally Quicken uses a regular typeface in its dialog boxes. If you prefer to see the text in bold, check this box.

- **Show Flyover Help in Toolbars.**   If you let your mouse pointer hover over one of the icons in Quicken's iconbar, a little yellow box appears and a description of what task that icon performs appears on the screen. This feature is turned on by default when you start Quicken. If you prefer not to use it, you can turn it off.

- **Remove Memorized Transactions Not Used in Last (fill in the blank) Months.**   When you memorize a transaction, the transaction stays memorized until you decide you no longer need it and you actually delete it from the Memorized Transaction list. Alternatively, you can choose this option and have Quicken boot that transaction off the memorized list after a designated number of months. (Memorized Transactions are discussed in Chapter 9, "Speed Up Your Register Entries with Memorized Transactions.")

- **Quick Tabs.**   *If Full-Window Mode* is selected, Quick Tabs appear along the left side of your Quicken screen each time you open a new window. You won't see Quick Tabs if the *Turn Quick Tabs Off* option is selected. If you are using Quick Tabs, you can check the *Alt-key Access to Quick Tabs* box. This feature assigns a number to each Quick Tab (visible on the Tab) and lets you access those tabs from the keyboard by holding down the Alt key and pressing the number of a Tab.

- **Mappings for Ctrl+Z/X/C/V.**   Quicken has its own uses for the key combinations Ctrl+Z, Ctrl+X, Ctrl+C, and Ctrl+V which override standard Windows uses for these keys. If you normally use Windows commands with these key combinations and prefer to return to those Windows commands, select *Undo/Cut/Copy/Paste.*

- **Working Calendar.**   By default, Quicken assumes you use a 365-day calendar that begins on January 1 and ends on December 31. Doesn't everybody? Actually, everybody doesn't. Occasionally businesses operate on a *fiscal* year, a year that for financial accounting purposes begins in a month other than January and proceeds for 12 months hence (April to March, for example). If you need Quicken to keep track of your records on a fiscal calendar you can specify that calendar here.

Customizing Checks

You can control the information that prints on your checks with Quicken's options for customization. Choose Edit, Options, and then click on Checks. In the Check Options window that appears (see fig. 24.3), you have a number of choices for making your checks look the way you want them to.

Fig. 24.3
Customize the appearance of your checks from this window

Click on any of the following choices that you want to activate, remembering that any choices you make on this screen can later be changed by opening this window again.

- Click on a date option to choose the style you prefer.

- **Allow Entry of Extra Messages on Check** gives you access to a message line in which you can type information that won't be visible through the transparent window in a window envelope.

- **Print Categories on Voucher Checks** enables Quicken to print information from split transactions on the lower portion of your check, under the perforation.

- **Warn if a Check Number is Re-used** posts an on-screen warning if you attempt to issue a check with a duplicate check number.

- **Change Date of Checks to Date When Printed** lets you print today's date on the checks even if you wrote them several days ago.

- **Artwork on Check Entry Screen** lets you control the image (if any) that you want printed on your checks.

Customize Your Quicken Register

Quicken has made an assumption about the way in which you want your register displayed on the screen. There are two lines for each entry, there is a description bar at the top of the register showing you what type of information goes in each section, the date precedes the number, the category field precedes the memo field—all of these options can be changed in the window you see if you choose Edit, Options, Register (see fig. 24.4).

Fig. 24.4
Change the appear-
ance of your registers
from this window.

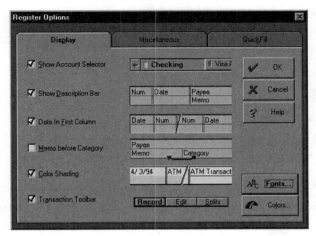

I don't like what's in the iconbar!

The icons in the iconbar are shortcuts, placed there by Quicken in order to make your life easier. If you don't use some of those icons though, they aren't doing you any good.

You can rearrange the order of icons on the iconbar by merely pointing to the icon you want to move, holding down your left mouse button, and dragging the icon to a new location on the bar. Presto!

And if you think that happened quickly, just try removing an icon from the iconbar. Don't think you want an icon anymore? Hold down the shift key and click the icon. Poof! It's gone!

You can replace icons in the iconbar with icons for tasks you like to perform, you can edit existing icons, and you can just clean house by removing the icons you don't ever use.

To alter the iconbar, follow these steps:

1 Choose <u>O</u>ptions from the <u>E</u>dit menu and the Options window appears (as shown earlier in fig. 24.1).

2 Click the <u>I</u>conbar button. The Customize Iconbar row of icons appears on-screen (see fig. 24.5).

Fig. 24.5
Fill your iconbar with buttons that fit your needs!

3 Notice in the Iconbar Display Options area of the window, both the Show Icons and Show Text boxes are checked. This means that the icons you see on your screen have both a picture and a one-word text description displayed on the button. You can select just Show Icons to display only the picture or select just Show Text to show only the word on the icon. Uncheck both of these boxes if you don't want to have icons displayed on your screen at all.

4 You can change an existing icon by clicking the icon in the Current iconbar display of the Customize Iconbar window. Both the Edit and Delete buttons become accessible to you when you click an icon. Remove an icon from the bar entirely by clicking on the icon you no longer need, then clicking the Delete button. Replace an icon on the bar with an icon that performs a different task by selecting the icon you no longer need and clicking the Edit button. A list appears of all the available Quicken commands that can be assigned to icons. Select the item you want from the list, then click OK to replace the old icon with your new, hand-picked icon.

5 Change the picture used for an icon by selecting the icon in the Current Iconbar window, clicking on the Edit button, and then clicking on the Change button. Pick from among a multitude of Quicken pictures for the new look for your icon.

One other neat iconbar trick you can perform is to place an icon on the bar that will open an account. Say you have both your personal finances tucked away in Quicken and also have a separate register for a business account. Switch back and forth easily between accounts by using the iconbar.

To place an access button to an account on the iconbar, follow these steps:

1 Choose Options from the Edit menu.

2 Click the Iconbar button. The Customize Iconbar window opens (as shown in fig. 24.3).

3 Click the New button.

4 In the list of available icons you can add to your iconbar, scroll down to the bottom of the list and select Use a Specific Account. Click OK and the Assign Account to Icon window appears (see fig. 24.6).

Fig. 24.6
Choose the account you want to be able to access from the iconbar.

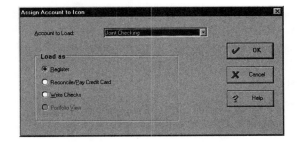

5 Choose whether you want this account to open as a register, a reconciliation or a credit card account, a portfolio view, or if you want to be able to write checks when the account opens. Choose the account you want this icon button to open. Then click OK.

6 In the Customize Iconbar window you can select this new icon, click the Change button, and not only select an appropriate graphic image for the icon but also change the text to read, for example, the name of your account.

From this point forward, when you click the icon for your account on the iconbar, Quicken opens the account you assigned to this icon.

25

Doing Your Banking Online

● **In this chapter:**

● **Getting starting with online banking**

● **Setting up an account for online banking**

● **You can suck information from the bank's computer**

● **Getting online information for your Quicken credit card**

● **How to transfer funds among accounts**

Forget the lines and the hassles—I'm banking from the comfort of home! . . . . ⊙

I magine a world in which you don't have to spend your lunch hour waiting in line at the bank, only to have the teller stick the "Next Teller Please" sign in your face as you finally make it to the front of the line. Things like direct deposit of paychecks and automatic teller machines have done a lot to alleviate the teller lines. Now there's a new way to relieve banking frustration: online banking.

You can use your computer to perform several banking functions that once were reserved for the teller lines—find out if checks have cleared, compare bank records to your own, and update your register with the latest transactions from your bank account. Best of all, you can perform these actions day or night, 24-hours a day.

The incentives for online banking are enormous: save time by not having to make a trip to the bank, save aggravation by not having to remember what days and hours the bank is open, and you don't even have to wait in line until it's your turn.

I'm convinced! How do I sign up?

There is an Online Service enrollment form with the materials that came with your Quicken software. Fill out this form, send it to your bank, and your bank will return to you a Welcome Kit, introducing the online features to you. Included with the Welcome Kit will be two numbers that you need: a 7-digit bank routing number, and a Personal Identification Number (PIN).

 Q&A *How do I find out if my bank is a participant in Quicken's online banking program?*

Select Financial, Directory from the Online menu. A screen displaying the participating banks appears. If you are interested in finding out more information about setting up an account with one of these institutions, click on the name of the bank for a telephone number and more information about the specific bank.

When you receive your Welcome Kit, you are ready to begin banking online. Make sure your modem is set up correctly (see Chapter 11, "Paying Bills Electronically" for specific information regarding setting up your modem and getting hooked up with your bank).

How do I set up accounts for online banking?

To get your Quicken account ready for online banking, follow these steps:

1 Choose <u>A</u>ccount from the <u>L</u>ists menu.

2 Select the account you plan to use to communicate with the bank (this will be a checking or savings account at that bank). Click the Edit button to open the Edit Bank Account window (see fig. 25.1).

Fig. 25.1

Click the Enable Online Ban<u>k</u>ing box to tell Quicken you plan to implement the Online Banking feature with this account.

3 Click the Enable Online Ban<u>k</u>ing check box to put a check in that box.

4 Click the Next button at the bottom of the window.

5 On this window, shown in figure 25.2, enter the name of your bank, the routing number, your bank account number, the type of account you are using, and your Social Security number. You cannot proceed beyond this screen without filling in the requested information.

6 Click Done to indicate you have finished entering your bank information.

On the Account list you can now see a bolt of lightning next to your account name (!) indicating that your account is available for online banking.

Fig. 25.2
Enter the name of your bank, routing number, account number, type of account, and your Social Security number on this screen. You should have received the bank routing number in your Welcome Kit that came from the bank.

I want to download my bank transactions—NOW!

All right, all right, don't be so impatient! You've gotten yourself set up with the bank and you're ready to communicate. One of the joys of doing online banking is that your bank is now open 24-hours a day. So when you want information, you don't have to wait until the tellers get there in the morning.

To access the online banking services through Quicken, follow these steps:

1 Make sure your modem is hooked up and your phone line is free.

2 Choose Online, Online Banking.

3 If you have more than one online service, select your financial institution from the drop-down list in the Online Banking window (see fig. 25.3).

4 Click on the name of the account you wish to access in the account list (see fig. 25.3).

Fig. 25.3
Open the Online
Window and open up
a world of armchair
banking opportunities.

*Click here to display
a list of the
institutions with
whom you have
on-line accounts*

*Click here to
connect with your
bank*

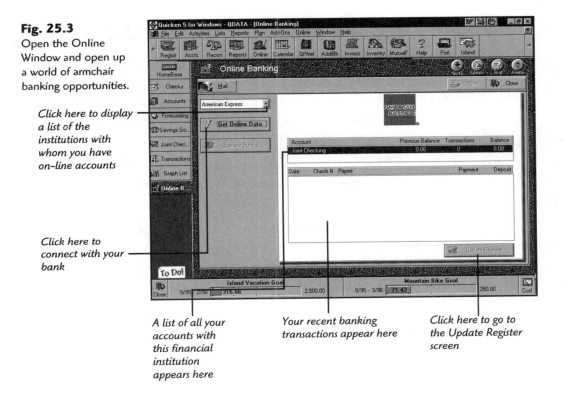

*A list of all your
accounts with
this financial
institution
appears here*

*Your recent banking
transactions appear here*

*Click here to go to
the Update Register
screen*

5 Click the Get Online Data button to connect with your financial
institution.

6 You are prompted to enter your Personal Identification Number (PIN).
Enter your PIN and then click OK. Quicken dials the bank's number and
collects data for all of your accounts at that establishment.

Now that you're connected to your bank, what's the next step? You can
review your transactions, you can update your register, you can get information about your credit card, you can even transfer funds if you have more
than one account at that financial institution.

Take a look at your account transactions

When you connect with your bank, Quicken grabs the transactions from your
account and makes them available to you on-screen by opening a new
window that displays all your transactions since the last statement.

You can review your transactions on-screen. Your transactions are sorted
by date.

Can I update my register with these new transactions?

Don't be satisfied with just looking at your transactions. Take advantage of the fact that you are viewing the real transactions as recorded at the bank. If you are viewing a checking account, what you see are the checks that have cleared your bank since your last statement.

- Quicken looks at the date, amount, and check number of each transaction in the bank's records and tries to match it up with one in your register.

- For transactions that match, Quicken fills in the payee and category information it gets from your register.

- If the bank's transaction doesn't match a transaction in your register, it is assumed the transaction is a new transaction.

- If a transaction is a duplication of one already in your register, click on the extra, unneeded transaction and click the Delete button to remove it from the list.

- If you agree with all of the transactions on-screen, you can click the Accept All button. For all matching transactions Quicken will mark your register with a **c** in the Clr column to indicate the transaction has cleared your bank (not to be confused with the **R** mark that signifies the transaction has been reconciled). For all new transactions, Quicken will add the transaction to your register and mark it with a **c** to indicate it has cleared.

- To choose only selected transactions for updating your register, click individual transactions, and then click the Mark button to mark the transactions you want to update. Click the Accept button to enter new transactions in your register and clear all marked transactions.

- When Quicken finishes, it automatically disconnects the modem link to your financial institution, clears the screen of your Online Banking window, and returns your view to the register that you just updated.

Can I get data for my Quicken credit card?

You can get information about your Quicken Credit Card online with the Quicken Online Banking feature. Begin in the same way as you did to get information about your checking account.

1 Make sure your modem is hooked up and your phone line is clear.

2 Choose Online Banking from the Online menu.

3 Once the Online Banking window is displayed, click on the drop-down list where your various online bank accounts are listed (as shown in fig. 25.3). From this list choose Quicken Credit Card.

4 Click the Get Online Data button. Quicken connects to the financial institution and gets the latest data regarding your credit card.

You can tie your online credit card information to your credit card register account by choosing the proper account from the list at the top of the online banking window. The techniques you just learned for comparing and updating information in your register with transactions from the online account apply to the Quicken Credit Card as well.

For more information about the Quicken Credit Card, see Chapter 14, "Managing Your Credit Cards."

I want to transfer funds between accounts

You can use Quicken's Online Banking feature to transfer funds between two accounts at the same financial institution. Follow these steps to transfer funds online:

1 Make sure your modem is hooked up and your phone line is free.

2 From the Quicken Online menu select Online Banking.

3 Choose the financial institution at which you bank from the drop-down list.

4 Click the Transfer Funds button.

5 Enter the amount of the transfer in the Transfer Funds Between Accounts window that appears.

6 Choose the accounts in the Transfer Money From and Transfer Money To fields.

7 Click the Transmit button.

Quicken calls your bank and requests the funds transfer. The transfer occurs and a Transmission Summary window appears. If you are satisfied with the information that appears in this window summarizing the transaction, click OK.

Quicken discontinues the modem connection and you're finished.

Index

PLUG YOURSELF INTO...

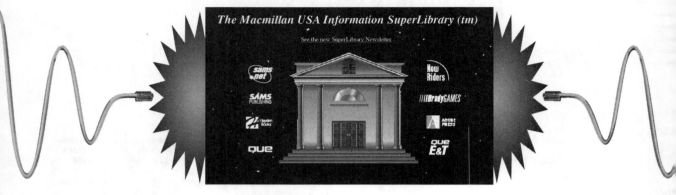

THE MACMILLAN INFORMATION SUPERLIBRARY™

Free information and vast computer resources from the world's leading computer book publisher—online!

FIND THE BOOKS THAT ARE RIGHT FOR YOU!
A complete online catalog, plus sample chapters and tables of contents!

- **STAY INFORMED** with the latest computer industry news through our online newsletter, press releases, and customized Information SuperLibrary Reports.

- **GET FAST ANSWERS** to your questions about Macmillan Computer Publishing books.

- **VISIT** our online bookstore for the latest information and editions!

- **COMMUNICATE** with our expert authors through e-mail and conferences.

- **DOWNLOAD SOFTWARE** from the immense Macmillan Computer Publishing library:
    - Source code, shareware, freeware, and demos

- **DISCOVER HOT SPOTS** on other parts of the Internet.

- **WIN BOOKS** in ongoing contests and giveaways!

TO PLUG INTO MCP:

WORLD WIDE WEB: **http://www.mcp.com**

FTP: ftp.mcp.com

Complete and Return this Card
for a *FREE* Computer Book Catalog

Thank you for purchasing this book! You have purchased a superior computer book written expressly for your needs. To continue to provide the kind of up-to-date, pertinent coverage you've come to expect from us, we need to hear from you. Please take a minute to complete and return this self-addressed, postage-paid form. In return, we'll send you a free catalog of all our computer books on topics ranging from word processing to programming and the internet.

Mr. ☐   Mrs. ☐   Ms. ☐   Dr. ☐

Name (first) ☐☐☐☐☐☐☐☐☐☐☐ (M.I.) ☐ (last) ☐☐☐☐☐☐☐☐☐☐☐☐☐☐☐☐☐

Address ☐☐☐☐☐☐☐☐☐☐☐☐☐☐☐☐☐☐☐☐☐☐☐☐☐☐☐☐☐☐☐☐☐☐☐

Address ☐☐☐☐☐☐☐☐☐☐☐☐☐☐☐☐☐☐☐☐☐☐☐☐☐☐☐☐☐☐☐☐☐☐☐

City ☐☐☐☐☐☐☐☐☐☐☐☐☐☐☐ State ☐☐ Zip ☐☐☐☐☐ ☐☐☐☐

Phone ☐☐☐ ☐☐☐ ☐☐☐☐ Fax ☐☐☐ ☐☐☐ ☐☐☐☐

Company Name ☐☐☐☐☐☐☐☐☐☐☐☐☐☐☐☐☐☐☐☐☐☐☐☐☐☐☐☐☐☐☐

E-mail address ☐☐☐☐☐☐☐☐☐☐☐☐☐☐☐☐☐☐☐☐☐☐☐☐☐☐☐☐☐☐☐

1. Please check at least (3) influencing factors for purchasing this book.

Front or back cover information on book .... ☐
Special approach to the content .... ☐
Completeness of content .... ☐
Author's reputation .... ☐
Publisher's reputation .... ☐
Book cover design or layout .... ☐
Index or table of contents of book .... ☐
Price of book .... ☐
Special effects, graphics, illustrations .... ☐
Other (Please specify): _____ ☐

2. How did you first learn about this book?

Saw in Macmillan Computer Publishing catalog .... ☐
Recommended by store personnel .... ☐
Saw the book on bookshelf at store .... ☐
Recommended by a friend .... ☐
Received advertisement in the mail .... ☐
Saw an advertisement in: _____ ☐
Read book review in: _____ ☐
Other (Please specify): _____ ☐

3. How many computer books have you purchased in the last six months?

This book only .... ☐   3 to 5 books .... ☐
2 books .... ☐   More than 5 .... ☐

4. Where did you purchase this book?

Bookstore .... ☐
Computer Store .... ☐
Consumer Electronics Store .... ☐
Department Store .... ☐
Office Club .... ☐
Warehouse Club .... ☐
Mail Order .... ☐
Direct from Publisher .... ☐
Internet site .... ☐
Other (Please specify): _____ ☐

5. How long have you been using a computer?

☐ Less than 6 months   ☐ 6 months to a year
☐ 1 to 3 years   ☐ More than 3 years

6. What is your level of experience with personal computers and with the subject of this book?

	With PCs	With subject of book
New	☐	☐
Casual	☐	☐
Accomplished	☐	☐
Expert	☐	☐

Source Code ISBN: 0-7897-0631-8

7. Which of the following best describes your job title?

Administrative Assistant ☐
Coordinator ☐
Manager/Supervisor ☐
Director ☐
Vice President ☐
President/CEO/COO ☐
Lawyer/Doctor/Medical Professional ☐
Teacher/Educator/Trainer ☐
Engineer/Technician ☐
Consultant ☐
Not employed/Student/Retired ☐
Other (Please specify): _____ ☐

8. Which of the following best describes the area of the company your job title falls under?

Accounting ☐
Engineering ☐
Manufacturing ☐
Operations ☐
Marketing ☐
Sales ☐
Other (Please specify): _____ ☐

9. What is your age?

Under 20 ☐
21-29 ☐
30-39 ☐
40-49 ☐
50-59 ☐
60-over ☐

10. Are you:

Male ☐
Female ☐

11. Which computer publications do you read regularly? (Please list)

_____
_____
_____
_____
_____
_____
_____
_____
_____
_____

Comments: _____
_____
_____

Fold here and scotch-tape to mail

NO POSTAGE
NECESSARY
IF MAILED
IN THE
UNITED STATES

BUSINESS REPLY MAIL
FIRST-CLASS MAIL PERMIT NO. 9918 INDIANAPOLIS IN

POSTAGE WILL BE PAID BY THE ADDRESSEE

ATTN MARKETING
MACMILLAN COMPUTER PUBLISHING
MACMILLAN PUBLISHING USA
201 W 103RD ST
INDIANAPOLIS IN 46209-9042